TERM PAPER RESOURCE GUIDE TO COLONIAL AMERICAN HISTORY

Roger M. Carpenter

Greenwood Press
An Imprint of ABC-CLIO, LLC

Santa Barbara, California • Denver, Colorado • Oxford, England

Library of Congress Cataloging-in-Publication Data

Carpenter, Roger M., 1956–
Term paper resource guide to colonial American history / Roger M. Carpenter.
p. cm.
Includes bibliographical references and index.
ISBN 978–0–313–35544–8 (hard copy : alk. paper) — ISBN 978–0–313–35545–2 (e-book)
1. United States—History—Colonial period, ca. 1600–1775—Chronology. 2. United States—History—Colonial period, ca. 1600–1775—Bibliography. 3. Report writing—Handbooks, manuals, etc.
I. Title.
E188.C285 2009
973.2—dc22 2009009048

13 12 11 10 9 1 2 3 4 5

This book is also available on the World Wide Web as an eBook.
Visit www.abc-clio.com for details.

ABC-CLIO, LLC
130 Cremona Drive, P.O. Box 1911
Santa Barbara, California 93116-1911

This book is printed on acid-free paper ∞

Manufactured in the United States of America

Contents

Introduction

Colonial history presents us with perhaps one of the most complex chapters of America's past. This complexity is often reflected in the classroom, where invariably, a student, given a writing assignment, will approach the instructor and say, "I do not know what to write about." This *Term Paper Resource Guide,* I hope, will give students a starting point in finding topics that match their interests. This book covers 100 important historical events, from earliest English attempts to establish a colony in North America in the 1580s to the ratification of the Constitution of the United States in 1791. This coverage is not exhaustive. Students should not read this list of entries and get the idea that colonial history can be neatly compacted into a given number of discrete events. I think of this guide as a starting point for research. Students should consult the guide but still attempt to develop their own research topics and interests, working with their instructors and librarians to determine the appropriateness of their topics, refine their research questions, and seek out primary and secondary sources.

Over the past decade, the Internet has become a much better research tool. Many colleges and universities offer Web sites that contain analysis of past events and often primary sources. However, keep in mind that not all Web sites are created equal. Some Web sites seek to promote a particular point of view, and if in doubt, students may wish to ask an instructor or librarian to give their evaluation of a site. I have attempted to list sources that students should be able to find quite easily, either in most libraries or on the World Wide Web. Recognizing that not all libraries and academic institutions have (or can afford) subscription-based databases such as JSTOR, Project Muse, and Eighteenth-Century Collections, I have avoided listing them, but if students have access to them, they should certainly use them.

USING THIS GUIDE

Each entry provides a brief overview of the event(s) in question. This is followed by a list of "Term Paper Suggestions," which are research questions that students may modify. The next section is "Alternative Term Paper Suggestions." These suggestions differ greatly from the term paper suggestions in that unlike the more traditional term paper, they ask students to create iMovies, PowerPoints, podcasts, and the like. They also sometimes ask students to assume the role of an advisor to a historic personage, or to make a counterhistorical argument. The next section is "Primary Sources." I have listed only primary source material that should be available in most libraries or on the World Wide Web. I have attempted whenever possible to list sources that can be found on the Internet. In particular, I would advise students searching for primary sources to visit sites such as Google Books (http://books.google.com), the Internet Archive (http://www.archive.org/index.php), Early Canada Online (http://www.canadiana.org, which has many documents pertaining to the United States), and Documenting the American South (http://docsouth.unc.edu/). The next section is "Secondary Sources." For the most part, I have attempted to include the most recent scholarship regarding each topic. "World Wide Web" is the next section, and each entry will have at least one Web site associated with it. I have attempted to list Web sites that are fairly stable, so many of the sites have an .edu or .org suffix, but there is a smattering of .com addresses. The last section is the "Multimedia Sources." Nearly every entry will have at least one multimedia source. For the most part, these consist of DVD videos, although a few are available only in VHS format. Another good Web source of videos portraying historical events is the popular www.youtube.com. However, as videos on this site are removed frequently, I was reluctant to list it consistently.

1. Roanoke, Virginia, "The Lost Colony," Is Founded (1584–1590)

The fate of the English colonists who attempted to settle Roanoke is perhaps the greatest mystery in American history. Seeking a suitable site for a settlement, English investors choose Roanoke Island in 1584, believing its sandbars, shoals, and contrary winds would make a Spanish attack on the colony difficult.

One hundred soldiers landed on the island in 1585 under the command of Ralph Lane. Lane expected the local Indians to feed his men, but in early 1586 the Indians ran short of maize and stopped provisioning the English. Lane attacked the Indians, thinking they could be terrorized into providing food, but the Indians fled the region, leaving the English to starve.

In 1587 another colonization effort led by John White arrived on the island. White returned to England later that year to secure supplies for the colony. However, the English, concerned about the Spanish Armada, embargoed all shipping, making it impossible for White to return to America.

When White did return to Roanoke in 1590, he found an abandoned settlement and the letters "CRO" carved into a post. White thought the letters were meant to be the word "Croaton," a reference to a nearby island. The sea captain leading the expedition, however, chose not to investigate.

There are many theories as to the fate of the colonists. Some argue that Indians either massacred the colonists or permitted them to live among them. Other sources suggest that some Roanoke colonists still survived among the coastal Algonquians at the time Jamestown was founded, but were killed on the orders of Chief Powhatan.

TERM PAPER SUGGESTIONS

1. Discuss English interest in North America in the late sixteenth century. Why are the English so interested in the Americas? Is it really all about the acquisition of gold and other forms of wealth? Discuss possible geopolitical

strategies that the English may have had in mind, especially as they were trying to counter Spanish expansion.

2. Discuss English expectations and treatment of Native Americans. Why would the English believe that the natives would willingly feed them? Why did Lane's strategy of frightening the Indians into feeding him and his men backfire? Why did he think it would work?
3. Examine the various theories that have been put forward to explain the disappearance of the Roanoke colonists. Make an argument for what you believe to be the strongest theory.
4. Read Richard Hakluyt's *Discourse of Western Planting* (it is very short). What do you believe is his most compelling argument for the English establishing colonies in North America? What is his least compelling argument?
5. Hakluyt suggested that a primary motivation for English colonization should be to spread their religion. Do you think this was actually a primary concern of the English? Why or why not?

ALTERNATIVE TERM PAPER SUGGESTIONS

1. It is 1584 and Sir Walter Raleigh has hired you and another individual to conduct a reconnaissance of what is now the eastern seaboard of the United States. Keeping in mind the English desire for security from Spanish attacks, and the need to find some sort of wealth in the New World, compose a recommendation for a site along the coast. To make things just a little more interesting, the other individual strongly recommends that the settlement be placed at Roanoke. You, of course, realize that is not a wise course of action, but you must make a strong counterargument so that Sir Walter will opt for your recommendation.
2. It is 1588 and you are the publicity agent for the company that is publishing Thomas Harriot's *A Briefe and True Report of the New Found Land of Virginia.* Many Englishmen are skeptical as to the value of having colonies in North America. Your job is to compose advertising copy that will make people want to buy this book and learn about the Americas. Think in terms of emphasizing the commodities that Harriot claims are plentiful in America but scarce in England.
3. It is 1590. John White has just returned from his failed attempt to find the Roanoke colonists. White is frustrated because the English public seems to care little about Roanoke or its colonists. White wishes to start a publicity

campaign to get the public interested in the fate of the colonists and to secure government funding for another attempt to find them. White is taking bids from several advertising firms. Prepare a PowerPoint presentation about why White should hire you and your firm to manage this campaign.

SUGGESTED SOURCES

Primary Sources

Burrage, Henry S., ed. *Early English and French Voyages, Chiefly from Hakluyt, 1534–1608.* New York: Scribner's, 1906. Contains accounts by John Barlowe, Ralph Lane, and Arthur White. Also available at Google Books.

Hakluyt, Richard. *Discourse of Western Planting* (1584). http://xroads.virginia.edu/~HYPER/HNS/Garden/hakluyt.html. Richard Hakluyt was an English writer (and armchair traveler) who collected, translated, and published stories from sailors about the New World. Hakluyt was one of the most voracious promoters of English overseas colonization. His *Discourse of Western Planting* is a brief summary of his arguments for English colonization of the Americas.

Harriot, Thomas. *A Briefe and True Report of the New Found Land of Virginia.* Originally published 1588. http://docsouth.unc.edu/nc/hariot/hariot.html. Harriot, a scientist and mathematician, made one voyage to Roanoke. The *Briefe and True Report* is one of the earliest descriptions of America in the English language.

Secondary Sources

Kupperman, Karen Ordahl. *Roanoke: The Abandoned Colony.* Lanham, MD: Rowman & Littlefield, 1984. Kupperman discusses the goals of English colonization, the plans for Roanoke as a military outpost, and the relations between the English and the coastal Algonquians.

Milton, Giles. *Big Chief Elizabeth: The Adventures and Fate of the First English Colonists in America.* New York: Picador, 2000. Milton covers the period from the first English explorations of the Americas to John Rolfe's marriage to Pocahontas. His section on Roanoke deals with the soldiers and colonists on the island, and the attempts by Sir Walter Raleigh to realize a profit from the colony.

Morgan, Edmund S. *American Slavery, American Freedom: The Ordeal of Colonial Virginia.* New York: Norton, 1975. One of the best histories of early

Virginia, Morgan includes a chapter on English motivations for colonization and a chapter on the Roanoke fiasco.

Stick, David. *Roanoke: The Beginnings of English America.* Chapel Hill: University of North Carolina Press, 1983. A thorough overview of the English attempt to settle Roanoke that offers differing theories regarding the disappearance of the colonists.

World Wide Web

"First English Settlement in the New World." http://statelibrary.dcr.state.nc.us/nc/ncsites/English1.htm. Overview of attempt to colonize Roanoke with links.

"Fort Raleigh National Historic Site." http://www.nps.gov/history/history/online_books/hh/16/hh16toc.htm. Overview of Fort Raleigh.

"Index of White Watercolors and De Bry Engravings." http://www.virtualjamestown.org/images/white_debry_html/jamestown.html. John White's watercolors are reproduced on this page along with engravings by Dutch artist Theodor de Bry. De Bry, unlike White, never visited the Americas and based many of his works on White's watercolors. Note the differences between the engravings and the watercolors.

Multimedia Source

In Search of History: Lost Colony of Roanoke. A&E, 2000. DVD. 50 minutes. Discusses some of the theories behind the disappearance of the Roanoke colonists.

2. Spanish Conquistadors Establish St. Augustine (1585)

In 1528 and 1539, Spain launched two separate expeditions, led by conquistadors Pánfilo Narváez and Hernando de Soto, that landed on what is now Florida's west coast. Not finding gold, silver, or anything else of value, the Spanish deemed both undertakings failures, dimming their enthusiasm for North American exploration. While the Spanish did claim Florida (a name they applied to what is now the entire southeastern United States), the unhealthy climate, hostile Indians, and lack of apparent wealth gave them little incentive to colonize it.

However, in the 1560s, French and Dutch pirates plundered Spanish treasure ships sailing the channel between Cuba and Florida. Needing to protect their ships, Spain gave Pedro Menéndez de Avilés the task of establishing naval bases in Florida in 1565. However, it turned out that French Huguenots also attempted to colonize Florida. Menéndez attacked their fort, and when the remaining Huguenots surrendered, Menéndez massacred them. Menéndez established St. Augustine and seven other posts in Florida, all with the twin goals of pacifying the local Indians and guarding Spanish ships against attacks by pirates. When Menéndez died in 1574, the Crown assumed control of the colonies.

Florida's reputation for disease and bad weather made it difficult to attract colonists. Instead, Spain sent missionaries to convert native peoples. As an incentive for the natives to accept the missionaries, the Spanish linked conversion to access to trade goods. This allowed the Spanish to use native peoples as military allies to shield Florida from the English colonies of South Carolina and, later, Georgia.

TERM PAPER SUGGESTIONS

1. Discuss the military rationale for the Spanish occupation of Florida. What strategies did the Spanish pursue to pacify the local Native Americans? Were these strategies effective? Why did the Spanish deal with the French Huguenots so harshly?
2. Discuss the expansiveness of Spain's claims of the present-day American Southeast. Considering that the Spanish referred to the entire Southeast as "Florida," what factors do you think made them unable to enforce their claims in regions such as Georgia and the Carolinas?
3. Both Pánfilo Narváez (the details of his expedition can be found in Cabeza de Vaca's narrative in *Spanish Explorers in the Southern United States*) and Hernando de Soto landed at Tampa Bay on Florida's west coast to begin their respective explorations of the Southeast. Why did they both choose the same spot? What did each expedition encounter in Florida? What was similar? What was different?

ALTERNATIVE TERM PAPER SUGGESTIONS

1. It is 1565 and Pedro Menéndez has hired you to write an advertising piece that will lure Spanish colonists to Florida. You must make Florida sound appealing, while remaining truthful about the shortcomings of the area, such as the climate and the hostile Indians.
2. Working with a classmate, select one side of this argument: It is 1565 and the Spanish government is very concerned about the attacks that French and Dutch pirates have launched against their treasure fleets. Florida has been suggested as the location for a possible naval base to try and thwart these pirates, but there have been objections due to the peninsula's climate and other factors. You may either (a) submit a report to the Spanish Crown as to why they need to establish a base in Florida or (b) submit a report that recommends not establishing a base in Florida. If you choose this option, you must name an alternative site and you must be ready to play up its virtues (military and otherwise).

SUGGESTED SOURCES

Primary Sources

Clayton, Lawrence A., Vernon James Knight, Jr., and Edward C. Moore, eds. *The De Soto Chronicles: The Expedition of Hernando De Soto to North America, 1539–1543.* 2 volumes. Tuscaloosa: University of Alabama Press, 1994. http://www.nps.gov/archive/deso/chronicles/index.htm. Contains several different accounts of the de Soto expedition.

Hodge, Frederick W., and Theodore H. Lewis, eds. *Spanish Explorers in the Southern United States.* New York: Scribner's, 1908. Also available online at Google Books. Contains "The Narrrative of Alvar Nuñez Cabeza de Vaca" and an account of the de Soto expedition by the Gentleman of Elvas.

Secondary Sources

Axtell, James. *The Indians' New South: Cultural Change in the Colonial Southeast.* Baton Rouge: Louisiana State University Press, 1997. Discusses the changes European colonization caused in the Southeast.

Weber, David J. *The Spanish Frontier in North America.* New Haven: Yale University Press, 1992. Perhaps the best book about Spain in North America. Has a good section on Florida.

Wright, J. Leitch. *The Only Land They Knew: The Tragic Story of the American Indians in the Old South.* New York: Free Press, 1981. Includes a section on Spanish Florida.

World Wide Web

"Historical Museum of Southern Florida." http://www.historical-museum.org/exhibits/sf/sf.htm. Offers text, images, and maps of the Spanish colonization of Florida.

"St. Augustine, America's Ancient City." http://www.flmnh.ufl.edu/staugustine/intro.htm. Offers a timeline and a capsule history of the city.

3. Spanish Colonize New Mexico (1598)

The failure of the Hernando de Soto (1539–1543) and Francisco Coronado expeditions (1540–1544) to discover mineral wealth north of Mexico resulted in dwindling Spanish interest in these territories. However, fearful that other European powers would seize these lands, and prodded by the Franciscans to claim more Indian souls for Christ, the Spanish decided to colonize what they called New Mexico. In the spring of 1598, Don Juan de Oñate led a colonizing expedition, consisting mainly of soldiers and a few missionaries, north from Mexico City to the northern Rio Grande Valley.

Oñate and his men settled among Pueblo people who did not resist the Spanish intruders at first. The Spanish made no plans to grow their own food or even to construct their own shelters. Instead, they evicted Native Americans from their villages, seizing their homes and foodstores. With the onset of winter Spanish soldiers confiscated blankets and clothing from the natives. In late 1598, a small contingent of Spanish soldiers attempted to extort supplies from the Acoma Pueblo. The Indians, fed up with the Spaniards, slaughtered the small group of soldiers.

Oñate led an assault on the Acoma Pueblo, seized 500 Pueblo Indians as prisoners and tried them for treason. Punishments ranged from 20 years slavery to having one foot amputated. Oñate's cruelty resulted in the Spanish having to conduct what amounted to an uneasy military occupation of the region.

Franciscan missionaries established missions within pueblo villages, forcing them to build churches. Pueblo peoples usually cooperated with the friars, largely because of the presence of Spanish soldiers.

TERM PAPER SUGGESTIONS

1. Between de Soto and Coronado's expeditions, and that of Oñate, Spain changed their official policy regarding Native Americans. Expeditions were no longer termed "conquests" but "pacifications." Assuming that Spanish explorers had followed the spirit of such orders, what could Pueblos and other native peoples have expected in terms of treatment?
2. A recurring aspect of very early European colonization of the Americas was the failure of expeditions to bring provisions, on the assumption that native people would provide them with food. Another example of this, besides the Oñate expedition, was the initial English attempt at Roanoke. Why did the leaders of these colonization attempts decide not to bring sufficient provisions? What made them think native people would (or could) feed them?
3. After Oñate, other governors of New Mexico had tense relations with the Franciscan missionaries. Examine the conflicts between the Franciscans and New Mexico governors. What was the source of these conflicts? Could they have been averted?
4. Franciscan missionaries expressed dismay that some of the Pueblo people they attempted to convert to Christianity sometimes deserted their communities and chose to live with the Apaches instead. Why did this upset the missionaries? Explore the differing views the Spanish held of Pueblo peoples and other, more nomadic peoples in the Southwest, such as the Apache and the Navajo.
5. The Spanish were fearful that other European powers would occupy and control the lands north of their colonies in present-day Mexico. Given European penetration of the Americas by 1600, that seems to have been a rather remote possibility. However, what did the Spaniards and other Europeans know about North American geography in 1598? Find maps from that period and try to imagine how they informed Spanish ideas regarding the Americas.

ALTERNATIVE TERM PAPER SUGGESTIONS

1. You have been appointed as Don Oñate's secretary. His first task for you is to compose a response to accusations of his mistreatment of the Indians. Oñate

directs you to put the best face on the reports of murder, rape, and pillaging, but he also forbids you to lie in your response. Good luck!

2. It is 1598, and you have been appointed to head up the Spanish intelligence service. The king has ordered you to prepare an assessment of the threat that other European powers offer to Spanish colonies in North America. The king specifically wants to know whether he should invest in an expedition to seize New Mexico. Using modern maps (which you have but no one else does) make your argument as to whether Spain should gain control of New Mexico.
3. You are a Franciscan missionary who has accompanied Oñate to New Mexico. You are tasked with converting Pueblo people to Christianity. Keeping in mind that the Pueblos know nothing about Christianity, your task is to prepare a heavily illustrated PowerPoint presentation that will introduce the religion to them.

SUGGESTED SOURCES

Primary Source

Bolton, Herbert Eugene, ed. *Spanish Exploration in the Southwest, 1542–1706.* New York: Scribner's, 1908. Also available online at Google Books. Includes accounts by Oñate and other colonists regarding the settlement of New Mexico, as well as narratives from earlier Spanish expeditions.

Secondary Sources

Cutter, Charles R. *The Protector de Indios in Colonial New Mexico, 1659–1821.* Albuquerque: University of New Mexico Press, 1986. Examines the role of the office of *Protector de Indios* in colonial New Mexico.

Forbes, Jack D. *Apache, Navajo, and Spaniard.* Norman: University of Oklahoma Press, 1994. Examines the nomadic native peoples of the Southwest, and why the Spanish regarded them differently than Pueblo peoples.

Gutiérrez, Ramón A. *When Jesus Came, the Corn Mothers Went Away: Marriage, Sexuality, and Power in New Mexico, 1500–1846.* Stanford, CA: Stanford University Press, 1991. Examines the affects of Spanish colonization on Pueblo life.

John, Elizabeth A. H. *Storms Brewed in Other Men's Worlds: The Confrontations of Indians, Spanish, and French in the Southwest, 1540–1795.* Norman: University of Oklahoma Press, 1996. A thorough history of colonial New Mexico.

Weber, David J. *The Spanish Frontier in North America.* New Haven, CT: Yale University Press, 1992. Perhaps the best book about Spain in North America. Has a good section on colonial New Mexico.

World Wide Web

"Cuartocentennial of Colonization of New Mexico." http://web.nmsu.edu/~publhist/cuatrocentennial.htm. Web site established by New Mexico State University. Includes weekly summaries of the Oñate and Aguilar expeditions.

4. Fur Trade Leads to Native Dependency on European Goods (1600 on)

During the earliest explorations of North America's eastern seaboard, Europeans found Native Americans willing to trade valuable furs for items such as nails, needles, knives, and other metal implements. Initially, the fur trade consisted of casual contacts between fishermen and native people.

Highly valued in Europe, furs gave native people the opportunity to obtain goods they both deemed practical and thought contained supernatural power. Copper pots, for example, served not only as cooking vessels but could be broken up and transformed into jewelry or useful items such as knives and arrowheads. Cagey traders, native peoples demanded European goods such as kettles, hatchets, knives, and woolen cloth. Later, as traders of various European nationalities began to compete with one another, they offered native peoples firearms and alcohol for their furs.

When European merchants realized the economic potential of the fur trade, large companies entered the market, many of them offering items manufactured specifically for the fur trade. The fur trade created a Native American dependency on European goods. Peoples who became dependent on trade goods lost the ability to make artifacts of wood and stone such as bows, arrows, and hatchets, instead trading furs for powder, shot, muskets, and metal implements that they could not manufacture or repair themselves. Many native people went from hunting for subsistence to hunting to satisfy the demands of the fur trade, and trapped out their territories. The fur trade may have been the greatest motivation for the exploration of the North American interior, as the quest for new sources of furs led Europeans into the heart of the continent.

TERM PAPER SUGGESTIONS

1. Think about the items that Europeans traded to Native Americans and then think about the items they replaced. How did items such as hatchets, knives, and cloth change native cultures?
2. In the eighteenth and nineteenth centuries, native prophets attempted to convince their people to return to the "old ways" and reject all European goods. All of these attempts failed. Were these efforts doomed to fail? Is it impossible for people to "go backward" technologically?
3. Ethnohistorian Calvin Martin (see *Keepers of the Game*) argued that the reason native people stepped up their hunting of fur-bearing animals was not because of a desire for European trade goods, but because they thought animals had declared war on them and were causing disease. Evaluate this controversial thesis.
4. Discuss how the fur trade altered life in Native American communities. For example, how did the day-to-day activities of native men change? How did the activities of native women change?
5. The fur trade did much to encourage the exploration of the North American interior. Explore this process. What did westward exploration mean for native people whose lands had been trapped out when fur traders and fur trading companies moved west?

ALTERNATIVE TERM PAPER SUGGESTIONS

1. You are a native person living on the Atlantic seaboard of what is now the United States in the sixteenth century. One day, a European ship appears and some sailors come ashore. They give you stockings, a hatchet head (hatchet without the handle), and a copper pot. Will you use these items in the way they were intended? Or will you manipulate them into something else? (Hint: see Heckewelder.)
2. You are a native person living in New England in the first decade of the seventeenth century. Your tribe has had contact with European fishermen and has engaged in trade, acquiring small items such as knives and fishhooks. However, you want to acquire other items that the Europeans have, such as cloth, firearms, and hatchets. Your tribe's leader has asked you to devise a trading strategy to get these items from the Europeans.

SUGGESTED SOURCES

Primary Sources

Calloway, Colin G., ed. *Dawnland Encounters: Indians and Europeans in Northern New England.* Hanover, NH: University Press of New England, 1991. This is a collection of primary sources pertaining to the first encounters in northern New England between native peoples and Europeans, with trade playing a major role.

Heckewelder, John. *History, Manners, and Customs of the Indian Nations Who Once Inhabited Pennsylvania and the Neighboring States.* Philadelphia: Historical Society of Pennsylvania, 1881. www.archive.org. Heckewelder was a Moravian missionary who recorded natives' stories about their first contacts with Europeans.

Thwaites, Reuben Gold, ed. *The Jesuit Relations and Allied Documents: Travels and Explorations of the Jesuit Missionaries in New France, 1610–1791.* 73 vols. Cleveland: Burrow's Brothers, 1896–1901. While they are rather extensive, *The Jesuit Relations* are one of the best sources regarding the early fur trade, and one of the best concerning Native American culture in this period. The last two volumes comprise the index. They are available online in PDF format from the Internet Archive at www.archive.org or in full text format from Creighton University at http://puffin.creighton.edu/jesuit/relations/.

Secondary Sources

Axtell, James. *After Columbus: Essays in the Ethnohistory of Colonial North America.* New York: Oxford University Press, 1988. Most of the essays deal with the fur trade, native dependency on European goods, and the beginnings of a "consumer revolution" among Native Americans.

Cronon, William. *Changes in the Land: Indians, Colonists, and the Ecology of New England.* New York: Hill & Wang, 1983. Cronon's innovative book examines the changes that took place in the landscape of New England thanks to the fur trade, and how native people became dependent on European goods.

Krech, Shepard. *The Ecological Indian: Myth and History.* New York: Norton, 1999. Krech argues that Native Americans were not the environmental paragons that modern-day conservationists have made them out to be, and places native interaction with the environment within the context of their culture.

Martin, Calvin. *Keepers of the Game: Indian-Animal Relationships and the Fur Trade.* Berkeley: University of California Press, 1978. Martin argues that as native peoples engaged Europeans in the fur trade, they also contracted European diseases. Martin further argues that native people blamed the animals for the diseases, believing that the animals were fighting back through magic.

Salisbury, Neal. *Manitou and Providence: Indians, Europeans, and the Making of New England, 1500–1643.* New York: Oxford University Press, 1982. Salisbury examines the early interactions of Europeans and Indians in New England, including the fur trade.

World Wide Web

"The Fur Trade: The Indian as Indispensable Partner." http://www.civilization.ca/cmc/exhibitions/hist/canp1/ca12beng.shtml. Online exhibit of fur trade artifacts and links to articles.

"The Fur Trade Era, 1650s to 1850s." http://www.wisconsinhistory.org/topics/shorthistory/furtrade.asp. Provides an overview of the fur trade, with links to biographies of prominent individuals.

"The Fur Trade in New France: Les Coureurs de Bois." http://www.civilization.ca/cmc/index_e.aspx?DetailID=4805. Examines the role of the "wood's runners," usually young men who became fur traders, often adopting the native way of life and living among them.

"The Fur Trade in New France: Voyageurs and Hired Men." http://www.civilization.ca/cmc/index_e.aspx?DetailID=4808. Maps out many of the fur trading routes, the items that were commonly used in the fur trade, and the dangers that fur traders often faced.

5. England Establishes the First Permanent North American Settlement at Jamestown, Virginia (1607)

In 1607, the Virginia Company of London established the first permanent English colony at Jamestown. Concerned that the Spanish may discover and destroy the colony, the English situated their stockade next to the James River and to a swamp teeming with disease-bearing mosquitoes. The colonists dumped their waste into the James, which also provided their drinking water. Racked with disease, the colonists died quickly. By January 1608, only 38 of the original 104 colonists survived. However, the Virginia Company (which suppressed bad news from the colony) sent more colonists.

In 1608–1609, John Smith commanded Jamestown and ordered all colonists to work the fields, and the population stabilized for a brief period. However, Smith suffered serious burns in a gunpowder accident and went back to England to recover.

In December 1609 a new influx of colonists raised Jamestown's population to 220 Englishmen and women. By June 1610, the remaining 60 survivors abandoned the fort, only to be compelled to return by a relief expedition from England. By 1620, the Virginia Company had transported about 20,000 Englishmen and women to the Chesapeake; however, the colony had a population of only about 1,000.

Virginia's difficulties stemmed from the disease environment as well as because the colony's population came largely from two disparate segments of English society. Jamestown had many people from the gentry, unwilling to work with their hands, and beggars who tried to avoid labor. Virginia would not turn a profit until the introduction of tobacco in 1616.

TERM PAPER SUGGESTIONS

1. Discuss the competition for American colonies among the major European powers in the seventeenth century. How did this competition influence decisions that were made regarding populating and establishing the site of the Jamestown colony?
2. Examine and discuss the plans of the Virginia Company of London. Compare the hopes of the investors in London with the experiences of the colonists in North America.
3. Jamestown's poor location was a primary reason for the colony's very high mortality rate. What prompted the English to select such a location? What factors did they take into consideration when they placed the colony several miles up the James River and next to a swamp?
4. Examine the response of Virginia's Native Americans (the Powhatan Confederacy) to the presence of the English. It has been argued that the leader of the Confederacy, Powhatan, seems to have adopted a policy of either keeping the English confined to Jamestown or attempting to make them into his allies. Does this seem to have been the case? Why or why not?

ALTERNATIVE TERM PAPER SUGGESTIONS

1. You are a public relations specialist for the Virginia Company of London. Richard Frethorne's letter (see Web sources) has been published in the London newspapers. Your job is to convince the press that the contents of Frethorne's letter are not true. Your bosses, however, have warned you that your response to the press and Frethorne's letter must be truthful.
2. You are a public relations specialist for the Virginia Company. You have been tasked with putting together an advertising campaign. You will prepare an advertising campaign, complete with a logo, a slogan, and a podcast designed to make Englishmen and women want to move to Virginia. Again, you cannot lie, but you can exaggerate a little and perhaps omit certain key facts.

SUGGESTED SOURCES

Primary Sources

Frethorne, Richard. *Richard Frethorne to his father and mother, March 20, April 2 and 3, 1623.* http://www.virtualjamestown.org/frethorne.html. One of the few surviving letters from an indentured servant describing conditions in the colony.

Tyler, Lyon Gardiner, ed. *Narratives of Early Virginia, 1606–1625.* New York: Scribner's, 1907. Also available at Google Books. Contains excerpts from primary sources from the establishment of the Virginia Company of London in 1606 to its dissolution in 1625.

Secondary Sources

Horn, James. *A Land as God Made It: Jamestown and the Birth of America.* New York: Basic Books, 2005. A very readable narrative history of Jamestown.

Milton, Giles. *Big Chief Elizabeth: The Adventures and Fate of the First English Colonists in America.* New York: Picador, 2000. Milton covers the period from the first English explorations of the Americas to John Rolfe's marriage to Pocahontas, and includes a good section on Jamestown.

Morgan, Edmund. *American Slavery, American Freedom: The Ordeal of Colonial Virginia.* New York: Norton, 1975. Perhaps the best book about colonial Virginia, from Roanoke to the Revolution.

Vaughan, Alden T. *American Genesis: Captain John Smith and the Founding of Virginia.* Boston: Little, Brown, 1975. Part biography of Smith and part narrative history of early Virginia.

World Wide Web

"Historic Jamestown." http://historicjamestowne.org/. Provides a history and information on the 400th anniversary of Jamestown.

"Jamestown Rediscovery." http://www.apva.org/jr.html. Provides a history and timeline for the Jamestown colony. Also provides constant updates of archaeological finds on the site of the colony and links to online exhibits.

"Virtual Jamestown." http://www.virtualjamestown.org/. Great Web site with letters written by the colonists, the complete works of John Smith, and up-to-date information on Jamestown archaeology.

Multimedia Sources

Death at Jamestown. PBS, 2001. 1 DVD. 60 minutes. Part of PBS's *Secrets of the Dead* series, this segment postulates that the high mortality rate in Jamestown may have been due to poisoning.

Invasion of the Coast. Warner Home Studio, 1994. VHS tape. 50 minutes. Part of the *500 Nations* series. Gives the native perspective of the landing of English colonists on the Atlantic coast.

The New World: Nightmare in Jamestown. National Geographic, 2005. 1 DVD. Historical overview with heavy emphasis on the hardships of English colonists at Jamestown.

Pocahantas: Ambassador to the New World. A&E Network, 1995. 1 DVD. 50 minutes. The story of Pocahontas, who helped the Jamestown colonists survive their early months in the New World.

6. Samuel de Champlain Instigates Hostilities between New France and the Iroquois (1609)

In 1609, French explorer Samuel de Champlain sought to establish close trade ties with the Huron and Algonquin peoples of Canada. The Hurons' location on the eastern shore of Lake Huron and their role as middlemen in the fur trade made them particularly important to the French. The Hurons traded maize and European goods acquired from the French to native peoples located to their north and west. They then exchanged these furs with the French in Quebec for metal goods and woolens. However, native peoples did not look upon a trading partnership as simply trade. Being a trading partner also meant that one became a military ally as well. In the summer of 1609, Champlain accompanied a native war party to what is now Lake Champlain, bordering present-day Vermont and New York. Toward dusk one evening, the Hurons encountered an Iroquois war party. Keeping Champlain out of sight, the Huron parlayed with the Iroquois and agreed to fight at first light. The Hurons and Mohawks constructed small enclosures within shouting distance of one another and spent the night dancing and hurling insults back and forth. The next morning, each side came out of its enclosures, wearing wooden armor. On a prearranged signal, Champlain came out of hiding, marched to the front of the Hurons, and fired his musket, killing three Mohawks. The Mohawks, never having before encountered firearms, fled the field. The Hurons and Algonquins celebrated their victory. Champlain, however, created a powerful enemy, and the Iroquois would harass New France until the demise of the colony in 1763.

TERM PAPER SUGGESTIONS

1. Research the technological and tactical changes that Champlain's skirmish with the Iroquois produced in Native American warfare.
2. Discuss the advantages and disadvantages to the French of having the Hurons and other native peoples as trade partners.
3. Discuss the role of the Hurons as middlemen in the fur trade. Is "middlemen" an accurate description of the Huron, or any other Native American tribe in this period?
4. Suppose that you are Samuel de Champlain. Unlike the real Champlain, you learn that the Hurons' enemies include the Iroquois, perhaps the most powerful people in eastern North America. How would you try to get out of going on the expedition yet still save face and maintain the alliance?

ALTERNATIVE TERM PAPER SUGGESTIONS

1. It is 1609 and you are Samuel de Champlain's assistant. In the wake of Champlain's battle with the Iroquois, there is criticism that he needlessly created an enemy for New France. Champlain wants you to start a blog that justifies his

actions and "spins" Iroquois hostility as a benefit, rather than a detriment to New France.

2. You are a Huron or an Algonquin Indian in 1609. From the perspective of 1609, what do you believe that Champlain's victory over the Iroquois means for your people in the future? Remember, you are writing this from the point of view of a person in 1609 who has no idea what the future holds.

SUGGESTED SOURCES

Primary Sources

de Champlain, Samuel. *Voyages of Samuel de Champlain,* ed. W. L. Grant. New York: Scribner's, 1907. A shorter version of Champlain's writings that includes his account of the battle with the Iroquois. It is also available at Google Books.

de Champlain, Samuel. *The Works of Samuel de Champlain,* 6 vols., trans. and ed. H. H. Langton and W. F. Ganong. Toronto: The Champlain Society, 1922–1936. Also available at the Champlain Society Web site, http://www.champlainsociety.ca/. The most complete available translations of Champlain's works.

Secondary Sources

Delage, Denys. *Bitter Feast: Amerindians and Europeans in Northeastern North America, 1600–1664,* trans. Jane Brierly. Vancouver: University of British Columbia Press, 1993. Delage includes an account of Champlain's clash with the Iroquois.

Eccles, W. J. *The Canadian Frontier, 1534–1760.* Albuquerque: University of New Mexico Press, 1983. Both of Eccles's works include accounts of Champlain's battles with the Iroquois.

Eccles, W. J. *The French in North America, 1500–1783.* Rev. ed. East Lansing: Michigan State University Press, 1998. A good overview of French colonization efforts in North America that makes reference to Champlain's fight with the Iroquois.

Fischer, David Hackett. *Champlain's Dream.* New York: Simon & Schuster, 2008. A very thorough biography of Samuel de Champlain

Steele, Ian K. *Warpaths: Invasions of North America.* New York: Oxford University Press, 1994. Steele's is perhaps one of the best compact military histories of colonial North American to 1765.

World Wide Web

"'The Iroquois were much astonished that two men should have been killed so quickly': Samuel de Champlain Introduces Firearms to Native Warfare, 1609." http://historymatters.gmu.edu/d/6594. Champlain's narrative of his fight with the Iroquois.

"Samuel de Champlain." http://www.civilization.ca/cmc/index_e.aspx?ArticleID=2919. Offers a biography and summary of Champlain's explorations.

"The Significance of Samuel de Champlain for the History of New York State." http://www.emsc.nysed.gov/ciai/chf/scholar/champlainscholar.html. New York Education Department offers an analysis of the long-term effects of Champlain's confrontation with the Iroquois.

7. John Rolfe Introduces Tobacco to Virginia (1616)

For the first nine years of its existence, the Jamestown, Virginia, colony barely survived, both demographically and economically. More than 1,700 Englishmen had immigrated to the Chesapeake by 1616, yet the colony had a population of only 350, as disease and warfare claimed the lives of most of the new arrivals. Jamestown also produced little of value. The colony shipped glass, potash, and iron back to England, but these commodities could be produced in the mother country, and the colony teetered toward economic ruin.

In 1612, colonist John Rolfe arrived in Virginia with tobacco seeds he acquired in the Caribbean. The native peoples in Virginia grew tobacco, but the English deemed it too strong. The Spanish marketed tobacco from their American colonies in England and reaped immense profits.

By 1616, Rolfe had developed a strain of tobacco that yielded a sweet, gentle smoke, and Virginia had found its economic salvation. Planters began to clear enormous tracts of land to grow tobacco, and because the crop was very labor intensive, they imported thousands of indentured servants to work the fields. In 1619, the Dutch imported the first Africans to Virginia, some of them becoming slaves, others indentured servants.

In the 1620s, tobacco sold in England for about ten times what it cost to produce and transport. The demand for indentured servants also created a population boom, as Virginia grew from only 350 colonists in 1616 to nearly 1,400 by 1622.

TERM PAPER SUGGESTIONS

1. Research and explain the workings of a Chesapeake tobacco plantation. How was land converted from forest to tobacco fields? How were laborers obtained and employed?
2. Research large plantation owners such as William Byrd and Landon Carter. How did they put together their plantations? What was their effect on Virginia society?
3. Discuss the lot of indentured servants. Why did many young Englishmen (and a few women) choose indentured servitude? What were their lives like in the Chesapeake?
4. Examine how tobacco became something of a craze in England. How do you explain tobacco's appeal?

ALTERNATIVE TERM PAPER SUGGESTIONS

1. Imagine that you are a doctor in England in the 1610s or 1620s. Many physicians are writing pamphlets praising tobacco as the new wonder drug that cures nearly everything. However, you know that is not correct, and that tobacco is, in fact, harmful. Write a brief pamphlet arguing why people should not use tobacco. Keep in mind you are writing this for a seventeenth-century audience that is very fond of tobacco.
2. You are an Englishman in the early seventeenth century who wishes to establish your own tobacco plantation in Virginia. Write out a plan as to how you will go about acquiring land and laborers and how you will use them.

SUGGESTED SOURCES

Primary Sources

Beverley, Robert. *The History and Present State of Virginia,* London, 1705. Reprinted 1855 and 1947. Available at Google Books. Written at a time when tobacco was still vitally important to the Virginia economy, Beverley's is one of the earliest histories of the colony.

Tyler, Lyon Gardiner, ed. *Narratives of Early Virginia, 1606–1625.* New York: Scribner's, 1907. Also available at Google Books. Contains excerpts from primary sources, including ones that point out the importance of tobacco in the colony's economy.

Secondary Sources

Breen, T. H. *Tobacco Culture: The Mentality of the Great Tidewater Tobacco Planters on the Eve of Revolution.* Princeton, NJ: Princeton University Press, 1985. Breen looks at the lifestyles of the large Virginia planters in the eighteenth century.

Milton, Giles. *Big Chief Elizabeth: The Adventures and Fate of the First English Colonists in America.* New York: Picador, 2000. Includes a section regarding Rolfe's experiments with tobacco.

Morgan, Edmond S. *American Slavery, American Freedom: The Ordeal of Colonial Virginia.* New York: Norton, 1975. Includes a section on the tobacco boom of the 1610s and 1620s.

World Wide Web

"Dry Drunk: The Culture of Tobacco in 17th- and 18th-Century Europe." http://www.nypl.org/research/chss/spe/art/print/exhibits/drydrunk/intro.htm. Articles and illustrations regarding tobacco in seventeenth- and eighteenth-century Europe.

8. Marriage of Pocahontas and John Rolfe Ushers in a Brief Period of Peace in Virginia (1616)

From its establishment in 1607, the Jamestown colony went through a period of simmering tensions with the local Powhatan peoples that at times settled into an uneasy peace and at others flamed into a full-scale conflict. In one 1610 incident, the English attacked and destroyed a local native village. In return, the Powhatans made it hazardous for the colonists to leave their stockade at Jamestown. In 1614, the English lured Powhatan's favorite daughter, Pocahontas, aboard a ship in the James River, where the English seized her as a hostage and held her prisoner to ensure her father's good behavior. The English instructed Pocahontas in Christianity during her captivity, baptizing her and rechristening her Rebecca. She also met John Rolfe, the colonist who introduced a profitable strain of tobacco to Virginia. The two began a relationship and married in 1616. Their marriage initiated a period of peace between the English and the Powhatan people. In June 1616, Rolfe and Pocahontas arrived in England, accompanied by one of Powhatan's advisors who had orders to report on all that he saw in England. The English viewed Pocahontas as being from an "American" royal family and received her in court, and she made quite an impression on London society. While in England, Pocahontas gave birth to a son, Thomas Rolfe. In 1617, the Rolfes made ready to return to Virginia, but before the ship cleared English waters, Pocahontas fell ill, and died a few days later at age 22. She was buried at Gravesend, England.

TERM PAPER SUGGESTIONS

1. Examine Pocahontas's conversion to Christianity. Was this a sincere conversion on her part? Or did she merely do what was expected on the part of her English captors?
2. John Rolfe composed a letter (which can be found in *Narratives of Early Virginia*) regarding his feelings for Pocahontas. Why does Rolfe feel the need to justify his feelings for Pocahontas?
3. Examine Pocahontas's reception at the English court. Why were the English so fascinated with her? Did the English really think of her as "royalty"?
4. Former Virginia governor John Smith had a meeting with Pocahontas during her tour of England. What did Pocahontas seem to think of Smith and England?

ALTERNATIVE TERM PAPER SUGGESTIONS

1. It is 1617, and you are the public relations assistant to the King of England, James I. He tells you that he wants Pocahontas's visit to England to have positive coverage in the press, and he really wants you to emphasize the relationship between him and "King" Powhatan, Pocahontas's father. Compose a press release, highlighting why the alliance between the English and the Virginia Algonquians is a natural one.

2. When John Rolfe and Pocahontas traveled to England, Powhatan (Pocahontas's father) sent one of his councilors, Uttamatomakkin, with them. Uttamatomakkin was to observe the English and report back to Powhatan his impressions of England. Write a report to Powhatan based on Uttamatomakkin's probable observations.

SUGGESTED SOURCES

Primary Source

Tyler, Lyon Gardiner, ed. *Narratives of Early Virginia, 1606–1625.* New York: Scribner's, 1907. Also available at Google Books. Includes Rolfe's letter explaining his reasons for marrying Pocahontas and John Smith's account of their meeting in England.

Secondary Sources

Kupperman, Karen Ordahl. *Indians and English: Facing Off in Early America.* Ithaca, NY: Cornell University Press, 2000. Offers a discussion of Pocahontas's marriage to John Rolfe and their visit to London.

Milton, Giles. *Big Chief Elizabeth: The Adventures and Fate of the First English Colonists in America.* New York: Picador, 2000. Milton discusses John Rolfe's marriage to Pocahontas.

Mossiker, Frances. *Pocahontas: The Life and Legend.* New York: De Capo Press, 1996. Biography of Pocahontas. Compares the real life Pocahontas to the one of legend.

Rountree, Helen C. *Pocahontas, Powhatan, Opechancanough: Three Indian Lives Changed by Jamestown.* Charlottesville: University of Virginia Press, 2006. Biographical account of Pocahontas, her father, and uncle, and how the arrival of the English altered the Powhatan peoples' way of life.

Townsend, Camilla. *Pocahontas and the Powhatan Dilemma.* New York: Hill & Wang, 2004. Biographical account of Pocahontas, using written sources and a good knowledge of the traditions of the Powhatan peoples.

World Wide Web

"Pocahontas: Icon at the Crossroads of Race and Sex." http://xroads.virginia.edu/~cap/POCA/POC-home.html. Includes a timeline and links to essays about Pocahontas.

"The Pocahontas Archive." http://digital.lib.lehigh.edu/trial/pocahontas/. The most extensive Pocahontas site on the Internet. Includes images, a timeline, a bibliography, and many links to works about Pocahontas.

"Virtual Jamestown—Pocahontas (c. 1595–1617)." http://www.virtualjamestown.org/Pocahontas.html. Biography and bibliography of works about Pocahontas.

Multimedia Sources

Pocahantas: Ambassador to the New World. A&E Network, 1995. 1 DVD. 50 minutes. Tells the story of Pocahontas, her efforts to smooth relations between natives and English, and her marriage to John Rolfe. Also known as *Pocahontas: Her True Story.*

Pocahontas Revealed. PBS, 2007. 1 DVD. 50 minutes. This site at http://www.pbs.org/wgbh/nova/pocahontas/ features images of Pocahontas and articles about archaeology at the Jamestown site.

9. Smallpox among the New England Indians Depopulates the Region (1616)

Perhaps the most important factor that enabled Europeans to eventually gain control of the Americas was disease. Separated from the rest of the world for several millennia, Native Americans lacked exposure to diseases such as smallpox. In Europe, with a population that had long experience with the disease, and thus had developed some antibodies, smallpox carried with it a mortality rate of about 30 percent. In North America, however, the native population had no prior exposure to the disease, and they experienced a mortality rate in excess of 90 percent. One of the most significant early disease epidemics took place in New England.

In 1604, French mariner Samuel de Champlain explored the region of present-day Cape Cod. Champlain's report and his map of the area show a region densely populated by native people, with many villages and cornfields. Some of Champlain's men were killed in an altercation with the natives over the ownership of an iron pot. Champlain's report on Cape Cod claimed that there were too many Indians in the region, and that any colony established there would have little success.

However, in 1620, English Separatists (Pilgrims) landed in the same area and found a land that had been almost totally depopulated. What had happened to the native population? In the years since Champlain, English fishermen often went ashore at Cape Cod to dry their catch. While they were ashore, they also traded with Native Americans, unwittingly passing pathogens (disease-causing organisms) on to them. Squanto, the Indian who assisted the Pilgrims, had been kidnapped by an English sea captain. When he returned to New England, he found that all of his people were dead. In some respects, the fate of native people in southern New England is the most dramatic example of the biological exchange between Europe and North America.

TERM PAPER SUGGESTIONS

1. Why were Native Americans so susceptible to European diseases? What accounted for the differing responses of native people and Europeans to pathogens such as smallpox?
2. Alfred Crosby used the term "Columbian Exchange" as a means of expressing that the trading (often unwittingly) of plants, animals, and pathogens was an interhemispheric phenomenon. Examine this idea and its effects beyond disease.
3. Native Americans did not live in a disease-free paradise and had their own share of maladies. What diseases did Amerindians pass on to Europeans?
4. Examine the native response to European diseases. Did Native American treatments help or harm a patient?
5. What would have been the long-term consequences to European colonization of the Americas if native people possessed immunity to Old World diseases?

ALTERNATIVE TERM PAPER SUGGESTIONS

1. It is 1620 and you have landed at Cape Cod with the Pilgrims. While exploring the area, the Pilgrims discover abandoned, deteriorating wigwams and unharvested fields of maize. Not recognizing how diseases work, the Pilgrims place you in charge of making sure a plague does not break out among them. What steps would you take as a public health officer to keep the Pilgrims healthy?

SUGGESTED SOURCES

Primary Sources

Bradford, William. *Bradford's History of Plymouth Plantation, 1606–1646,* ed. William T. Davis. New York: Scribner's, 1908. Contains suppositions that there had been some sort of epidemic among the natives. Also available at Google Books.

Heath, Dwight, ed. *Mourt's Relation: A Journal of the Pilgrims at Plymouth.* Carlisle, MA: Applewood Books, 1986. *Mourt's Relation* is a journal of the Pilgrims' first year at Plymouth, originally published in London in 1622. Edward Winslow is thought to be the author. Contains accounts of the Pilgrims' first explorations ashore.

Secondary Sources

Cook, Noble David, and W. George Lovell, eds. *"Secret Judgments of God": Old World Disease in Colonial Spanish America.* Norman: University of Oklahoma Press, 1991. Examines the effects of disease and the collapse of the Native American population.

Crosby, Alfred W., Jr. *The Columbian Exchange: Biological and Cultural Consequences of 1492.* Westport, CT: Greenwood Press, 1972. A classic in the field of early American history. Crosby was the first historian to recognize that the great biological exchange that began with Columbus's landfall is still going on today.

Crosby, Alfred W. *Ecological Imperialism: The Biological Expansion of Europe, 900–1900.* Cambridge: Cambridge University Press, 1986. A continuation of Crosby's *Columbian Exchange* that deals with biological exchanges not just in the Americas but on a global scale.

Diamond, Jared. *Guns, Germs, and Steel: The Fates of Human Societies.* New York: Norton, 1997. Diamond takes a global approach, but there is information about the Americas in his book.

Fenn, Elizabeth A. *Pox Americana: The Great Smallpox Epidemic of 1775–82.* New York: Hill & Wang, 2001. Fenn argues that North America suffered a continent-wide pandemic between 1775 and 1782. She also provides interesting information as to how smallpox was spread and treated.

Kiple, Kenneth F., and Stephen V. Beck. *Biological Consequences of the European Expansion, 1450–1800.* Brookfield, VT: Ashgate Publishing, 1997.

Contains 15 essays examining the impact of European pathogens on the Americas.

McNeil, William H. *Plagues and Peoples.* New York: Doubleday, 1977. One of the first works to examine the impact of disease on human history.

World Wide Web

"Colombian Exchange." http://daphne.palomar.edu/scrout/colexc.htm. Web site that deals with not only the exchange of diseases between hemispheres, but plants and animals as well.

10. Dutch Import the First African Slaves to Jamestown, Virginia (1620)

Virginia's tobacco boom of the 1610s forced planters to confront a labor shortage, a problem virtually unheard of in England. Virginia had plenty of land but lacked the hands to put all of it into production. Tobacco planters imported indentured servants, usually poor young single Englishmen, in an effort to satisfy their need for laborers, but still fell short. The Virginia Company used inducements to lure investors and servants, such as the headright system, which granted 50 acres of land to any persons who paid their own passage to North America, and an additional 50 acres for paying the way of another passenger. Additionally, servants who completed their term of indenture would be granted 50 acres. Despite these efforts, Virginia still suffered from labor shortages.

In 1619, a Dutch slave ship docked at Jamestown. The Dutch dominated the transatlantic slave trade in the early seventeenth century and imported slaves to their own sugar colonies in the Caribbean as well as those of Spain and Portugal. The English had little experience with slavery. Indeed, while the Dutch sold the twenty-odd Africans they imported to Jamestown, their English purchasers seemed uncertain as to their legal status. Some remained slaves, while others became indentured servants and eventually gained their freedom. Until the mid-seventeenth century, indentured servants continued to outnumber slaves. In the disease-ridden environment of the mid-seventeenth-century Chesapeake, most new arrivals—whether servants or slaves—seldom survived beyond five years. While purchasing a slave meant that a planter had the slaves' labor for the duration of his lifetime, the disease-ridden environment made such a purchase a poor investment.

TERM PAPER SUGGESTIONS

1. Discuss the English decision to use slavery in Chesapeake. Was this a local decision, or was it made by the British government?
2. Discuss the spread of slavery throughout the British Empire. The British had no prior experience with slavery. How did slavery spread from the sugar islands of the Caribbean, and the American South, to England?
3. Consult the book by Breen and Innes, and discuss the role of freed black people in seventeenth-century Virginia. How were they regarded by their neighbors and the colonial government?
4. Discuss the role of indentured servants in early Virginia. Why did there not seem to be enough of them to fulfill tobacco planters' need for labor?

ALTERNATIVE TERM PAPER SUGGESTIONS

1. It is 1619, and you are an English tobacco planter in the Chesapeake. Compose an editorial and argue in favor of either slaves or indentured servants. Your arguments should address the economic advantages and disadvantages of each form of labor. Do not use moral arguments. Your fellow planters would not understand them.
2. It is 1619 and you have been hired by a Dutch firm to promote the sale of slaves to Chesapeake planters. Begin a blog that promotes the supposed advantages of African over English labor. Make sure you anticipate (and respond to) some of the doubts planters may have regarding African slaves.

SUGGESTED SOURCES

Primary Sources

Equiano, Olaudah. *The Interesting Narrative of the Life of Olaudah Equiano, or Gustavus Vassa, the African. Written by Himself. Two Volumes.* London: Author, 1789. Available online at "Documenting the American South," http://docsouth.unc.edu/neh/equiano1/menu.html.

Equiano, Olaudah. *The Interesting Narrative and Other Writings.* New York: Penguin Classics, 2003. Olaudah Equiano's autobiographical work is considered one of the classic slave narratives and one of the few firsthand accounts of the middle passage written from a slave's perspective.

Tyler, Lyon Gardiner, ed. *Narratives of Early Virginia, 1606–1625.* New York: Scribner's, 1907. Also available at Google Books. Collection of extracts from primary source documents. Contains accounts of the arrivals of the first slaves to Virginia.

Secondary Sources

Berlin Ira, *Many Thousands Gone: The First Two Centuries of Slavery in North America.* Cambridge, MA: Harvard University Press, 1998. One of the best histories of slavery in America.

Breen, T. H., and Stephen Innes, *"Myne Owne Ground": Race and Freedom on Virginia's Eastern Shore, 1640–1676.* New York: Oxford University Press, 1980. Looks at free Africans, mostly former servants, who achieved freedom in mid-seventeenth-century Virginia.

Jordan, Winthrop D. *White over Black: American Attitudes toward the Negro, 1550–1812.* New York: Norton, 1968. Looks at how first colonists, then Americans, thought of slavery.

Worldwide Web

"The African American: A Journey from Slavery to Freedom." http://www.liu.edu/cwis/cwp/library/aaslavry.htm. Comprehensive Long Island University Web site that contains synopses of the Middle Passage, the advent of slavery in British North America, and the creation of Slave Codes. It also contains links to additional readings.

"Africans in America." http://www.pbs.org/wgbh/aia/home.html. Another PBS Web site that also contains many of the features found in "Slavery and the Making of America." However, it contains more detail regarding slavery in the colonial period.

"Slavery and the Making of America." http://www.pbs.org/wnet/slavery/. Companion Web site for the 2004 PBS program of the same name. Contains an overview of the history of slavery in British North America and the United States.

Multimedia Sources

Africans in America. PBS, 1998. 2 DVD. PBS series that uses historical images and interviews with leading scholars to illuminate the history of the slave trade and slavery from 1450 to 1865.

Slavery and the Making of America. PBS, 2004. 4 DVD. Using historical images and reenactments, this PBS series traces the history of slavery from 1619 to the end of the Civil War.

11. Pilgrims Establish Plymouth Bay Colony (1620)

In the 1610s, English separatists living in the Netherlands, who had fled their homeland in 1608, influenced by John Smith's *History of New England* and the map that accompanied it, decided after much debate to settle in North America. Lacking funds for such a move, they contracted with English merchants, who provided transportation in return for receiving a share of the commodities the colony would produce. The investors required the Separatists, who referred to themselves as "saints," to take other would-be colonists with them, whom they called "strangers." After surviving an uncomfortable trip on the *Mayflower,* which had remarkably few fatalities, the Separatists reached Cape Cod in November 1620. The Pilgrims spent their first month in New England aboard the *Mayflower,* sending reconnaissance parties ashore to seek a suitable spot for a settlement. In December the colonists established Plymouth on the site of a deserted Indian village and began constructing their first shelters. But over the winter, 51 of the 102 colonists perished from exposure, disease, and hunger. Fearful that the local Indians would take advantage of their weakness, the Separatists buried their dead at night in unmarked graves. In the spring, the colonists began planting crops and unexpectedly received help from the local Wampanoag peoples, who established communications with them through an English-speaking Indian named Squanto. The Wampanoag leader, Massasoit, fearful because his people had been devastated by European diseases, yet his Narragansett neighbors had not been, signed a treaty of alliance with the Separatists that endured for a half century.

TERM PAPER SUGGESTIONS

1. Examine the arguments the Separatists gave for establishing a colony in North America. Do you think their goals were unrealistic? Explain why or why not.
2. Examine the rather unusual career of Squanto. How did Squanto come to learn English and to know so much about the English? Discuss his motives for assisting the English.
3. Some scholars have argued that the foundations of American identity originated with the establishment of the New England colonies. Discuss this idea. Why would the New England colonies be "more American" than, say, colonies in Pennsylvania or the Chesapeake?
4. Discuss why the Separatists wished to leave the Netherlands. Did they have good reason to leave, in your view?
5. The voyage of the *Mayflower* has assumed a prominent place in American history, but also a certain mythology has grown around it. Examine the voyage of the *Mayflower* and the stories associated with it.

ALTERNATIVE TERM PAPER SUGGESTIONS

1. It is 1621, and the new governor of the colony, William Bradford, has appointed you to be Plymouth's "Blogger in Chief." Your mission is to establish a blog, informing people in England about how well the colony is doing. However, you must make the colony very appealing to the separatists' co-religionists, while minimizing its appeal to other denominations.
2. You are a Quaker, newly arrived in Plymouth Bay Colony. Because of your religious affiliation, the Separatists make it very clear that you are not welcome. Establish a blog that gives your side of the story to people back in England.

SUGGESTED SOURCES

Primary Sources

Bradford, William, *Bradford's History of Plymouth Plantation, 1606–1646,* ed. William T. Davis. NY: Scribner's, 1908. Also available at Google Books. Written by the governor of the Plymouth Colony for most of its first three decades, Bradford's *History* is a key primary source.

Heath, Dwight, ed. *Mourt's Relation: A Journal of the Pilgrims at Plymouth.* Carlisle, MA: Applewood Books, 1986. *Mourt's Relation* is a journal of the Pilgrims' first year at Plymouth, originally published in London in 1622. Edward Winslow is thought to be the author.

Secondary Sources

Deetz, James, and Patricia Scott. *The Times of Their Lives: Life, Love & Death in Plymouth Colony.* New York: W. H. Freeman, 2000. Examines aspects of everyday life in Plymouth Colony.

Demos, John. *A Little Commonwealth: Family Life in Plymouth Colony.* New York: Oxford University Press, 1970. Demos's study examines family life and society in Plymouth Colony.

Langdon, George D. *Pilgrim Colony: A History of New Plymouth.* New Haven, CT: Yale University Press, 1966. A history of Plymouth from its 1620 founding to the dissolution of the colony in 1691.

Philbrick, Nathanial. *Mayflower: A Story of Courage, Community, and War.* New York: Viking, 2006. Covers the history of the Separatists from the time they left England for Holland, describes their voyage to New England, and ends with King Philip's War in the 1670s.

World Wide Web

"Pilgrim Hall Museum." http://www.pilgrimhall.org/. A museum in Plymouth, Massachusetts, that has the largest repository of items used by the Pilgrims. It also contains links to many sites.

"Plimoth Plantation." http://www.plimoth.org/. Web site for Plimoth Plantation, a living history museum that recreates the first Pilgrim village located in Plymouth, Massachusetts.

"The Plymouth Colony Archive Project." http://www.histarch.uiuc.edu/plymouth/index.html. Contains links to primary source documents, as well as scholarly articles. Much of the scholarship on this site focuses on the material culture of Plymouth Colony.

Multimedia Sources

Desperate Crossing: The Untold Story of the Mayflower. The History Channel, 2006. 1 DVD. 133 minutes. Uses original illustrations and reenactments to tell the story of the Pilgrim's voyage to North America.

Invasion of the Coast. Warner Home Studio, 1994. VHS tape. 50 minutes. Part of the *500 Nations* series. Gives the native perspective of the landing of English colonists on the Atlantic coast.

The Mayflower Pilgrims. Janson Media, 2003. 1 DVD. 43 minutes. Uses reenactments and on location footage to tell the story of the Pilgrims.

12. Opechancanough and the Virginia-Powhatan War (1622)

In1618, Powhatan, the leader of the Indian confederacy that bore his name, died. Leadership of the Powhatan confederacy passed to his half-brother or uncle (the sources vary) named Opechancanough. At the time, Virginia and the Powhatans enjoyed a peaceful relationship that began when the English seized Powhatan's favorite daughter Pocahontas as a hostage, and solidified it even further when English colonist John Rolfe married her following her conversion to Christianity. However Opechancanough—who had once been taken prisoner by John Smith, the leader of the Jamestown colony—nursed resentments toward the English, but maintained the pretense that he would uphold the peace. Realizing the English needed more land to grow tobacco, Opechancanough invited them to take any lands further inland, knowing that they would establish scattered plantations, which would be more difficult to defend. In March 1622, the Powhatan Confederacy launched a devastating attack against Virginia, killing 347 Englishmen, or about a quarter of the colony's population, in a single day.

The survivors fled to the safety of Jamestown. After recovering from the initial shock, the English realized that they now had justification to exterminate the Indians. Launching attacks against Indian villages, the English had a great deal of success. At one point, they proposed a "peace" but poisoned the 200 or so Indians who showed up for the conference. Opechancanough, however, did not attend this meeting and continued to wage war against Virginia for another decade. In 1632, the Powhatans signed a peace agreement that forced them to surrender thousands of acres, opening more land to English settlement.

TERM PAPER SUGGESTIONS

1. Examine relations between the Powhatans and the English colonists. How did Opechancanough's approach to the English differ from that of Powhatan?
2. Discuss the dispersion of the Virginia colony. Why were the colonists taken in by Opechancanough? Why did they not anticipate or prepare for an attack by the Powhatans?

3. Could the Virginia-Powhatan War be considered a template for later wars between Native Americans and European colonists? In which way was this war similar to and different from other conflicts between natives and Europeans?
4. Examine the English reaction to the Powhatan attack. After they got over the initial shock, the English were elated that they now had just cause to exterminate the Indians. What does it tell us that the English were thinking in terms of extermination and not simply winning the war?
5. Discuss the long-term implications of the Powhatan attack on the Virginia colony. Did Opechancanough have good reason to believe that he could defeat the colony in 1622?

ALTERNATIVE TERM PAPER SUGGESTIONS

1. You are a Powhatan Indian in Virginia in 1622. People in England are aghast at the uprising in Virginia. Opechancanough has given you the job of starting a blog, aimed at convincing the English that the Indians' attack on the colonists was justified.
2. In the wake of Opechancanough's attack, you have been appointed the military commander of Virginia. Draft a plan showing how you plan to defeat Opechancanough.

SUGGESTED SOURCES

Primary Source

Tyler, Lyon Gardiner, ed. *Narratives of Early Virginia, 1606–1625.* New York: Scribner's 1907. Also available at Google Books. Extracts from primary sources dealing with the early history of Virginia, including the 1622 Indian war.

Secondary Sources

Axtell, James. "The Rise and Fall of the Powhatan Empire." In *After Columbus: Essays in the Ethnohistory of Colonial North America.* New York: Oxford University Press, 1988. Essay that traces the history of the Powhatan confederacy from their first contacts with the English to the 1644 war.

Gleach, Frederic W. *Powhatan's World and Colonial Virginia: A Conflict of Cultures.* Lincoln: University of Nebraska Press, 1997. Examines the contacts between the English and the Powhatans.

Rountree, Helen C. *Pocahontas's People: The Powhatan Indians of Virginia through Four Centuries.* Norman: University of Oklahoma Press, 1990. A history of the Powhatan people from the seventeenth century to the present.

Rountree, Helen C. *Pocahontas, Powhatan, Opechancanough: Three Indian Lives Changed by Jamestown.* Charlottesville: University of Virginia Press, 2006. Seventeenth-century Powhatan history wrapped around the lives of three key individuals.

Rountree, Helen C. *The Powhatan Indians of Virginia: Their Traditional Culture.* Norman: University of Oklahoma Press, 1989. A cultural history of the Powhatans.

World Wide Web

"The Anglo-Powhatan Wars." http://www.virginiaplaces.org/nativeamerican/anglopowhatan.html. Overview of the Anglo-Powhatan wars of 1622 and 1644.

"The Tyme Appointed." http://www.history.org/Foundation/journal/Autumn05/tyme.cfm. Very detailed article regarding Opechancanough's attacks of Virginia.

Multimedia Source

Pocahontas Revealed. PBS, 2007. 1 DVD. 50 minutes. History of the Powhatans and Jamestown, using archaeology, historical images, and reenactments.

13. Dutch Establish American Colonies at New Amsterdam and Fort Orange (1626)

After Henry Hudson's 1609 exploration of the river that now bears his name, the Dutch established a fur trading post at Fort Nassau, later named Fort Orange (present day Albany, New York) in 1614. Fort Orange had only about 50 Dutchmen, mostly traders and soldiers, in its early years. Fearing that either the English or the French could easily sail up the Hudson River and seize Fort Orange and its store of furs, the Dutch established the port of New Amsterdam on Manhattan Island (present-day New York City) to defend the entrance to the mouth of the river. The Dutch faced severe difficulties in attracting colonists. The Netherlands was the economic powerhouse of seventeenth-century Europe, and young people there had far more attractive options than going to the wilds of North America to make their fortunes. Needing a sizable population of farmers in the vicinity of New Amsterdam to feed the colony, the Dutch offered colonists a number of incentives, but few Dutchmen came.

In the vicinity of Fort Orange, the Dutch dealt with the Mohawks, the easternmost of the powerful Iroquois League as their primary trading partners. Around New Amsterdam, the Dutch forced smaller, weaker groups of Algonquians to move. The Dutch West India Company controlled the colony and attracted few colonists. However, they were somewhat more successful after they allowed individual colonists to enter into the fur trade. One of the most diverse colonies in North America, New Netherland became something of a haven for religious dissidents, attracting a good number of English colonists dissatisfied with New England's theocracy.

TERM PAPER SUGGESTIONS

1. Compare and contrast Dutch colonization efforts with those of the English, French, and Spanish. Why did the Dutch have a difficult time attracting colonists? Is there something they could have done differently?
2. Discuss the differences between Fort Orange and New Amsterdam in dealing with Native Americans. What accounts for these differences between the two Dutch outposts?
3. While other European colonizers seem to place a great deal of importance on their colonies in the Americas, the Dutch seem to have treated theirs almost as an afterthought. Why did the Netherlands not pour more resources into their North American colonies?
4. The Dutch West India Company attempted at first to monopolize the fur trade in New Netherland, but quickly gave up on this and threw the trade open to individual colonists. Why did the Dutch West India Company do this?

ALTERNATIVE TERM PAPER SUGGESTIONS

1. The Dutch West India Company has hired you to head their advertising department. The company is having difficulty attracting settlers and employees for its venture in North America. Your job is to write scripts for a series of

television commercials designed to persuade young people in the Netherlands to settle in North America or to come to work for the West India Company.

2. The Dutch West India Company has just given large investors (called Patroons) enormous land grants in North America. For these Patroons to realize a profit, they do not intend to sell the land, but to rent it out to would-be colonists. Your job, as the public relations person for the company, is to design a series of ads, aimed at young people in the Netherlands, extolling the virtues of renting land in America, as opposed to owning it or pursuing opportunities elsewhere in the Dutch commercial empire.

SUGGESTED SOURCES

Primary Source

Jameson, J. Franklin, ed. *Narratives of New Netherland, 1609–1664.* New York: Scribner's, 1909. Extracts from primary documents dealing with New Netherland. Also available at Google Books.

Secondary Sources

Rink, Oliver A. *Holland on the Hudson: An Economic and Social History of Dutch New York.* Ithaca, NY: Cornell University Press, 1992. A history of Dutch society in New Netherland.

Shorto, Russell. *The Island at the Center of the World: The Epic Story of Dutch Manhattan, the Forgotten Colony that shaped America.* New York: Vintage Books, 2005. Emphasizes the importance of New Netherland in the context of the Dutch commercial empire.

World Wide Web

"The New Netherland Museum and the Half Moon." http://www.newnetherland.org/. The New Netherland Museum is located in Albany, New York. Site contains links to documents and a brief history of New Netherland.

"The New Netherland Project." http://www.nnp.org/. The New Netherland Project translates, transcribes, and publishes seventeenth-century Dutch documents in the New York state archives.

Multimedia Source

The Dutch Frontier. Ambrose, 2000. 1 DVD. 30 minutes. Episode four of the *America: Discovery to Revolution* series. Examines the history of

New Netherland from Henry Hudson's explorations in 1609 to the seizure of the colony in 1664 by the English.

14. English Puritans Begin Their "Great Migration" and Establish Massachusetts Bay Colony (1630)

A decade after the Pilgrims founded Plymouth Colony, a larger contingent of English Puritans began what came to be known as the "Great Migration," a decade-long process that saw Massachusetts Bay Colony become one of England's most important overseas possessions. Wealthier and better organized than the Plymouth colonists, the Puritans learned much about New England from the writings of John Smith and their religious brethren already in the region. Believing England beyond redemption and destined to be punished by God, many Puritans liquidated their immovable property and immigrated to North America, sometimes as entire church congregations and villages. In his departure sermon abroad the *Arabella,* their leader, John Winthrop, outlined the Puritan goal of establishing a "City on a Hill," an earthly example for the world of a model godly community.

The Puritans had the advantage of being able to transport most of their wealth to North America, and they brought with them enough supplies to establish their colony. Nevertheless, they suffered though a hungry winter in 1630–1631. However, the colony quickly recovered and expanded inland rapidly, as new immigrants continued to arrive before the Great Migration ended in 1640. Adjacent to Plymouth Colony, Massachusetts occupied far more land, and its geographic location hemmed in and halted the expansion of the older colony.

The Massachusetts colony would not remain intact, however. While the Puritans sought to worship outside the confines of the Anglican Church in England, their movement fractured in New England, leading to the founding of the colonies of Rhode Island and Connecticut.

TERM PAPER SUGGESTIONS

1. Analyze and explain the Puritan's unhappiness with the Church of England.

2. While many Puritans went to North America, many did not. What were their motives for remaining in England?
3. While the Puritans migrated to the same region of North America as did the Pilgrims, their migration went much more smoothly and was far better organized. Explain how this came about.
4. The Puritans viewed their migration to North America as "an errand into the wilderness" where they would create a shining example for the rest of the world that John Winthrop referred to as "A City on the Hill." Did they achieve this? Or did the rest of the world simply not care?

ALTERNATIVE TERM PAPER SUGGESTIONS

1. You are a Puritan writer in seventeenth-century New England. You have been given a time machine that will let you travel to the early twenty-first century. Your task is to write a blog, trying to convince present-day Americans to come with you back to colonial New England. You have to make it sound good, but remember, you must always be truthful.
2. It is 1640, and John Winthrop, the governor of Massachusetts Bay Colony, is troubled that migration to the colony has slowed to a trickle. Winthrop has dispatched you to England to start an ad campaign to convince people to move to Massachusetts. If you wish, you can change this assignment by arriving in England, finding that you like it much better than Massachusetts, and you can start an ad campaign trying to convince New Englanders to return to England. Of course, your boss, John Winthrop, is going to be really angry with you!

SUGGESTED SOURCES

Primary Source

Winthrop, John. *Winthrop's Journal, "History of New England" 1630–1649.* Ed. James Kendall Hosmer. 2 vols. New York: Scribner's, 1908. The journal of Puritan leader John Winthrop. Also available on Google Books.

Secondary Sources

Anderson, Virginia DeJohn. *New England's Generation: The Great Migration and the Formation of Society and Culture in the Seventeenth Century.* New York: Cambridge University Press, 1991. Examines the migration and the creation of a Puritan society in New England.

Bremer, Francis J. *John Winthrop: America's Forgotten Founding Father.* New York: Oxford University Press, 2003. Biography of Puritan leader John Winthrop that includes a substantial section on the Great Migration.

Cressy, David. *Coming Over: Migration and Communication Between England and New England in the Seventeenth Century.* New York: Cambridge University Press, 1987. Deals with the Great Migration and the importance of English ties to the colonists.

World Wide Web

"Greatmigration.org. A Survey of New England, 1620–1640." http://www.greatmigration.org/index.html. Seeks to provide an accounting of every person who immigrated to New England between 1620 and 1640.

"Pilgrims and Puritans: Background." http://xroads.virginia.edu/~CAP/PURITAN/purhist.html. Explains the differences in religious views between Pilgrims and Puritans.

"Puritanism in New England." http://www.wsu.edu/~campbelld/amlit/purdef.htm. Offers a good outline of the beliefs of Puritans and of the government of the New England colonies.

Multimedia Source

The Puritan Frontier. Ambrose, 2000. 1 DVD. 30 minutes. Uses illustrations, narration, and reenactments to tell the story of the Great Migration and the Puritans of Massachusetts.

15. France Regains Quebec and Jesuits Attempt to Convert Native Americans (1632)

In 1608, French navigator Samuel de Champlain established Quebec as the first permanent French outpost in North America. Twenty years later, in 1628, English privateers sailed up the St. Lawrence River and forced the lightly populated colony to surrender. Four years later, in 1632, the English returned Quebec to France.

When France regained Canada, Cardinal Richelieu, regent for King Louis XIV, directed that only the Jesuit order could send missionaries among the native peoples of North America. Richelieu based his decision on the failure of the Recollects (a French offshoot of the Franciscan order) to convert significant numbers of New France's natives in the 1620s. The Recollects had little success among the Montagnais peoples, and one of them, Gabriel Sagard, attempted, without success, to convert the Hurons.

Well financed and educated, the Jesuits had several advantages over the Recollects, including extensive training in missionary work. The Jesuits also made the decision that it would be best to first convert Native Americans to Christianity. Unlike the English Puritans who attempted to convert native people to Christianity and English culture in their praying towns, the Jesuits decided the process of "civilizing" the natives could wait.

Remarkably (but not uniformly) successful as missionaries, the Jesuits converted large numbers of natives. However, the Jesuits also faced hostility, often being accused of being demons, particularly when European diseases devastated native communities. On the other hand, examples of Jesuit stoicism such as that of Isaac Jogues, who survived capture and torture by the Iroquois, greatly impressed the natives.

TERM PAPER SUGGESTIONS

1. Discuss the conversion strategies employed by the Jesuits. Which ones seem to have worked and which ones did not? Discuss why certain strategies worked and why others failed.
2. Discuss native opposition to the Jesuits. Discuss the role of native shamans in opposing the Jesuits and their teachings.
3. Why did the French decide to send missionaries to New France rather than large numbers of colonists? Compare the French colonization strategy to that of the English.
4. Discuss the Jesuits and their thoughts regarding Puritan missionaries in New England.

ALTERNATIVE TERM PAPER SUGGESTIONS

1. You are a Jesuit missionary in New France. The natives have a number of questions for you. One of their questions is that they do not understand the difference between Jesuit missions (Catholic) and New England Praying Towns (Puritans). Keep in mind that, when you explain the difference, your

faith must appear more viable than the Puritans'. However, also keep in mind that you cannot lie.

2. You are a Jesuit missionary in New France. In a letter to France, discuss how you use elements of European culture or technology to awe Native Americans into listening to your sermons.

SUGGESTED SOURCES

Primary Sources

Sagard, Gabriel. *Sagard's Long Journey to the Country of the Hurons,* trans. and ed. George M. Wrong. Toronto: The Champlain Society, 1939. Sagard was a Recollect (not a Jesuit) who was one of the first missionaries to the Hurons, working among them in the 1620s. Available from the Champlain Society at http://www.champlainsociety.ca/. Click on the button labeled "Champlain Society Digital Archives" and browse for authors.

Thwaites, Reuben Gold, ed. *The Jesuit Relations and Allied Documents: Travels and Explorations of the Jesuit Missionaries in New France, 1610–1791.* 73 vols. Cleveland: Burrow's Brothers, 1896–1901. While they are rather extensive, *The Jesuit Relations* are the best source concerning the Jesuits and their missions, and one of the best concerning Native American culture in this period. The last two volumes comprise the index. Almost the entire *Jesuit Relations* are available at the Internet Archive at www.archive.org. The entire set is available at Early Canada Online at http://www.collectionscanada.gc.ca/jesuit-relations/index-e.html and in full text format from Creighton University at http://puffin.creighton .edu/jesuit/relations/.

Secondary Sources

Axtell, James. *The Invasion Within: The Contest of Cultures in Colonial North America.* New York: Oxford University Press, 1985. Axtell examines the collision of cultures and deals with the influence of the Jesuits extensively.

Delage, Denys. *Bitter Feast: Amerindians and Europeans in Northeastern North America, 1600–1664.* Vancouver: University of British Columbia Press, 1993. A history of native peoples and Europeans, including the Jesuits, in seventeenth-century North America.

Parkman, Francis. *The Jesuits in North America in the Seventeenth Century.* Boston: Little, Brown & Co., 1867. Very readable account. Although Parkman admired the Jesuits' courage, his anti-Catholic tendencies sometimes appear in this volume.

World Wide Web

"How Stuff Works Video Center: French Jesuit Missionaries." http://videos.howstuffworks.com/hsw/5367-colonial-frontier-french-jesuit-missionaries-video.htm. Brief video about the Jesuits and the settlement of New France.

"The Jesuit Relations and the History of New France." http://www.collectionscanada.gc.ca/jesuit-relations/index-e.html. Online collection from the Library and Archives Canada/Bibliothèque et Archives Canada. Places the Jesuit Relations online, including Reuben Gold Thwaites's translations. Includes essays on a number of topics such as exploration and missionary efforts among native people.

"Native American Nations: The Jesuits in North America in the Seventeenth Century." http://www.nanations.com/jesuits_in_north_america.htm. Contains summaries of Jesuit contacts with various native peoples, and excerpts from their writings.

Multimedia Source

Black Robe. MGM, 1991. 1 DVD. One hour, 41 minutes. While *Black Robe* is a fictional tale, many incidents from the *Jesuit Relations* find their way into the film. The film does have some problems, particularly when dealing with aspects of Iroquois culture.

16. Maryland Is Established as a Haven for English Catholics (1634)

In 1632, King Charles I, the titular head of the Church of England, but suspected by many to be a closet Catholic, awarded Cecilius Calvert, better known as Lord Baltimore, some 12 million acres north of the Potomac River. Charles I did this to reward Lord Baltimore, who had been a loyal political supporter of the king during his battles with Parliament. Baltimore, whose political career came to an end in the 1620s as a result of his conversion to Catholicism, had long been seeking a refuge for his fellow English

Catholics. Baltimore did consider starting a colony in Newfoundland in the 1620s, but spending the winter of 1628 there disabused him of the notion that it would be suitable as the site of a settlement.

In 1634, Leonard Calvert, Lord Baltimore's younger brother, set out with two shiploads of colonists, both Catholic and Protestant. Baltimore's hope was that the colony would demonstrate that Catholics and Protestants could live in harmony. However, from the beginning most of the colonists were not Catholics, but Protestants. A good number of colonists did not even emigrate from England. Many were colonists from Virginia who moved north of the Potomac, seeking better lands for growing tobacco. Land was a primary incentive to go to Maryland, and Lord Baltimore, compared with other colonial proprietors, was exceedingly generous. Colonists who brought five adult males with them could receive 1,000 acres. Families could receive 100 acres for each spouse and an additional 50 for each child.

TERM PAPER SUGGESTIONS

1. Examine religious strife in England in the 1620s and 1630s. Was creating a Catholic colony actually a viable solution?
2. Examine the settlement of Maryland. Was the colony successful? Did it succeed as a haven for English Catholics?
3. Compare the "headright" systems of Maryland and Virginia. What were the significant differences between the two systems? Which one was a better deal for new colonists?
4. Why would Maryland draw colonists from Virginia? Tobacco was the primary economic activity in both colonies. Why would Virginians go to Maryland to grow tobacco?

ALTERNATIVE TERM PAPER SUGGESTIONS

1. You are an English Protestant, and you have chosen to immigrate to Maryland. Your friends and family want to know why you have chosen to go to the "Catholic colony." Construct an argument as to why Maryland is a better choice for you than either Virginia or New England.
2. You are an English Catholic, and you are going to immigrate to Maryland. However, once aboard ship, you discover that there are a number of Protestants on board and, like you, they are bound for Maryland. You are upset

because you thought this was going to be a Catholic colony. Compose a letter of protest to Lord Baltimore.

SUGGESTED SOURCES

Primary Sources

Archives of Maryland Online. http://www.msa.md.gov/megafile/msa/speccol/sc2900/sc2908/html/volumes.html. Tremendous resource. Digitized version of the colonial Maryland archive.

Hall, Clayton Colman, ed. *Narratives of Early Maryland, 1633–1684.* New York: Scribner's, 1910. Available at Google Books and the Internet Archive at www.archive.org. Collection of primary sources dealing with early Maryland.

Secondary Sources

Carr, Lois Green, Russell R. Menard, and Lorena S. Walsh. *Robert Cole's World: Agriculture and Society in Early Maryland.* Chapel Hill: University of North Carolina Press, 1991. Using the life of colonist Robert Cole as a template, the authors reconstruct life in colonial Maryland.

Main, Gloria L. *Tobacco Colony: Life in Early Maryland, 1650–1720.* Princeton University Press, 1982. Examines the tobacco culture of Maryland.

World Wide Web

Historic St. Mary's City. http://www.stmaryscity.org/. Web site for the first capital of Maryland. Includes a history of Maryland as well as links to articles about the Calvert family and archaeology in St. Mary's City. Historic St. Mary's City also has a living history museum.

17. Roger Williams Is Expelled from Massachusetts for His Dissenting Religious Views and Founds the Colony of Rhode Island (1636)

Arriving in Massachusetts in 1631, Roger Williams, a friend of Massachusetts Governor John Winthrop, did not share more orthodox Puritan notions that the roles of church and state should be combined. Williams became perhaps the first person in American history to argue for the concept of the separation of church and state, arguing that the power of the state extended to the physical beings of humans and their property, and that the church profaned the sacred when it entered into the secular sphere. In particular, Williams disagreed with the notion that secular authorities should enforce church laws, including those regarding attendance and financial support. Williams also ran afoul of the Massachusetts authorities when he argued that the colony had no legal standing to appropriate Native American lands. Fed up with Williams, Massachusetts Governor John Winthrop made plans to deport him to England in the winter of 1636. Williams fled to the Narragansett people who sheltered him and some of his followers for the winter. In the spring of 1636, Williams purchased land from the Indians that would become Providence, the capital of the new colony of Rhode Island. Rhode Island developed a reputation for being the contrarian colony, becoming the last to ratify the Articles of Confederation, the governing document of the United States during and in the years immediately after the American Revolution. It later became the only one of the original 13 states not to send a representative to the Constitutional Convention and was the last state to ratify the Constitution.

TERM PAPER SUGGESTIONS

1. Examine the issues surrounding Roger Williams's planned expulsion from Massachusetts. Why did the colonial authorities regard Williams's ideas as threatening to the colony?
2. Williams is sometimes identified as the first person to argue for the separation of church and state. Is this an accurate assessment? Would we agree with Williams's argument today, or was it one that could only be applicable to his place and time?
3. Williams went to great lengths to protect Native American land rights in colonial New England. Yet his advocacy of Native American rights did not spare Rhode Island during King Philip's War in the 1670s. Why did Native Americans not differentiate between Rhode Island and the other New England colonies?
4. Could Williams be considered a Puritan? He ran afoul of other Puritan clergy, yet, like them, he opposed the attempts of the Quakers to enter New England in the latter part of the seventeenth century.

ALTERNATIVE TERM PAPER SUGGESTIONS

1. It is 1636 and Massachusetts Governor John Winthrop has asked you to "talk some sense" into Roger Williams. What sort of arguments would you use to convince Williams that in Massachusetts, church and state should be one and the same?
2. It is 1636, and you are a follower of Roger Williams. Start a blog explaining why you support him and why you oppose the authorities of Massachusetts.

SUGGESTED SOURCES

Primary Sources

Williams, Roger. *The Complete Writings of Roger Williams.* Ed. Perry Miller. 7 vols. New York: Russell & Russell, 1964. The complete writings of Roger Williams.

Williams, Roger. *The Correspondence of Roger Williams.* Ed. Glenn W. LaFantasie. Providence, RI: Brown University Press/Rhode Island Historical Society, 1988. The correspondence of Rhode Island's founder.

Secondary Sources

Daniels, Bruce C. *Dissent and Conformity on Narragansett Bay: The Colonial Rhode Island Town.* Middletown, CT: Wesleyan University Press, 1983. A history of Rhode Island that includes its contrarian tradition.

Gaustad, Edwin S. *Roger Williams.* New York: Oxford University Press, 2005. Recent biography of Roger Williams.

James, Sidney V. *Colonial Rhode Island: A History.* New York: Scribner's, 1975. History of Rhode Island from its founding by Roger Williams to the American Revolution.

Miller, Perry. *Roger Williams: His Contribution to the American Tradition.* Indianapolis, IN: Bobbs-Merrill, 1953. Older biography of Williams by one of the twentieth century's most prominent historians of New England.

World Wide Web

Roger Williams Family Association. http://www.rogerwilliams.org/. Organization for descendants of Roger Williams but includes a biography and information regarding the founding of Providence and the settlement of Rhode Island.

18. Harvard College Is Established (1636)

In 1636, Massachusetts established Harvard College to train their next generation of Puritan clerics. Taking its name from John Harvard who willed the institution his library, the college's primary mission was to stock New England's pulpits with ministers. The first Harvard students studied Latin, Greek, Hebrew, and theology. After 1650, the college offered courses in literature and the sciences. Perhaps the adding of these additional courses was a little too much for some Puritans. Connecticut Puritans, fearful that Harvard was too liberal, founded Yale College in 1718, when Elihu Yale contributed some goods, books, and a portrait of George I to the college.

For the most part, colonial colleges focused on training clergy. They infused their curriculums with theology and trained students in classical philosophy. In nearly every region of Colonial America, the colleges reflected the will of the dominant church. Thus in New England, Harvard and Yale focused on training Puritan clergy. William & Mary, established in 1693 in Virginia, focused on training Anglican clergy, but attracted few students from the northern colonies. In 1754, another Anglican institution, King's College (later Columbia University), was established in New York City. While the curriculum was very similar to Harvard and Yale, the institution's theological emphasis was understandably different.

More colleges would be established in British North America in the wake of the eighteenth-century religious upheaval known as the Great Awakening. Nearly all of them would be founded by different religious denominations.

TERM PAPER SUGGESTIONS

1. Why did colleges emphasize teaching theology from a particular religious perspective? Did any of the colonial colleges allow some leeway in this regard? Which ones, and why?
2. Graduates of Anglican institutions (such as William & Mary and King's College) tended not to enter the ministry. What were the reasons for this?
3. Colleges formed in the wake of the Great Awakening—such as the College of Rhode Island (now Brown) and King's College (now Columbia)—had a religious affiliation and mission. The College of Philadelphia (now the

University of Pennsylvania), however, had a secular mission. What accounted for this difference between the College of Philadelphia and other colleges founded in the same period?

ALTERNATIVE TERM PAPER SUGGESTIONS

1. It is 1700 and you are living in New York. The governor of the colony knows you are a smart person, so he calls you up and gives you the job of founding a new college. He instructs you that it cannot be anything like the Puritan colleges in New England, nor can it be too Anglican, since New York has a fairly diverse population. He wants you to prepare a PowerPoint presentation that outlines the proposed curriculum. Good luck!
2. It is 1636, and you are a young person in Massachusetts. Harvard College is recruiting its first class and you have chosen to apply. Compose a well-written application essay for the college. Point out how you, the colony, and, of course, the Congregational Church will benefit from a Harvard education.

SUGGESTED SOURCES

Primary Source

New England's First Fruits. New York: Reprinted for Joseph Sabin, 1865. Available at Google Books. Reprint of an anonymously authored 1636 pamphlet that called for the establishment of a college in Massachusetts.

Secondary Sources

Axtell, James. *The School upon a Hill: Education and Society in Colonial New England.* New Haven: Yale University Press, 1974. Examines formal and informal education in colonial New England, including Harvard.

Cremin, Lawrence A. *American Education: The Colonial Experience, 1607–1783.* New York: HarperCollins, 1972. Addresses the development of educational institutions in the colonies, the role of religion, and the role of the various Christian denominations in founding many of the first colleges and universities in what would become the United States.

World Wide Web

"Colonial Colleges: The First Five." http://www.suite101.com/article.cfm/5871/78837. Article about the founding of Harvard, William & Mary, Yale,

Princeton, The College of Philadelphia (University of Pennsylvania), and Columbia.

19. Pequot War (1637)

In 1637, Indians killed two English traders on the Mystic River in southeastern Connecticut. Puritan authorities accused the Pequots, who lived at the mouth of the Connecticut and Mystic Rivers and controlled the wampum trade, of committing the murders. Made from whelk's shells and highly valued by inland native peoples, wampum became the medium of exchange in the New England fur trade. The New England colonies demanded that the Pequot surrender large quantities of wampum, turn over some children as hostages, and give up the murderers of the traders. The Pequot refused, asserting they did not commit the murders. The New England colonies declared war on the Pequot, and sought native allies for the conflict. The powerful Narragansetts sided with the English, as did the Mohegans.

In May 1637, New English soldiers, backed by their native allies, attacked the Pequot's major village on the Mystic River. The English set the village on fire, shooting down any Pequot who attempted to escape. The savagery of the English assault horrified their native allies, who claimed the English mode of war killed too many men, leaving few people to be absorbed as captives. The Puritans' Native American allies adopted most of the Pequot women and children who survived the attack. The Puritans sold the men into slavery and deported them to the West Indies. New England clergymen celebrated their victory over the Pequot. However, Puritans in England harshly criticized their New England brethren, arguing that more should have been done to Christianize the Indians instead of killing them.

TERM PAPER SUGGESTIONS

1. While the stated aims of the English were to punish the Pequots for the murder of the English traders, what other motives would the English have had for warring against the Pequots?

2. Examine the motives of the Native American leaders Uncas and Miantonomo. Why did they choose to side with the English against another group of native people?
3. Explain the differing attitudes of Puritans in England and Puritans in New England regarding the outcome of the Pequot war. What accounted for these differences?
4. The Pequot War represents a departure for New England colonists. For the most part, their relations with native peoples had been friendly since 1620. What caused the New England colonists to change their policies, at least regarding the Pequot?

ALTERNATIVE TERM PAPER SUGGESTIONS

1. It is 1637 and the Pequot War has just ended. Puritans in England have read accounts of the war and are very critical of the unchristian manner in which the New England colonists behaved. Massachusetts Bay colony has hired you to write a blog to defend the colony's actions during the war.
2. It is 1638 and you are one of the Pequot survivors who somehow escaped death or enslavement. Write a blog, explaining to people in England the misconduct of their own colonists.

SUGGESTED SOURCES

Primary Sources

Bradford, William. *Bradford's History of Plymouth Plantation, 1606–1646,* ed. William T. Davis. New York: Scribner's, 1908. Also available at Google Books. Contains references to Plymouth Colony's participation in the war.

Gardner, Lion. *A Relation of the Pequot Warres.* Ed. W. N. Chattin Carlton. Connecticut: Acorn Club, 1901. Available at http://digitalcommons.unl.edu/etas/38/. Lion Gardner, a soldier in the Pequot War, wrote down his recollections in about 1660.

Mason, John. *A Brief History of the Pequot War: Especially of the Memorable Taking of their Fort at Mistick in Connecticut in 1637.* Ed. Paul Royster. Boston: Kneeland & Green, 1736. Available at http://digitalcommons.unl.edu/etas/42/. Mason was the commander of the Connecticut forces in the Pequot War.

Underhill, John. *Newes from America; Or, A New and Experimentall Discoverie of New England; Containing, A Trve Relation of Their War-like Proceedings These Two Yeares Last Past, with a Figure of the Indian Fort, or Palizado.* Ed. Paul Royster. London: Printed by J. D. for Peter Cole, 1638. First-hand account by the militia captain who led the assault on the Pequot Fort. Available at http://digitalcommons.unl.edu/etas/37/.

Vincent, Philip. *A True Relation of the Late Battell fought in New England, between the English and the Salvages: With the Present State of Things There.* Ed. Paul Royster. London: Printed by M. P. for Nathanael Butter and John Bellamie, 1637. Available at http://digitalcommons.unl.edu/etas/35/

Winthrop, John. *Winthrop's Journal, "History of New England," 1630–1649.* Ed. James Kendell Hosmer. 2 vols. New York: Scribner's, 1908. Also available at Google Books. Contains references to Massachusetts Bay Colony's participation in the war.

Secondary Sources

Cave, Alfred A. *The Pequot War.* Amherst: University of Massachusetts Press, 1996. Best current account of the Pequot War.

Jennings, Francis. *The Invasion of America: Indians, Colonialism, and the Cant of Conquest.* Chapel Hill: University of North Carolina Press, 1975. Jennings explores the motivations of the New England colonists in launching the war.

Oberg, Michael LeRoy. *Uncas: First of the Mohegans.* Ithaca, NY: Cornell University Press, 2003. Biography of the Mohegan leader Uncas, who sided with the English in both the Pequot War and King Philip's War.

World Wide Web

Mashantucket Museum and Research Center. http://www.pequotmuseum.org/. Web site for the Pequot tribal museum, which is perhaps one of the best tribal museums. Contains information about the Pequot people and the Pequot War.

The Society of Colonial Wars in the State of Connecticut. http://www.colonialwarsct.org/1637.htm. Contains a narrative of the war, a timeline, and biographies of key personalities.

Multimedia Sources

Massacre at Mystic. The History Channel, 2006. 3 DVD. 60 minutes. Part of the History Channel's *10 Days That Unexpectedly Changed America,* this film uses reenactments to recreate the destruction of the Pequot's fort on the Mystic River.

Mystic Voices: The Story of the Pequot War. The Cinema Guild, 2006. 1 DVD. 116 minutes. Film that explores the Pequot War using narration and historical reenactments.

20. Massachusetts Bay Colony Banishes Anne Hutchinson for Her Dissenting Religious Views (1638)

In their efforts to create a godly community on Earth, New England Puritans sought to control not only the social behavior of their church members, but their religious thought as well. Lacking clergymen of other denominations to bicker with, the Puritans turned on each other in religious disputes. The Puritan insistence on literacy, and the belief that one should read the Bible in order to establish one's own relationship with the Almighty, meant that members of a congregation may interpret the "Good Book" differently.

In 1635, Anne Hutchinson claimed that most New England clergy preached a doctrine of good works versus the more Calvinistic notion of grace. Hutchinson began holding prayer meetings at her home in Boston, attracting hundreds of followers. In 1636, Hutchinson's followers voted John Winthrop out of the governorship of the colony (the only year between 1630 and 1649 that Winthrop did not serve as the colony's governor). Alarmed at Hutchinson's unorthodox teachings, more orthodox Puritans returned Winthrop to office in the next year's election.

Back in office, Winthrop moved quickly to place Hutchinson on trial for having disturbed the peace of the commonwealth. Under questioning, Hutchinson claimed that she had received a revelation from God. Puritans believed that revelations ended with the Bible, and the colony charged Hutchinson as a heretic. Soon after, Massachusetts banished Hutchinson and her followers from the colony. For his part, Winthrop continued to assert that God opposed Hutchinson's teachings, pointing to a miscarriage she suffered and her death in New Netherland in 1643 at the hands of Indians.

TERM PAPER SUGGESTIONS

1. Examine the religious and secular culture of Massachusetts Bay Colony. Why did the colonial government consider Hutchinson a threat? Was she placed on trial for religious reasons, secular reasons, or both?
2. Read the transcript from Anne Hutchinson's trial (see either of the Web sites listed here). Who do you think got the better of the exchange between Anne Hutchinson and Massachusetts Governor John Winthrop? Can you point out errors by both Hutchinson and Winthrop?
3. Analyze Hutchinson's assertion that New England clergy had veered away from the Calvinistic doctrine of salvation through grace to a doctrine of salvation through good works. Was she correct? What counterarguments would New England ministers have offered to Hutchinson?
4. The incidents in Anne Hutchinson's life after her trial, her miscarriage and her death at the hands of Indians in New Netherland, became fodder for Puritan sermons regarding the judgment of God. What does this tell us about the uses of the pulpit in New England, not only for religious instruction, but for political and social commentary?

ALTERNATIVE TERM PAPER SUGGESTIONS

1. It is 1638 and Anne Hutchinson has decided that rather than defend herself, she is going to hire you as her lawyer. Your assignment is to plan a defense that you think will allow Hutchinson to prevail in court.
2. Anne Hutchinson has hired you as her publicity agent. One of your tasks will be to start a blog, not only defending her, but attacking the leadership of the colony as well. You have to be gentle criticizing the powers that be in Massachusetts. After all, *you* do not want to be charged with disturbing the peace of the commonwealth!

SUGGESTED SOURCES

Primary Source

John Winthrop, *Winthrop's Journal, "History of New England" 1630–1649.* Ed. James Kendall Hosmer. 2 vols. New York: Scribner's, 1908. Also available at Google Books. The journal of Massachusetts Bay Colony Governor John Winthrop includes several mentions of Anne Hutchinson, most of them uncomplimentary.

Secondary Source

LaPlante, Eve. *American Jezebel: The Uncommon Life of Anne Hutchinson, the Woman Who Defied the Puritans.* New York: HarperCollins, 2004. The most recent and very readable biography of Hutchinson.

World Wide Web

"Anne Hutchinson." http://www.annehutchinson.com/. Includes a biography of Hutchinson, her creed, and the transcript of her trial.

"The Trial of Anne Hutchinson." http://pbskids.org/wayback/civilrights/features_hutchison.html. A PBS Kid's site that, nevertheless, offers a concise account of the events leading up to Hutchinson's trial.

21. John Eliot Establishes "Praying Towns" to Convert the Native Peoples of New England to Christianity (1640s)

In the wake of the Pequot War, English Puritans harshly criticized their New England brethren for their lackluster missionary efforts among Native Americans. Puritan minister John Eliot initiated a missionary effort among Native Americans, learning their language and translating the Bible into Algonquin. Believing that Christianity went hand in hand with English civilization, Eliot established 14 "praying towns," villages in eastern Massachusetts and Connecticut that had been set aside for native converts. Eliot believed that native converts would backslide and never become civilized if they lived among unconverted natives. Living in a praying town required that natives accept Christianity and discard nearly every aspect of their own culture and become English. Native men gave up hunting and fishing and engaged in dawn to dusk agricultural labor like English male colonists. Native women converts could no longer work in the fields, but had to care for the home and spin cloth, much like English women.

For the most part, the native peoples who moved to the praying towns came from small weakened groups who had seen their communities devastated by European diseases. These people were looking for ways to make sense of their disrupted world. While many "Praying Indians," as they came to be known, may have sincerely wished to convert, some went to praying towns out of love of place. The first praying town, Natick, translates into "my land." Eliot also translated the Bible into the Massachusetts language, and while he attempted to teach native people how to read their own language, it is thought that no more than 15 percent of the Praying Indians became literate.

TERM PAPER SUGGESTIONS

1. Examine the missionary efforts of the New England Puritans. Compare their efforts to those of the French and the Spanish. Which nation seemed to have the most effective missionaries?
2. Examine the praying town movement. Why did some native peoples choose to move to praying towns? How effectively did they acculturate to the English way of life?
3. Why did the New England Puritans wait until after the Pequot War to initiate attempts to convert Native Americans? How effective was the criticism of their co-religionists in England in this regard?
4. Native people often blended their traditional beliefs with teachings of Christian missionaries. Do you see any evidence that the praying town Indians did this? How did Puritan clergy respond?
5. Did New England Puritans accept native converts as full members of the Church? Did they consider them to be true Christians? Think about the way native converts were treated as you respond to this question.

ALTERNATIVE TERM PAPER SUGGESTIONS

1. You are a Native American person in 1650 Massachusetts. You have decided that you are going to move to a praying town. Explain your reasons for this decision. Your explanation should refer to the changes that have taken place in New England since the arrival of the English and their affects on the Native American population.
2. You are a Native American person in 1650 Massachusetts. You are opposed to moving to a praying town. Explain your opposition, citing events that have taken place since the English arrived in New England.

SUGGESTED SOURCES

Primary Sources

Eliot, John. *The Christian Commonwealth: or, The Civil Policy of the Rising Kingdom of Jesus Christ.* Ed. Paul Royster. London: Liverwell-Chapman, 1659. John Eliot discusses the founding of Christian communities in the "wilderness." Available at http://digitalcommons.unl.edu/libraryscience/19/.

Eliot, John. *The Day Breaking If Not the Sun Rising of the Gospell With the Indians in New-England.* London: Rich Cotes for Fulk Clifton, 1647. Available at Google Books. John Eliot promoting his success in converting native people to Christianity. He published tracts like this to solicit donations for his mission.

Secondary Sources

Axtell, James. *The Invasion Within: The Contest of Cultures in Colonial North America.* New York: Oxford University Press, 1985. Has a very good section on the New England praying towns comparing Puritan conversion efforts among native peoples with those of the French Jesuits in Canada.

Bross, Kristina. *Dry Bones and Indian Sermons: Praying Indians in Colonial America.* Ithaca, NY: Cornell University Press, 2004. Argues that Native American converts used literacy and Christianity for their own purposes.

Morrison, Dane. *A Praying People: Massachusetts Acculturation and the Failure of the Puritan Mission, 1600–1690.* New York: Peter Lang, 1995. Morrison argues that the Massachusetts people attempted to acculturate and that their failure to do so was primarily the fault of the Puritans.

O'Brien, Jean M. *Dispossession by Degrees: Indian Land and Identity in Natick, Massachusetts, 1650–1760.* Cambridge: Cambridge University Press, 1997. Argues that native people had motives other than religion for going to praying towns.

World Wide Web

"Mass Moments." http://www.massmoments.org/moment.cfm?mid=57. A history of Natick, Massachusetts, the first of the praying towns.

"The Praying Towns." http://www.nativetech.org/Nipmuc/praytown.html. Offers an overview of the history of the praying towns as well as the rules of conduct that John Eliot gave to the residents.

22. Miantonomi Urges New England's Native Peoples to Unite (1642)

An important Narragansett leader, Miantonomi (also known as Miantonomo), allied himself with the English during the Pequot War. Knowing the English had designs on Indian lands, and disgusted with their mode of warfare, which emphasized killing over the taking of prisoners, Miantonomi became one of the first Native American leaders to argue that native people had to unite in order to resist European expansion.

Miantonomi argued that native people had to formulate a common identity as Indians, rather than as members of disparate tribes, and think of themselves as one people. Miantonomi pointed out the English shared a common identity, and he invoked the image of a peaceful, precontact New England as he argued for native unity. New England colonial governments, alarmed about Miantonomi's activities, looked for ways to eliminate him.

The treaty that ended the Pequot War awarded Miantonomi hunting territory in Connecticut. However, Mohegans led by Uncas attacked Narragansett hunters. Miantonomi informed Massachusetts Bay Colony of his intent to punish the Mohegans. Weighed down by armor given him by a colonist, the Mohegans easily captured Miantonomi during a battle. While a prisoner, Miantonomi and Uncas discussed the possibility of joining forces. But in the end, Uncas turned Miantonomi over to the Connecticut authorities.

The Connecticut officials, however, were not sure what to do. On the one hand, they wanted to be rid of Miantonomi, regarding him as a troublemaker, but at the same time, they did not want his blood on their hands. They handed Miantonomi back over to Uncas. With colonial representatives looking on, Uncas's brother buried a hatchet in Miantonomi's skull, killing the first native leader to propose a pan-Indian movement.

TERM PAPER SUGGESTIONS

1. Examine Miantonomi's call for Indian unity and compare it to later calls for unity by Pontiac and Tecumseh. Why did these efforts fail?

2. Why did Uncas and the Mohegans consistently side with the English (they did so in the Pequot War and again during King Philip's War)? Were they opposed to Indian unity? Or did they have other reasons?
3. Why did the Connecticut authorities turn Miantonomi over to Uncas and the Mohegans? If they wished for him to be executed, why did they simply not do it themselves?
4. After reading Miantonomi's speech urging native unity, evaluate how effective it was. Did the English truly have anything to be alarmed about, or did they overreact by having Miantonomi killed?

ALTERNATIVE TERM PAPER SUGGESTIONS

1. You are a blogger in 1642 Massachusetts. Governor John Winthrop is concerned about Miantonomi's effort to unite native people and wants you to write a blog, directed at native people, trying to convince them that unity is a bad idea and that they should ignore Miantonomi.
2. You have been hired by Miantonomi as a diplomat. Your job is to convince Uncas and the Mohegans that native unity will be to their advantage. Write a speech to be delivered before them.

SUGGESTED SOURCES

Primary Sources

Bradford, William. *Bradford's History of Plymouth Plantation, 1606–1646.* Ed. William T. Davis. New York: Scribner's, 1908. Also available at Google Books. Bradford offers his views regarding the dispute between Uncas and Miantonomi.

" 'So Must We Be One. . . , Otherwise We Shall Be All Gone Shortly': Narragansett Chief Miantonomi Tries to Form an Alliance Against Settlers in New England and Long Island, 1640s." http://historymatters.gmu.edu/d/6227. Text of Miantonomi's speech urging native unity.

Winthrop, John. *Winthrop's Journal, "History of New England," 1630–1649.* Ed. James Kendell Hosmer. 2 vols. New York: Scribner's, 1908. Also available at Google Books. Winthrop offers details regarding the colonists' concerns about Miantonomi's activities, about his questioning, and his murder by Uncas.

Secondary Sources

Jennings, Francis. *The Invasion of America: Indians, Colonialism, and the Cant of Conquest.* Chapel Hill: University of North Carolina Press, 1975. Jennings includes an account of Miantonomi and his push for native unity.

Oberg, Michael Leroy. *Uncas: First of the Mohegans.* Ithaca, NY: Cornell University Press, 2003. A biography of Miantonomi's chief rival. Contains a good bit of information regarding Miantonomi.

World Wide Web

"Miantonomo." http://www.famousamericans.net/miantonomo/. Comprehensive biography of Miantonomi.

23. Opechancanough Leads a Second War against Colonists in Virginia (1644–1646)

In 1632, Virginia colonists and the Powhatan confederacy reached an agreement that ended their decade-long war. The resulting treaty forced Virginia's Native Americans to yield large tracts of land along the Potomac and Rappahannock rivers to the colony. Over the next dozen years, colonists established plantations along these waterways. In April 1644, with the English more widely dispersed than they had been in 1622, and believing them weakened by the Civil War in England, Opechancanough launched his second war against the colonists in Virginia. In some respects, Opechancanough's warriors enjoyed more success than in 1622, killing over 400 colonists in the initial assault. These first attacks did not have the same devastating effect as they had in 1622, however. The English population of Virginia now numbered nearly 10,000 (five times what it had been in 1622), and they greatly outnumbered the Indians. The English struck back, destroying native villages along the rivers, driving many of the survivors into the interior. The English captured Opechancanough, now reputably 100 years old, in 1646. Despite having to be carried on a litter and being nearly blind, the English jailed Opechancanough in Jamestown, placing him on public display. An enraged soldier drew the assignment of guarding Opechancanough and shot him dead. Opechancanough's murder signaled the end of the Powhatan confederacy and broke Indian power in Virginia. Virginia colonists placed its few remaining native peoples on small reservations (the first in what would become the United States), where they were surrounded by a large English population.

TERM PAPER SUGGESTIONS

1. Discuss the Powhatan people's point of view in 1644. Short of going to war against the colonists, what other avenues could they have pursued?
2. Discuss the founding of reservations after Opechancanough's second war and the laws Virginia colonists enacted to control the native population.
3. Why do you think Opechancanough believed the English Civil War would have an effect on the ability of the Virginians to fight a war against the Indians?

ALTERNATIVE TERM PAPER SUGGESTIONS

1. You are a Powhatan Indian leader who is opposed to Opechancanough's plans for a war against the colonists. Prepare a podcast in which you outline an alternative course of action. Keep in mind that leaving their homeland is a course that will not appeal to most Powhatan peoples.
2. You are a member of the Virginia House of Burgess (their legislature) in 1646. You are part of a committee that is tasked with drawing up the terms of the peace agreement with the Powhatans. What terms would you offer the Powhatans?

SUGGESTED SOURCES

Primary Source

Beverley, Robert. *History and Present State of Virginia.* Chapel Hill: University of North Carolina Press, 1960. Reprint of the 1705 edition. Beverley includes firsthand accounts of Opechancanough's second war.

Secondary Sources

Axtell, James. "The Rise and Fall of the Powhatan Empire." In *After Columbus: Essays in the Ethnohistory of Colonial North America.* New York: Oxford University Press, 1988. Axtell discusses Opechancanough's war.

Gleach, Frederic W. *Powhatan's World and Colonial Virginia: A Conflict of Cultures.* Lincoln: University of Nebraska Press, 1997. Gleach includes an entire chapter on the 1644 war.

Rountree, Helen C. *Pocahontas's People: The Powhatan Indians of Virginia through Four Centuries.* Norman: University of Oklahoma Press, 1990. Has an entire chapter on Opechancanough and the 1644 war.

Rountree, Helen C. *Pocahontas, Powhatan, Opechancanough: Three Indian Lives Changed by Jamestown.* Charlottesville: University of Virginia Press, 2006. The seventeenth-century history of the Powhatan peoples as seen through the lives of three prominent individuals.

Rountree, Helen C. *The Powhatan Indians of Virginia: Their Traditional Culture.* Norman: University of Oklahoma Press, 1989. Includes information about Opechancanough.

Worldwide Web

"The Anglo-Powhatan Wars." http://www.virginiaplaces.org/nativeamerican/anglopowhatan.html. Overview of the Anglo-Powhatan wars of 1622 and 1644

"The Tyme Appointed." http://www.history.org/Foundation/journal/Autumn05/tyme.cfm. Very detailed article regarding Opechancanough's attacks of Virginia.

24. Iroquois Initiate the "Beaver Wars" (1649)

In the 1620s and 1630s, Dutch traders at Fort Orange (present-day Albany, New York) became the primary providers of European goods to the Iroquois League. Initially, the Iroquois faced competition from the Mahican for the Dutch trade at Fort Orange. The Iroquois defeated the Mahicans in a brief war, driving them away from the Dutch. More liberal than other European traders, the Dutch had few qualms about providing the Iroquois with firearms.

By the 1640s, the Iroquois exhausted the supply of beaver pelts in their territory, leaving them nothing to offer Dutch traders. Also, contact with the Dutch led to the outbreak of European diseases that killed many

Iroquois. Needing a new source of furs, as well as to replace their dead with captives, the Iroquois launched a series of wars that attempted to seize control of fur trading routes controlled by other native peoples.

The Huron on the east shore of Lake Huron traded maize to upper Great Lakes Indians for furs, which they traded to the French. The Iroquois hoped to replace the Huron as "middlemen" and funnel furs away from their French enemies and to their Dutch (later English) trade partners at Fort Orange.

In 1649, a large Iroquois force destroyed two Huron villages, dispersing the survivors throughout the Great Lakes. The Iroquois spent the next half century at war with other native peoples in the region, attempting to gain control of the trade. In the process, they seriously weakened themselves. When the French invaded Iroquoia in the 1680s and 1690s, the Iroquois launched a diplomatic initiative that resulted in the Grand Settlement of 1701.

TERM PAPER SUGGESTIONS

1. Examine French diplomacy toward the Iroquois League. Could it have been possible for the French to avert the Beaver Wars?
2. Why did the Iroquois not succeed in their half-century attempt to gain control of the fur trade? Why did other events beyond their control preclude this?
3. The Iroquois were much better armed than the Hurons and other native peoples. Why did the French not take steps to ensure that their partners in the fur trade had the means to defend themselves?
4. Examine the effects of the Beaver Wars on Iroquois society. What changes did the half century of nearly continuous war bring to the Iroquois League?

ALTERNATIVE TERM PAPER SUGGESTIONS

1. You are an Iroquois diplomat in 1645. You have been given the task of contacting the Huron and proposing an agreement that will allow them to funnel furs to the Iroquois and cut the French out of the fur trade. What kind of arguments are you going to make to encourage the Huron to agree to this scheme?
2. You are a Huron diplomat in 1645. An Iroquois diplomat has proposed that the Huron should provide furs to the Iroquois. You reply that you already

have a satisfactory agreement with the French. Enumerate the advantages of the Huron agreement with the French.

SUGGESTED SOURCES

Primary Source

Thwaites, Reuben Gold, ed. *The Jesuit Relations and Allied Documents: Travels and Explorations of the Jesuit Missionaries in New France, 1610–1791.* 73 vols. Cleveland: Burrow's Brothers, 1896–1901. The Jesuit Relations are the single best primary source for anything connected to the Beaver Wars. Keep in mind that most of the Jesuits' writings are not favorable regarding the Iroquois.

Secondary Sources

Brandao, Jose Antonio. *"Your Fyre Shall Burn No More": Iroquois Policy Towards New France and Its Native Allies to 1701.* Lincoln: University of Nebraska Press, 1997. A reevaluation of the Beaver Wars. A little less than half of the book consists of tables evaluating the outcome of military encounters between the Iroquois and their native foes.

Dennis, Matthew. *Cultivating a Landscape of Peace: Iroquois-European Encounters in Seventeenth Century America.* Ithaca, NY: Cornell University Press, 1993. Covers the Beaver Wars and Iroquois diplomacy with both the French and the Dutch.

Hunt, George T. *The Wars of the Iroquois: A Study in Inter-tribal Trade Relations.* Madison: University of Wisconsin Press, 1940. Perhaps the classic work regarding the Iroquois and the Beaver Wars. Hunt's older interpretation stresses the economic incentives of the Iroquois while ignoring traditional motivations.

Richter, Daniel K. *The Ordeal of the Longhouse: The Peoples of the Iroquois League in the Era of European Colonization.* Chapel Hill: The University of North Carolina Press, 1992. Covers the Beaver wars and internal conflicts within the Iroquois confederacy.

World Wide Web

"Beaver Wars." http://www.ohiohistorycentral.org/entry.php?rec=483. Contains a narrative of the Beaver Wars and a bibliography.

25. English Parliament Institutes the Navigation Acts (1650s)

In the mid-seventeenth century, England and the Netherlands vied for naval and commercial supremacy. In an effort to deny the Dutch access to English markets and to initiate the closed, state-directed economic system known as mercantilism, the English Parliament passed the first of the Navigation Acts. Before the Navigation Acts, foreign vessels had access to ports in the English colonies. The Navigation Acts ended that, requiring that ships be built in England or one of her colonies, be owned by English merchants or investors, and be commanded by an English captain. Additionally, three-quarters of the crew had to be composed of English subjects.

High-value or enumerated commodities, such as sugar and tobacco, could only be shipped from the colonies to England. Colonial ships were free to trade nonenumerated commodities with whomever they wished. The Act also forbade the importation of European goods directly to the colonies, requiring them to first be imported to England, where they would be assessed a duty, and then reexported to British North America. The shipping costs and the duties increased the prices of other nations' products, making them noncompetitive in the colonial marketplace.

The Navigation Acts were later amended in the 1660s and would continue to be revised into the eighteenth century. They had the effect of expanding the English navy, allowing them to eventually control the Atlantic Ocean, and they helped transform England into a commercial and maritime power.

TERM PAPER SUGGESTIONS

1. Why did the English government embrace mercantilism in the seventeenth and eighteenth centuries? What were the limitations of this economic system?
2. Discuss the effects that the Navigation Acts would have had on particular colonies. For which colonies would the Acts have created hardships? Which colonies would have been affected very little by the Acts?

ALTERNATIVE TERM PAPER SUGGESTIONS

1. It is 1651, and Parliament is ready to pass a Navigation Act. However, they are concerned about how this act will be received in the colonies. You have been hired by Parliament to start an ad campaign, using any medium you choose, such as full-page ads in colonial papers, podcasts, or iMovies, to convince the colonists that the Navigation Acts are the greatest thing since sliced bread (which, by the way, has not been invented yet).
2. You are a tobacco grower in Virginia. Draft a letter of protest to Parliament. Point out how the Navigation Acts will cause hardship for you.
3. How would mercantilism have affected individual colonists? You are a tobacco planter in eighteenth-century Virginia and you are beginning to tire of Jamaican rum (Jamaica is an English colony). Instead, you would like a nice French wine, and you order a bottle. Trace the journey and the tariffs that have to be paid as the bottle of wine makes its journey from France to you.

SUGGESTED SOURCES

Primary Sources

"Charles II, 1660: An Act for the Encourageing and Increasing of Shipping and Navigation." *Statutes of the Realm: volume 5: 1628–80* (1819), pp. 246–250. http://www.british-history.ac.uk/report.aspx?compid=47266. Text of the 1660 Navigation Act after the Restoration of the Crown.

"Charles II, 1663: An Act for the Encouragement of Trade." *Statutes of the Realm: volume 5: 1628-80* (1819), pp. 449–452. http://www.british-history.ac.uk/report.aspx?compid=47343. Revision of the 1660 Act.

"October 1651: An Act for Increase of Shipping, and Encouragement of the Navigation of this Nation." *Acts and Ordinances of the Interregnum, 1642–1660* (1911), pp. 559–562. http://www.british-history.ac.uk/report.aspx?compid=56457&strquery=559. Contains the text of the first Navigation Act addressing the American colonies.

Secondary Sources

Bliss, Robert M. *Revolution and Empire: English Politics and the American Colonies in the Seventeenth Century.* Manchester: Manchester University Press, 1990. Argues that the Navigation Acts were a result of a period of increased British interest in their North American colonies.

McCusker, John J. "British Mercantilist Policies and the American Colonies." In *The Cambridge Economic History of the United States: The Colonial Era.* Vol. 1. Ed. Stanley L. Engermand and Robert E. Gallman. New York: Cambridge University Press, 1996. A good overview of British efforts to control the economies of their colonies in North America.

Price, Jacob M. "The Transatlantic Economy." In *Colonial British America: Essays in the New History of the Early Modern Era.* Ed. Jack P. Greene and J. R. Pole. Baltimore, MD: Johns Hopkins University Press, 1984. Examines the economic value of the colonies to England.

World Wide Web

"Mercantilism and the American Revolution." http://freepages.history.rootsweb.ancestry.com/~cescott/mercan.html. Postulates that the American Revolution was, in part, a reaction against the mercantile system.

"The Navigation Acts." http://www.usgennet.org/usa/topic/colonial/book/chap10_6.html. Discusses how the Navigation Acts affected each colony.

"The Navigation Acts." http://www.sagehistory.net/colonial/topics/navacts.htm. Brief article on the history of the Navigation Acts.

26. Massachusetts Bay Colony Persecutes Quakers (1657–1659)

English Puritans came to North America seeking religious freedom for themselves, but not for others. Governed for most of their first two decades by ruling bodies who interwove religious and civil powers, the New England colonies (with the notable exception of Rhode Island) insisted on social order and stifled religious dissent to achieve it. Massachusetts Bay Colony dealt harshly with religious dissidents, going so far as to exile individuals who deviated from the orthodox view. For example, the authorities banished dissenter Anne Hutchinson from the colony and planned to deport Roger Williams to England before he fled and founded Rhode Island.

In the late 1650s, Quakers appeared in Plymouth and Massachusetts Bay colonies, spreading their religious message of an "inner light," sometimes by disrupting Church services. New England punished them with whippings, ear cropping, and banishment. Their stoicism under punishment (always carried out in public) caused ordinary Puritans to question their government. Banished Quakers sometimes returned, and the authorities responded by branding them and banishing them again. If Quakers returned yet a third time, Massachusetts authorities hanged them. In 1659, the government sentenced three Quakers to be hanged in Boston; however, Massachusetts citizens caused such an uproar that 100 soldiers had to be called out to maintain order on the day of their execution. The authorities hanged two of the Quakers and set a third, Mary Dyer, free but ordered her to leave the colony. When Dyer returned six months later, the court condemned her to death. The public punishments inflicted on the Quakers generated an enormous amount of public sympathy, forcing the New England colonial governments to defend their actions. Nevertheless, after 1660, New England grudgingly had to be more accepting of religious toleration.

TERM PAPER SUGGESTIONS

1. Discuss the efforts of Puritan authorities to bar other religious beliefs from New England. Was this a realistic goal?
2. Discuss the Quakers and their motives for going to as well as for returning to New England. Knowing they could have been put to death, why do you think they persisted in this?
3. Read the references to the Quakers in Morton's *New England's Memorial.* Then read the versions of events by George Bishop and John Clarke. In modern terms, would their differences in religious observance cause problems today?

ALTERNATIVE TERM PAPER SUGGESTIONS

1. The governor of Massachusetts is concerned about the unrest that the execution of Quakers has caused among the citizens of the colony. The governor has asked you to prepare a podcast, designed to demonstrate to the populace that executing the Quakers was the only recourse the government had.
2. George Fox, the founder of the Quaker movement, has appointed you his minister of propaganda. You are to make an iMovie, sort of like an infomercial (that tries to look like a talk show) that will be beamed into Massachusetts. You will have various guests on, all following a script designed to get

Puritans to question their government and to consider tolerating Quakers. Good luck!

SUGGESTED SOURCES

Primary Sources

Bishop, George. *New-England judged, by the spirit of the Lord: In two parts. First, containing a brief relation of the sufferings of the people call'd Quakers in New-England, from the time of their first arrival there, in the year 1656, to the year 1660 . . . In answer to the declaration of their persecutors apologizing for the same, MDCLIX. Second part, being a farther relation of the cruel and bloody sufferings of the people call'd Quakers in New-England, continued from anno 1660, to anno 1665. Beginning with the sufferings of William Leddra, whom they put to death.* London, 1703. http://www.archive.org/details/newenglandjudged00bishuoft. George Bishop, a Quaker and former soldier, wrote this account denouncing Massachusett's Puritan authorities for the hangings of his co-religionists.

Clarke, John. "Ill Newes from New-England, or a Narrative of New Englands Persecution." In *Collections of the Massachusetts Historical Society,* fourth ser., vol. two. http://books.google.com/books?id=6jATAAAAYAAJ&pg=PA1&dq=John+Clarke+new+england&lr=&as_brr=1&client=firefox-a#PPA1,M1. Contains Clarke's (a Baptist) arguments against religious authoritarianism in Massachusetts. It also has an account of his experiences visiting the colony with two of his Quaker friends.

Morton, Nathaniel. *New England's Memorial.* Available at the Internet Archive (www.archive.org), as part of *Chronicles of the Pilgrim Fathers.* Morton's *Memorial* is a contemporaneous history, first published in the seventeenth century, and gives the reader the negative view that many Puritans had of the Quakers.

Secondary Sources

Bonomi, Patricia U. *Under the Cope of Heaven: Religion, Society, and Politics in Colonial America.* New York: Oxford University Press, 1986. Contains an overview of religious conflict in early America and a good section on the Quakers.

Hall, David D. *Worlds of Wonder: Days of Judgment: Popular Religious Belief in Early New England.* Cambridge, MA: Harvard University Press, 1989. Has an interesting take on the Puritan view of the Quakers.

World Wide Web

"Mary Dyer, Quaker Martyr, Hangs." http://colonial-america.suite101.com/article.cfm/quaker_martyr_new_england_1660. Summarizes Mary Dyer's testimony in New England court.

"Quakers in Brief" or "Quakerism made Easy." http://people.cryst.bbk.ac.uk/~ubcg09q/dmr/intro.htm. Overview of the Quaker movement from the seventeenth to the twentieth centuries.

"The Quakers: Hostile Bonnets and Gowns." http://www.mayflowerfamilies.com/enquirer/quakers.htm. Good overview of the Puritan prosecution of Quakers.

Multimedia Source

Saints & Strangers. Vision Video, 2002. 1 DVD. 59 minutes. Uses live action to emphasize the role of the Congregationalist, Quaker, Baptist, and Anglican denominations in early America.

27. Slave Codes Are Developed (1660s–1700)

By the mid-seventeenth century, Chesapeake planters noticed that, for the first time, most newly imported English servants and African slaves survived their first year in North America. The changing disease environment in the colonies and improving economic conditions in England resulted in fewer English servants and helped prompt a large-scale shift to African slaves as the primary labor force. Slaves cost more than indentured servants, but a planter could keep a servant from only four to seven years versus a lifetime for an African slave. Before 1650, Chesapeake planters regarded the indentured servant as a better investment, since both slaves and indentured servants were likely to live only a few years.

The change in the disease environment meant that, despite their higher initial price, slaves were now the better long-term investment. However, the English, unlike other European nations, had no tradition of slavery, so the American colonists had to invent their own slave codes. With no guidelines, colonial legislatures enacted laws that defined slaves as property, permitting masters, with few exceptions, to do as they would with their slaves. As property, slaves could not give testimony in court.

Furthermore, the law defined slavery as a lifetime status, unless a master manumitted them, and colonial governments later placed restrictions on manumission. This meant that planters not only had access to a slave's labor for life but also that of their children. One obstacle to slavery was the notion that Christians could not enslave other Christians, but in 1667 Virginia's courts ruled that religion did not alter one's legal status and Maryland followed suit four years later.

TERM PAPER SUGGESTIONS

1. Winthrop Jordon (see secondary sources) argued that the transition from servants to racialized slavery was an "unthinking decision." However, Edmund Morgan suggested that the factors that led planters to opt for slaves over servants indicates that this was very much a conscious decision. Do you think it was a conscious decision, and why?
2. Discuss the factors that led to a decrease in English indentured servants immigrating to the Chesapeake. Was slavery the only option for Chesapeake planters? Were there other sources of labor available?
3. Why did English colonists in the Chesapeake devise harsh slave codes? Slavery at the time was unknown in England. What precedents did the colonists draw on as examples for their code?

ALTERNATIVE TERM PAPER SUGGESTIONS

1. It is 1650, and planters in the Chesapeake are a little uneasy that the supply of indentured servants has started to diminish and have not yet fully embraced the notion of buying African slaves (who have a higher initial purchase price). The planters have selected you to launch a public relations campaign to encourage young Englishmen to seek their fortunes in the Chesapeake. You may exaggerate, you may leave out a few key facts, but you cannot lie. Design your campaign as a series of podcasts, complete with testimonials from "real colonists" about the wonders that await new immigrants in Virginia.
2. It is the 1670s, and you and a classmate(s) are part of a committee that the House of Burgess (Virginia's governing body) appoints to draft a set of slave codes. What would your slave code include that Virginia's did not? What would you leave out? Why? Do you think it could have worked in the seventeenth century?

SUGGESTED SOURCES

Primary Sources

Equiano, Olaudah. *The Interesting Narrative of the Life of Olaudah Equiano, or Gustavus Vassa, the African. Written by Himself.* 2 vols. London: Printed and sold by the author, 1789. http://docsouth.unc.edu/neh/equiano1/menu.html. Equiano's *Interesting Narrative* is perhaps the most important piece of antislavery literature and the first description of the Middle Passage written from the perspective of a slave.

"Selected Virginia Statutes Relating to Slavery." http://www.virtualjamestown.org/slavelink.html. Links to the text of every Virginia slave law authored between 1629 and 1705.

Secondary Sources

Berlin, Ira. *Many Thousands Gone: The First Two Centuries of Slavery in North America.* Cambridge, MA: Harvard University Press, 1998. Perhaps the best examination of African American slavery.

Countryman, Edward, ed. *How Did American Slavery Begin?* New York: Bedford/St. Martin's, 1999. Essays by five historians seeking to explain the origins of American slavery.

Dunn, Richard P. "Servants and Slaves: The Recruitment and Employment of Labor." In *Colonial British America: Essays in the New History of the Early Modern Era.* Ed. Jack P. Greene and J. R. Pole. Baltimore, MD: Johns Hopkins University Press, 1984. This essay examines the acquisition and divergence in labor systems between the different colonies in British North America.

Jordan, Winthrop D. *White over Black: American Attitudes Toward the Negro, 1550–1812.* New York: Norton, 1977. Jordan argues that the English choice to adopt a system of racialized slavery in the Americas was an "unthinking decision."

Morgan, Edmund S. *American Slavery, American Freedom: The Ordeal of Colonial Virginia.* New York: Norton, 1975. One of the classic works of the history of early Virginia, Morgan examines tension that slavery created and how the planter class came to see slavery as essential to their freedom.

World Wide Web

"Africans in America." http://www.pbs.org/wgbh/aia/home.html. Companion Web site for the PBS presentation.

"Slavery and the Making of America." http://www.pbs.org/wnet/slavery/. Companion Web site for the PBS presentation.

Multimedia Sources

Africans in America. PBS, 1998. 2 DVD. 360 minutes. PBS series that uses historical images and interviews with leading scholars to illuminate the history of the slave trade and slavery from 1450 to 1865.

Slavery and the Making of America. PBS, 2004. 4 DVD. 240 minutes. Using historical images and reenactments, this PBS series traces the history of slavery from 1619 to the end of the Civil War.

28. Massachusetts Churches Approve the Halfway Covenant (1662)

After a generation in New England, Puritan churches faced the problem of declining church membership. Church membership had been predicated not only on baptism but also on the ability of members to relate, in front of the congregation, a narrative of their conversion experience. In other words, they had to describe the moment that they realized that they were one of the "elect." But by the 1660s, church membership declined, particularly among males. Much of the decline was attributed to the inability of baptized church members to relate a conversion experience. Puritan clergy, taking this as a sign of some sort of moral failing on the part of their flocks, preached a species of sermon known as the "jeremiad," named for the Old Testament prophet Jeremiah, that bewailed the loss of religion and the failure of the current generation of Puritans to live up to the standards set by their forefathers. Historians have referred to this, as well as the decline of things religious in Puritan life at the time, as evidence of "declension."

To solve the problem of declining membership, New England churches adopted the "halfway covenant." Infants would be baptized, would be allowed to take communion, and could take part in the Lord's supper, with the expectation that they would have a conversion experience and be admitted to full membership as adults. However, many of the halfway members never had, or related, a conversion experience.

TERM PAPER SUGGESTIONS

1. In the view of first generation Puritans, why did the apparent decline of religious fervor become a cause for concern?
2. Why did the Puritans place such importance on church membership? How did it differ in their view from church attendance?
3. Was the first generation of Puritans born in America truly less religious than their parents? Is there something about Puritanism that may have made them reluctant to make a public declaration of faith?

ALTERNATIVE TERM PAPER SUGGESTIONS

1. It is 1662. You are a Puritan who has been a member of the church for years. The synod discussing the halfway covenant has asked for public comment on the measure. Write out your comments either for or against the covenant.
2. It is 1662. You are a Puritan and a parent. Offer an opinion as to whether the halfway convenant will benefit your children.

SUGGESTED SOURCES

Primary Sources

Cotton, John. *Milk for Babes. Drawn Out of the Breasts of Both Testaments. Chiefly, for the Spirituall Nourishment of Boston Babes in Either England: But May Be of Like Use for Any Children.* London: J. Cole for Henry Overton, 1646. http://digitalcommons.unl.edu/etas/18/. A beginning catechism for children and young people by a noted Puritan clergyman.

Scottow, Joshua. *Old Mens Tears For their own Declensions, Mixed with Fears of their and Posterities further falling off from New-England's Primitive Constitution.* London: Benjamin Harris and John Allen, 1691. http://digitalcommons.unl.edu/scottow/1/. A classic Puritan jeremiad.

Wigglesworth, Michael. *God's Controversy with New-England (1662).* http://digitalcommons.unl.edu/etas/36/. Poem written about the time of the halfway covenant that reflects the belief that the current generation of New England colonists were not as religious as their forbearers.

Secondary Sources

Hall, David D. *Worlds of Wonder, Days of Judgment: Popular Religious Belief in Early New England.* Cambridge, MA: Harvard University Press, 1989. Discusses the halfway covenant.

Miller, Perry. *Errand into the Wilderness.* Cambridge, MA: Harvard University Press, 1956. The section about the Puritans discusses the halfway covenant.

Pope, Robert G. *The Half-Way Covenant: Church Membership in Puritan New England.* Princeton, NJ: Princeton University Press, 1969. Argues that not all New England churches adopted the halfway covenant.

World Wide Web

"Puritanism in New England." http://www.wsu.edu/~campbelld/amlit/purdef.htm. Good brief overview of Puritan belief and practice.

"Religion: Half-Way Covenant." http://www.u-s-history.com/pages/h1166.html. Brief entry on the halfway covenant and its effect on Puritan New England.

29. Maryland Makes Slavery an Inheritable Status (1664)

When the Dutch first began importing Africans into England's Chesapeake colonies in 1619, the Africans' legal status was uncertain. Some were enslaved but most were given a status akin to that of an indentured servant. However, they were treated differently. For example, when an English indentured servant impregnated a female African servant, the Englishman was forced to do penance at a church, while the woman was tied to a post and whipped. Legally, there was a great deal of uncertainty as to the status of Africans because there was nothing like slavery in English common law. This, however, should not be taken to mean that slavery did not exist in the English colonies; English sugar planters in the Caribbean copied Spanish colonists and adopted the practice of slavery. However, it was not until 1664 that the colony of Maryland formally adopted a slave code that was quickly copied by the other colonies in British North America.

In September, the Maryland assembly passed the "Act Concerning Negroes & other Slaves." The new law stipulated that African slaves in the colony would "serve Durante Vita," that is, their entire lives. It also made slavery an inheritable status and explicitly linked slavery to skin color, stating, "all Children born of any Negro or other slave shall be

Slaves as their fathers were for the term of their Hues." In other words, as long as they were black, they would remain enslaved.

TERM PAPER SUGGESTIONS

1. Compare the status of slaves throughout the seventeenth century world with the law devised by the Maryland assembly? How did slavery differ in other areas of the world? In which respects was it similar?
2. Is there anything in British law that the Maryland assembly may have used as a guide? Why did they choose to make slavery an inheritable status? Why did they emphasize color as a factor in determining who was or was not a slave?
3. Why did English colonists choose to go to slavery rather than continue the practice of treating Africans as indentured servants?

ALTERNATIVE TERM PAPER SUGGESTIONS

1. You are the public relations secretary for the governor of Maryland in 1664. Before passing a measure that will make slavery an inheritable status, he wants you to put together a public relations campaign. The governor anticipates that there will be some people who will object to the new measure, and he wants you to make a series of podcasts that point out the benefits of the new law.
2. You are a slave in 1664 Maryland who is opposed to the proposed new law that will link slavery to race and make it an inheritable status. You are going to begin a public relations campaign against the measure. Make a podcast and compose a full-page newspaper advertisement that you hope will turn many colonists against the measure. Good luck!

SUGGESTED SOURCES

Primary Source

Archives of Maryland Online. http://aomol.net/megafile/msa/speccol/sc2900/sc2908/html/volumes.html. Volume one contains the "Act Concerning Negroes & other Slaves" on page 28.

Secondary Sources

Berlin, Ira. *Many Thousands Gone: The First Two Centuries of Slavery in North America.* Cambridge, MA: Harvard University Press, 1998. Perhaps the best examination of African slavery in North America.

Countryman, Edward, ed. *How Did American Slavery Begin?* New York: Bedford/St. Martin's, 1999. Essays by five historians seeking to explain the origins of American slavery.

Dunn, Richard P. "Servants and Slaves: The Recruitment and Employment of Labor." In *Colonial British America: Essays in the New History of the Early Modern Era.* Ed. Jack P. Greene and J. R. Pole. Baltimore, MD: Johns Hopkins University Press, 1984. Examines the acquisition and divergence in labor systems between the different colonies in British North America.

Jordan, Winthrop D. *White over Black: American Attitudes Toward the Negro, 1550–1812.* New York: Norton, 1977. Jordan argues that the English choice to adopt a system of racialized slavery in the Americas was an "unthinking decision."

World Wide Web

"Africans in America." http://www.pbs.org/wgbh/aia/home.html. Companion Web site for the PBS presentation.

"Slavery and the Making of America." http://www.pbs.org/wnet/slavery/ Companion Web site for the PBS presentation.

Multimedia Sources

Africans in America. PBS, 1998. 2 DVD. 360 minutes. PBS series that uses historical images and interviews with leading scholars to illuminate the history of the slave trade and slavery from 1450 to 1865.

Slavery and the Making of America. PBS, 2004. 4 DVD. 240 minutes. Using historical images and reenactments, this PBS series traces the history of slavery from 1619 to the end of the Civil War.

30. English Capture New Amsterdam (1664)

For much of the first half of the seventeenth century, England and the Netherlands vied for commercial and naval supremacy in the Atlantic Ocean. The presence of New Netherland, lodged between the Chesapeake colonies and New England, was of particular concern to the English. Dutch traders used the colony as a base to conduct (what the English regarded as) illegal trade with both New England and Virginia. The English also wanted access to the valuable fur trade of the interior. In 1664, the Dutch were surprised when three English warships sailed into the waters around New Amsterdam, and the New Englanders who settled on Long Island also marched onto the city. Despite urgings and threats from New Netherland Governor Peter Stuyvesant, the Dutch colonists did not resist, giving the English a bloodless conquest. Renaming the newly captured colony "New York," the English now were able to link their northern and southern seaboard colonies. The surrender terms of 1664 were generous, permitting the Dutch colonists to keep their own laws and customs. The Dutch briefly recaptured New Amsterdam from the English in 1673 but were forced to part with it in the peace settlement. Because the majority of the Dutch colonists cooperated with the Netherlands forces, the English rescinded their earlier guarantees and placed the colony under English law.

TERM PAPER SUGGESTIONS

1. Explore the reasons behind the Anglo-Dutch conflicts of the seventeenth century. These wars had their roots in economic competition between the two countries. Could such a conflict happen today?
2. Why did the Dutch population of New Amsterdam not resist the English invasion? Could the openness of the Dutch West India Company in allowing foreigners to settle in their colony have had something to do with its swift surrender?
3. Why were many Dutch colonists unwilling to fight the English in 1664 but were willing to assist Netherlands forces when they retook the colony in 1673?

ALTERNATIVE TERM PAPER SUGGESTIONS

1. It is 1664, and you are the head of the English espionage service. Draw up a set of instructions for English agents in New Amsterdam. Give them detailed instructions for assessing the Dutch defenses. They are also to start rumors to sap the will of the population to defend New Amsterdam.
2. It is 1664 and you are the military assistant of New Netherland Governor Peter Stuyvesant. When the English fleet arrives, Stuyvesant orders you to draft a plan for the colony's defense, which he wants in the form of a PowerPoint presentation, complete with maps.

SUGGESTED SOURCES

Primary Source

Jameson, J. Franklin, ed. *Narratives of New Netherland, 1609–1664.* New York: Scribner's, 1909. Available at Google Books. Includes the surrender documents of New Netherland and Governor Stuyvesant's report on the surrender.

Secondary Sources

Rink, Oliver A. *Holland on the Hudson: An Economic and Social History of Dutch New York.* Ithaca, NY: Cornell University Press, 1992. A history of Dutch society in New Netherland.

Shorto, Russell. *The Island at the Center of the World: The Epic Story of Dutch Manhattan, the Forgotten Colony that shaped America.* New York: Vintage Books, 2005. Emphasizes the importance of New Netherland in the context of the Dutch commercial empire.

World Wide Web

"The New Netherland Project." http://www.nnp.org/. The New Netherland Project translates, transcribes, and publishes seventeenth-century Dutch documents in the New York state archives.

Multimedia Source

"Illuminating New York's Dutch Past." In production as of July 2008. See http://www.nnp.org/2009/info.html.

31. John Locke Writes the Fundamental Constitutions of Carolina (1669)

Carolina (which today includes both North and South Carolina and parts of Georgia) was the first colony established by England following the restoration of King Charles II. He established the Carolinas as a proprietary colony and granted a charter to eight prominent men, named, appropriately, the Lords Proprietors. The proprietors initially promised a representative government, religious toleration, and land grants for would-be colonists. However, they asked the famous political philosopher John Locke to prepare a governing document for the colony. While Locke is often lauded for his influence on American political thought, his plan for Carolina essentially produced a plan for a feudal regime.

Locke's plan gave the proprietors and "nobles" control over 40 percent of the colony's land. All executive positions would be held by proprietors and nobles. Election to the colony's parliament would be restricted to men who owned at least 500 acres.

In practice, however, "Barbados men," primarily the sons of established sugar planters, spearheaded the settlement of the colony while the proprietors attempted, unsuccessfully, to govern Carolina from London. However, the proprietors did succeed in attracting large numbers of colonists by offering each immigrant 150 acres of land in exchange for a minimal annual quitrent of one-half pence per acre. The colony quickly grew from 200 colonists in 1670 to more than 6,000 in 1700.

TERM PAPER SUGGESTIONS

1. Why did the Crown wish to establish a colony to the south of Virginia? What would the immediate benefits have been to Virginia? What geopolitical considerations did the English have in mind?
2. Examine why the Lords Proprietors could not control their colony. Why did they lose control of the Carolinas to the "Barbados Men"? What were the difficulties in asserting their legal rights to the colony?
3. John Locke is often recognized in the United States for his influence on the generation of American politicians who wrote the Declaration of Independence and drafted the Constitution. Why did Locke opt for a feudal form of government in Carolina?
4. South Carolina developed much more quickly than North Carolina. Examine the differences between colonial South and North Carolina in terms of the colonists they attracted and the economic activities of each colony.

ALTERNATIVE TERM PAPER SUGGESTIONS

1. It is 1669 and the Lords Proprietors of the Carolina colony have hired you to conduct a public relations campaign to promote settlement in their new colony. Using podcasts and full-page newspaper ads, put together a campaign that will make Englishmen think the Carolinas is the place to be.

2. It is 1680 and there is concern that the northern portion of the Carolinas is not being settled quickly enough. Put together an advertising campaign to lure English colonists. Point out the profitable economic enterprises they can engage in.

SUGGESTED SOURCES

Primary Source

Salley, Alexander S., Jr., ed. *Narratives of Early Carolina, 1650–1708.* New York: Scribner's, 1911. Available at Google Books and the Internet Archive at www.archive.org. A summary of the *Fundamental Orders* can be found in Daniel Defoe's "Party-Tyranny."

Secondary Source

Craven, Wesley Frank. *The Colonies in Transition, 1660–1713.* New York: Harper & Row, 1968. Craven discusses the differing plans of the Carolina proprietors versus those of Barbados planters who got there first.

World Wide Web

"The Fundamental Constitutions of Carolina: March 1, 1669." http://www.yale.edu/lawweb/avalon/states/nc05.htm. The full text of John Locke's proposed governing document for the Carolina colony.

"John Locke: His American and Carolinian Legacy." http://www.johnlocke.org/about/legacy.html. The full text of Locke's Fundamental Orders.

32. English Merchants Establish the Hudson's Bay Company (1670)

In the 1660s, French *Coureur de bois* (wood's runners) Pierre-Esprit Radisson and his brother-in-law, Médard Chouart des Groseilliers, explored the areas of Lakes Michigan and Superior, traded with native peoples, and obtained a large quantity of fur. However, they did not have a license to trade, so French authorities confiscated their furs when they returned to Montreal and briefly incarcerated Groseilliers. While in the Great Lakes region, Radisson and Groseilliers discovered that Hudson's Bay offered an advantageous trade route. They quickly realized that if fur trading posts could be established there, they would benefit from lower transportation costs because the furs could be supplied by sea. They would have access to the vast, untapped fur trapping territories of the Canadian Shield, a region that stretched from the St. Lawrence River to Hudson's Bay and veered north and west of the bay into the Arctic, and have the willing cooperation of the Cree people, who were not only numerous but desperately needed European goods.

Unable to interest the French in their scheme, Radisson and Groseilliers traveled to Boston. An English investor took them to England and arranged for them to present their plan to King Charles II. Using the plan outlined by Radisson and Groseillers, London merchants organized the Hudson's Bay Company (HBC) in 1670. Despite company rules against fraternization with the Indians, many company men married into Cree families. Establishing their trading posts (called factories), the HBC dominated the fur trade in North America well into the nineteenth century, competing first with French trading concerns, and later with American trading concerns in the Old Northwest and the Great Plains, and they even had a presence in California when the United States acquired it after the Mexican War.

TERM PAPER SUGGESTIONS

1. The English had strategic as well as economic reasons for establishing the Hudson's Bay Company. Explore the strategic advantages the English realized.
2. Examine the expansion of the Hudson's Bay Company. What advantages did the company possess that allowed it to expand into territories that would later become part of the United States?
3. How did the Hudson's Bay Company affect the history of the United States? Think of this question primarily in terms of the fur trade and the exploration of the American West.

ALTERNATIVE TERM PAPER SUGGESTIONS

1. You are a French investor who realizes that Radisson and Groseilliers have devised a plan that would give the British an enormous economic advantage in the fur trade. Devise a PowerPoint presentation designed to convince the

French authorities to heed their plan. Do not be shy about mentioning how Hudson's Bay would benefit the English.

2. Imagine you are Pierre Radisson and you have to speak to an audience of businessmen (potential investors in the Hudson's Bay Company) and British officials about the benefits that England will realize from the Hudson's Bay Company. Prepare a PowerPoint presentation that emphasizes not only the economic advantages (this is for the businessmen) but what may be found as a result of further exploration of the North American interior. Use seventeenth-century maps to illustrate your presentation. Keep in mind that geographic knowledge was not quite what it is today.

SUGGESTED SOURCES

Primary Sources

"Charter and Supplemental Charter of the Hudson's Bay Company." http://www.gutenberg.org/etext/6580. Original Charter of the Hudson's Bay Company.

"Exploration, the Fur Trade, and the Hudson's Bay Company." http://www.canadiana.org/hbc/intro_e.html. Contains biographies and links to primary source documents.

Secondary Sources

Dickason, Patricia Olive. *Canada's First Nations: A History of Founding Peoples from Earliest Times.* Norman: University of Oklahoma Press, 1992. Includes discussion of Radisson's founding of the Hudson's Bay Company.

Eccles, W. J. *The Canadian Frontier, 1534–1760.* Albuquerque: University of New Mexico Press, 1983. Includes discussion of the founding of the Hudson's Bay Company.

Newman, Peter C. *Empire of the Bay: The Company of Adventurers that Seized a Continent.* New York: Penguin, 2000. Well, maybe they did not quite seize a continent, but the Hudson's Bay Company exerted enormous influence over the fur trade after its founding.

Ray, Arthur J. *Indians in the Fur Trade: Their Role as Hunters, Trappers, and Middlemen in the Lands Southwest of Hudson Bay, 1660–1870.* Toronto: University of Toronto Press, 1974. The fur trade could not run without Native American labor.

Van Kirk, Sylvia. *Many Tender Ties: Women in Fur-Trade Society, 1670–1870.* Norman: University of Oklahoma Press, 1980. Van Kirk examines the role of women in the fur trade.

World Wide Web

"Empire of the Bay." http://www.pbs.org/empireofthebay/. Companion Web site for the PBS presentation. Includes maps, timeline, transcript, and short biographies of key individuals.

33. Carolina Is Founded and Soon Becomes Only Mainland Colony Where Slaves Outnumber Free Men (1670s)

The establishment of the Carolina colony (today's North and South Carolina plus part of Georgia) led to an influx of settlers, not from England as its proprietors expected, but from the sugar colony of Barbados. Small and crowded, Barbados offered few opportunities for new colonists, whereas Carolina offered large swaths of land for settlement. Realizing that they could not grow sugar in the Carolinas, and knowing they could not compete with Virginia's established tobacco plantations, the "Barbados men" engaged in several different types of economic activity. At first, Carolina relied heavily on the Indian trade, specifically the trade in Indian slaves, who would be shipped to the Caribbean. The deerskin trade also contributed to the colony's economic stability, but Carolinians realized that the long-term growth of their colony would have to rely on commodities more stable than Indian slaves or deerskins. The colonists took to growing food and raising livestock and became a primary exporter of foodstuffs to English sugar colonies. Closer to the Caribbean than the New England colonies, Carolina had a competitive advantage in providing food to the sugar islands. However, Carolina found its economic salvation in a subtropical crop, rice. Most English planters knew almost nothing about how to grow rice, but slaves imported from Africa did. Planters built dikes in the tidewater swamps to keep saltwater out of the rice paddies. Because of rice, Carolina became England's only North American colony where most of the population was enslaved. Another crop that was enormously important to Carolina was indigo, which produced a dark blue dye that was very much in demand in England.

TERM PAPER SUGGESTIONS

1. Examine colonial Carolina's economy. Other southern colonies relied heavily on slavery to provide a labor force. Carolina, however, used slaves to a far greater extent than the other colonies. Why? What impact did this have on Carolinian society?
2. Examine Carolina's slave codes (see the Web resources listed here). Give the reasoning behind these codes. Keep in mind the reasoning would be from the perspective of a seventeenth-century colonist.
3. Examine Carolina's drive toward economic stability. Which commodities did Carolina export before rice and indigo?

ALTERNATIVE TERM PAPER SUGGESTIONS

1. Imagine you are an English colonist who has just arrived in seventeenth-century Carolina. You plan to start a rice plantation, but you know nothing about rice. Your economic success is completely dependent on your African slaves and their knowledge of the crop. Write a long letter to your relatives in England and explain your anxieties about your lack of knowledge of the crop and of your reliance on your slaves.
2. You live in seventeenth-century England, but you want to immigrate to Carolina and become a rice planter. However, you have no money. You decide to try and find individuals to invest in your scheme for a rice plantation. Prepare a PowerPoint presentation complete with maps, charts, and graphs that you will show to would-be investors. Remember, you have to convince them that they will get rich if they invest in your rice plantation, so lay it on heavy and thick!

SUGGESTED SOURCES

Primary Sources

"Colonial and State Records of North Carolina." http://docsouth.unc.edu/csr/index.html/volumes. "Documenting the American South" is a project of the University of North Carolina. This part of the Web site will eventually contain the published colonial and state records of North Carolina. As of March 2009, 24 of the 26 volumes of the colonial documents were available online, with the other two due soon.

Lawson, John. *A New Voyage to Carolina; Containing the Exact Description and Natural History of That Country: Together with the Present State Thereof. And a Journal of a Thousand Miles, Travel'd Thro' Several Nations of Indians. Giving a Particular Account of Their Customs, Manners, &c.* London: n.p., 1709. http://docsouth.unc.edu/nc/lawson/lawson.html. John Lawson was appointed the surveyor for Carolina in 1701. His *New Voyage* is one of the best firsthand accounts of the flora, fauna, and peoples of the region.

Salley, Alexander S., Jr., ed. *Narratives of Early Carolina, 1650–1708.* New York: Scribner's, 1911. Available at Google Books and the Internet Archive at www.archive.org. Valuable resource that contains a number of edited primary sources from the first years of the Carolina colony.

Secondary Sources

Axtell, James. *The Indians' New South: Cultural Change in the Colonial Southeast.* Baton Rouge: Louisiana State University Press, 1997. Examines the changing world of native peoples in the southeast, including the Carolinas.

Corkran, David H. *The Carolina Indian Frontier.* Columbia: University of South Carolina Press, 1970. Examines the role of native peoples in the colonial period.

Crane, Verner W. *The Southern Frontier, 1670–1732.* New York: Norton, 1981. Examines the transformation of South Carolina into a slave society.

Littlefield, Daniel C. *Rice and Slaves: Ethnicity and the Slave Trade in Colonial South Carolina.* Baton Rouge: Louisiana State University Press, 1981. Emphasizes that Carolina's wonder crop, rice, went hand in hand with the stepped up importation of slaves into the colony.

Merrell, James H. *The Indians' New World: Catawbas and Their Neighbors from European Contact Through the Era of Removal.* Chapel Hill: University of North Carolina Press, 1989. Merrell examines the changes in Carolina from the perspective of its native peoples.

Weir, Robert M. *Colonial South Carolina: A History.* Milwood, NY: KTO Press, 1983. A history of colonial South Carolina.

Wood, Peter. *Black Majority: Negroes in Colonial South Carolina from 1670 Through the Stono Rebellion.* New York: Knopf, 1974. A history of African American slaves in the Carolinas from the founding of the colony to about 1740.

World Wide Web

"Rice, Indigo, and Fever in Colonial South Carolina." http://www.geocities.com/Athens/Aegean/7023/indigo.html. Good overview of agricultural development and of the role of disease in slowing the colony's growth.

"South Carolina Slave Laws Summary and Record." http://www.slaveryinamerica.org/geography/slave_laws_SC.htm. Offers a brief article about slavery in South Carolina, with sources, and a summary that traces the development of Carolina's slave codes.

34. King Philip's War in New England (1675–1676)

In 1661, Massasoit, the Wampanoag leader who signed a peace treaty with the Pilgrims in 1621, passed away. His son Wamsutta, known to the English as Alexander, succeeded him. The Wampanoag faced considerable pressure to surrender their lands to the growing numbers of English colonists. Wamsutta ceased his father's practice of selling land. Acting on reports that Wamsutta planned to launch a war against New England, colonial authorities summoned him to Plymouth for questioning in 1663. On the way home from his interrogation, Wamsutta fell ill and died, and many Wampanoag concluded that the English poisoned him.

Wamsutta's brother, Metacom, known to the English as King Philip, replaced his brother as the leader of the Wampanoag. Metacom secretly prepared for war against the English. Unbeknownst to Philip, his secretary, John Sassamon, a Harvard-educated Indian, also worked as a spy for the English. Just before Christmas 1674, Sassamon warned the colonists that Philip had made preparations for war. Shortly thereafter, Sassamon was murdered and colonial authorities executed three Wampanoag men for the crime, igniting the conflict.

The natives destroyed a dozen English towns. However, the winter of 1675–1676 gave the colonists a respite. The Indians ran out of food and ammunition and many surrendered.

In the late summer of 1676, an Indian allied with the English shot and killed Philip, ending the rebellion. The English dismembered Philip's remains and sold his wife and child into slavery. King Philip's War marked the end of native resistance in southern New England.

TERM PAPER SUGGESTIONS

1. Discuss the period from 1661 (Massasoit's death) to 1674 (John Sassamon's murder). Why did tensions between the colonists and the Indians increase? Does it appear that either side sought ways to decrease friction?
2. Discuss the role of the Praying Indians in the conflict. Why did many of them remain loyal to the English? Why did the English often refuse to use them as military allies?
3. What were some of the long-term effects of King Philip's War? How did the war contribute to a "crisis of confidence" among the English?
4. Because of the timing of both King Philip's War in Massachusetts and Bacon's Rebellion in Virginia, many colonists thought it likely that two wars were part of a larger conspiracy against them. Examine this idea.

ALTERNATIVE TERM PAPER SUGGESTIONS

1. It is 1675 and Metacom (King Philip) has hired you as a public relations consultant during his war with the New England colonies. Using a blog on the Internet, your job is to sway public opinion in England and convince a majority of people that the colonists are wrong in prosecuting this war against the Indians.
2. You are a Praying Indian during King Philip's War. You must either remain loyal to the English or join King Philip. You cannot remain neutral. Which side would you join? Why? What qualms would you have about your decision (other than the possibility that you might choose the losing side!)?

SUGGESTED SOURCES

Primary Sources

Lincoln, Charles Henry, ed. *Narratives of the Indian Wars, 1675–1699.* New York: Scribner's, 1913. Despite the title, nearly all of the narratives in this collection deal with King Philip's War. Available at Google Books and at the Internet Archive at www.archive.org.

Rowlandson, Mary, and Neal Salisbury, eds. *The Sovereignty and Goodness of God: With Related Documents.* New York: Bedford/St. Martin's Press, 1997. (Originally published 1682 as *The Narrative of the Captivity and Restoration of Mrs. Mary Rowlandson.*) Considered the classic Indian captivity narrative. Still in print under different titles, and many different versions can be found at Google Books and at the Internet Archive at www.archive.org.

Slotkin, Richard. *So Dreadful a Judgment: Puritan Responses to King Philip's War, 1676–77.* Middletown, CT: Wesleyan University Press, 1979. A good collection of primary source accounts.

Secondary Sources

Drake, James D. *King Philip's War: Civil War in New England, 1675–1676.* Amherst: University of Massachusetts Press, 2000. Drake argues that King Philip's War was not so much an Indian war, as it was a civil war in New England, with the colonists and Indians opposed to one another.

Lepore, Jill. *The Name of War: King Philip's War and the Origins of American Identity.* New York: Vintage, 1999. Lepore takes an expansive approach, examining not only the conflict itself but also how Americans choose to remember and commemorate it. Lepore also looks at the mythologizing of King Philip on the American stage in the nineteenth century.

Philbrick, Nathaniel. *Mayflower: A Story of Courage, Community, and War.* New York: Penguin, 2006. Philbrick includes a very good section on King Philip's War.

Schultz, Eric B., and Michael J. Tougias. *King Philip's War: The History and Legacy of America's Forgotten Conflict.* Woodstock, VT: Countryman Press, 2000. A detailed account of the war.

World Wide Web

"King Philip's War, 1675." http://www.colonialwarsct.org/1675.htm. The Society of Colonial Wars in Connecticut maintains this Web site, which gives an overview of the conflict and a timeline.

"King Philip's War: The Causes." http://www.pilgrimhall.org/philipwar.htm. Causes and effects of the conflict.

Multimedia Source

History of King Philip's War. Bride Media, 2000. VHS. 26 minutes. Using interviews with scholars and Native Americans, this presentation gives a brief overview of King Philip's War.

35. Bacon's Rebellion in Virginia (1676)

In the 1670s, Virginia's elite held the best lands in the eastern part of the colony and most of the political offices. In April 1676, small land holders in the western part of the colony, upset with what they regarded as the colonial government's inadequate responses to Indian attacks on the frontier, formed their own militia. Nathaniel Bacon, a wealthy, newly arrived planter, assumed command of the frontier militias. Bacon and his men attacked Indians indiscriminately, often killing native peoples who were at peace with the colony.

When ordered to appear in Jamestown by Governor William Berkeley (related to Bacon through marriage), Bacon arrived with a force of 500 men, demanding that he be granted a commission to lead his militia against local Indians. Instead, Berkeley arrested Bacon, charging him with treason. Then, hoping to diffuse tensions, Berkeley pardoned Bacon. Bacon and his men, however, still demanded a commission and the authority to wage war against Indians on the frontier. Berkeley agreed, fled Jamestown, and attempted to recruit an army to oppose Bacon. Rather than fight Indians, Bacon and his men instead sacked the plantations of colonists who remained loyal to Berkeley. The revolt came to an abrupt halt with Bacon's death (attributed to fevers or dysentery) in October 1676.

During the rebellion, both Berkeley and Bacon offered freedom to slaves and servants if they would join their forces. It has been argued that Bacon's Rebellion was instrumental in the adoption of slave codes. Fearful that poor whites and African slaves would again work together to overthrow the government, the colony adopted a set of laws that placed blacks at the bottom of the colonial hierarchy.

TERM PAPER SUGGESTIONS

1. Examine the factors that led to Bacon's Rebellion. What actions could the colonial government have taken to prevent the revolt?
2. What led to conflict with native peoples on Virginia's western frontier? Was Governor Berkeley reluctant to fight a war against the Indians? How did Berkeley propose to pacify the frontier? Why did Bacon find these proposals inadequate?
3. Virginia's elite had long worried about the possibility of a rebellion. Examine the makeup of Bacon's followers. Were the fears of the elites justified?

4. Some scholars have argued that Bacon's Rebellion was a precursor of sorts for the American Revolution 100 years later. Evaluate this argument.
5. In his declaration of rebellion, Bacon takes care to note that the rebellion was directed at Governor William Berkeley, not the English government. Why did Bacon make such a distinction?

ALTERNATIVE TERM PAPER SUGGESTIONS

1. You are Governor William Berkeley's public relations secretary in 1676. Governor Berkeley has directed you to put together a podcast to be broadcast to the rebels. You are to try and convince the rebels that the governor has proposed many reforms and that they should not follow Nathaniel Bacon.
2. As Governor Berkeley's public relations person, you also have to address the concerns of the governor's allies, the eastern elites. Many of them are concerned about the governor's offer of freedom to slaves and servants who join him to fight Bacon. They want to know how slavery will be reestablished once the crisis has passed. Prepare a PowerPoint presentation that will be shown *only* to the elites.

SUGGESTED SOURCES

Primary Sources

Andrews, Charles M., ed. *Narratives of the Insurrections, 1675–1690.* New York: Scribner's, 1915). Available at Google Books and at the Internet Archive at www.archive.org. Contains firsthand accounts of Bacon's Rebellion.

"Bacon's Rebellion: The Declaration (1676)." http://historymatters.gmu.edu/d/5800. Contains the text of Bacon's declaration of rebellion against the governor of Virginia.

Beverley, Robert. *The History and Present State of Virginia.* London: R. Parker, 1705. http://docsouth.unc.edu/southlit/beverley/menu.html. Beverley included accounts of Bacon's Rebellion that he gleaned from eyewitnesses.

Secondary Sources

Morgan, Edmund S. *American Slavery, American Freedom: The Ordeal of Colonial Virginia.* New York: Norton, 1975. Morgan offers a solid detailed account of Bacon's Rebellion and its aftermath.

Steele, Ian K. *Warpaths: Invasions of North America.* New York: Oxford University Press, 1994. Contains a chapter that examines Virginia's seventeenth-century conflicts with Native Americans, including Bacon's Rebellion.

Webb, Stephen Saunders. *1676: The End of American Independence.* Syracuse, NY: Syracuse University Press, 1995. Webb argues that Bacon's Rebellion introduced an era of more direct involvement by the English Crown and Parliament in governing their North American colonies.

Wertenbaker, Thomas Jefferson. *Torchbearer of the Revolution: The Story of Bacon's Rebellion and its Leader.* Princeton, NJ: Princeton University Press, 1940. This older work argues that Bacon's Rebellion was a sort of template for the American Revolution a century later.

World Wide Web

"Bacon's Rebellion." http://www.virginiaplaces.org/military/bacon.html. Provides an overview to Bacon's Rebellion and offers links to other sites.

"Robert Beverley on Bacon's Rebellion." http://www.let.rug.nl/~usa/D/1651-1700/bacon_rebel/bever.htm. Excerpt from Beverley's *History and Present State of Virginia* (1705).

Multimedia Source

Africans in America. PBS, 1998. 2 DVDs. 180 minutes. Includes an account of Bacon's Rebellion and an analysis of its aftermath.

36. Pueblo Revolt (1680)

After the failure of the Hernando de Soto and Francisco Coronado expeditions, the Spanish moved slowly in colonizing Mexico's northern frontier, not settling present-day New Mexico until 1598. The Spanish brought Franciscan friars with them, who converted Pueblo peoples to Christianity. Many of the conversions were forced, and the Pueblo people had to wear Spanish clothing and learn the Spanish language. In addition, they were forced to build missions and churches. The Pueblos offered little resistance and the Spanish regarded them as pliable, docile people. However in the 1670s, a series of droughts and Spanish failure to protect Pueblos from Apache and Navajo raiders led to a resurgence of native religion. Native religious leaders blamed the Pueblos' misfortunes on the Spanish. In response, the Spanish rounded up a number of Pueblo religious leaders, whipping most of them and executing five. One of the leaders who had been whipped, a Tewa man named Popé, hatched a plan to drive the Spaniards out of New Mexico. Popé put together a conspiracy that included most of the Pueblo villages. The plan employed runners carrying knotted ropes from one Pueblo to another to signal when to start the attack. Stunned by the attack, the Spanish retreated to Santa Fe. The Pueblos drove the Spanish out of the town, forcing them to withdraw to central Mexico. With the Spaniards gone, Pueblo peoples practiced "debaptism," plunging into rivers to wash the Christianity off of them, and dismantled the churches the friars forced them to build. The Spanish did not return to New Mexico until 1692, and the Pueblo Revolt is the most successful rebellion ever mounted by Native Americans against Europeans.

TERM PAPER SUGGESTIONS

1. Review the conditions that contributed to the Pueblos' decision to rebel.
2. Examine the role of Pueblo leaders such as Popé. What actions taken by Pueblo leaders contributed to the success of the revolt? What actions (or lack thereof) on the part of the Spanish contributed to their defeat?
3. Examine the disparate nature of the Pueblo villages in the seventeenth century. How did the Pueblo leadership encourage peoples with ofttimes competing interest to work together to eject the Spanish?
4. Read the testimony of Indians (see under "Primary Sources," *Revolt of the Pueblo Indians of New Mexico*). Do the Spanish interrogators seem to understand why the Pueblos revolted? What lessons do you think they learned?

ALTERNATIVE TERM PAPER SUGGESTIONS

1. It is 1680 and you are a trusted lieutenant of the Pueblo leader Popé. Popé is concerned about securing the support of other native leaders. He has tasked you with creating a PowerPoint presentation that will sway native people who are sitting on the fence.
2. Popé has appointed you his minister of propaganda. You are to create podcasts to be broadcast in Spain promoting the native point of view. One thing

you must do is to try to set the Spanish secular authorities and the Franciscan priests against each other.

SUGGESTED SOURCES

Primary Sources

Espinosa, J. Manuel, ed. *The Pueblo Indian Revolt of 1696 and Franciscan Missions in New Mexico: Letters of the Missionaries and Related Documents.* Norman: University of Oklahoma Press, 1988.

Hackett, Charles Wilson, ed. *Revolt of the Pueblo Indians of New Mexico and Otermín's Attempted Reconquest, 1680-1682 [volume 9—excerpt],* Trans. Clair Shelby Charmion. Albuquerque: The University of New Mexico Press, 1942. http://www.americanjourneys.org/aj-009b/summary/index.asp. Excerpts from primary documents pertaining to the revolt.

Secondary Sources

Gutiérrez, Ramón A. *When Jesus Came, the Corn Mothers Went Away: Marriage, Sexuality, and Power in New Mexico, 1500–1846.* Stanford, CA: Stanford University Press, 1991. Gutiérrez's history of the Southwest includes chapters on the Pueblo Revolt and the Spanish reconquest in 1692.

Knaut, Andrew L. *The Pueblo Revolt of 1680: Conquest and Resistance in Seventeenth Century New Mexico.* Norman: University of Oklahoma Press, 1997. Account of the planning, execution, and aftermath of the Pueblo Revolt.

Roberts, David. *The Pueblo Revolt: The Secret Rebellion That Drove the Spaniards Out of the Southwest.* New York: Simon & Schuster, 2004. Interesting look at the Pueblo Revolt that includes assessments of its impact on native peoples today.

Weber, David J. *The Spanish Frontier in North America.* New Haven, CT: Yale University Press, 1992. Perhaps the best history of Spanish inroads in North America.

Weber, David J., ed. *What Caused the Pueblo Revolt of 1680?* New York: Bedford/St. Martin's, 1999. Essays by five historians that examine the hows and whys of the 1680 Pueblo revolt.

World Wide Web

"Archives of the West to 1806." http://www.pbs.org/weta/thewest/resources/archives/one/pueblo.htm. This is the companion Web site for the PBS series *The West.* It contains letters from Franciscan missionaries who survived the revolt.

"The Pueblo Revolt of 1680." http://www.nativepeoples.com/article/articles/121/1/The-Pueblo-Revolt-of-1680/Page1.html. Article about the Pueblo Revolt.

"Trouble for the Spanish: The Pueblo Revolt of 1680." http://www.neh.gov/news/humanities/2002-11/pueblorevolt.html. Essay about the Pueblo Revolt.

Multimedia Source

The Pueblo. Schlessinger Media, 1994. 1 DVD. 30 minutes. Explores Pueblo history and culture.

37. William Penn Establishes the Colony of Pennsylvania (1682)

Led by a preacher named George Fox, the Society of Friends, known by their opponents as "Quakers," appeared in England in the seventeenth century. The Quakers did not have clergymen or ministers, and they argued that everyone could come to God by heeding their "inner light." They asserted that all humans were "spiritual equals" and disdained societal conventions, often using the familiar term "thou" instead of the more formal "you." They advocated pacifism and refused to serve in the military, which the Crown considered treason. Not surprisingly, the Quakers were persecuted in England.

However, a prominent Quaker, William Penn, sought to create a haven for them. Wealthy and the son of an important British naval officer, Penn converted to Quakerism while a young man. Upon his father's death, he approached the Crown regarding the repayment of debts the Crown owed his father. Rather than money, the Crown instead offered Penn the largest land grant England ever gave a single individual, the present state of Pennsylvania.

Penn wished for his colony to be a haven to his co-religionists, but he also wanted to make a profit. His Frame of Government vested most of the power in himself, but permitted religious liberty to all and allowed for the immigration of non-English settlers and non-Quakers. Believing that wars between native peoples and English colonies in New England and the Chesapeake were the result of misunderstandings, Penn learned the Delaware language before signing treaties with them to purchase their land.

TERM PAPER SUGGESTIONS

1. A supporter of Penn and the Quaker movement was King James II. Why would James (the titular head of the Anglican Church) be willing to help the Quakers? What does his support tell us about English politics and religion at the time?
2. Pennsylvania, unlike the New England colonies, did not have an established Church. How did this policy benefit the colony?
3. Examine Penn's Indian policy. Was it a success? Compare Pennsylvania's relations with native peoples with those of other colonies.
4. One of the consequences of Penn's liberal policy regarding immigration is that Pennsylvania attracted settlers from countries throughout Western Europe. How did this affect Pennsylvania and the Quakers in the eighteenth century?

ALTERNATIVE TERM PAPER SUGGESTIONS

1. You have been hired by William Penn to promote immigration to Pennsylvania. The advertising campaign has two slogans, and the one you use depends on the audience. One slogan is "The Best Poor Man's Country in the World" and the other is "The Holy Experiment." Using one of these slogans, prepare a PowerPoint presentation for an audience of perspective colonists.
2. Penn has sought you out as his advisor regarding Indian affairs. Prepare a PowerPoint briefing for Penn and his associates that reviews relations between Native Americans and other English colonies in North America. Focus on what these colonies did right and what they did wrong. Offer Penn at least three courses of action.

SUGGESTED SOURCES

Primary Sources

"Frame of Government of Pennsylvania, May 5, 1682." http://www.yale.edu/lawweb/avalon/states/pa04.htm. Text of Penn's original plan of government for his colony.

Myers, Albert Cook, ed. *Narratives of Early Pennsylvania, West New Jersey, and Delaware, 1630–1707.* New York: Scribner's, 1912. Collection of edited documents related to early Pennsylvania. Also available at Google Books.

Soderlund, Jean R., ed. *William Penn and the Founding of Pennsylvania: A Documentary History.* Philadelphia: University of Pennsylvania Press, 1983. Collection of documents related to early Pennsylvania.

Secondary Sources

Dunn, Maples Mary. *William Penn, Politics, and Conscience.* Princeton, NJ: Princeton University Press, 1967. Part biography, this work examines Penn's role in the designing of Pennsylvania's government.

Dunn, Richard S., and Mary Maples Dunn. *The World of William Penn.* Philadelphia: University of Pennsylvania Press, 1986. A biography of William Penn.

Illick, Joseph. *Colonial Pennsylvania: A History.* New York: Scribner's, 1976. A history of Pennsylvania from its founding to the American Revolution.

Levy, Barry. *Quakers and the American Family: British Settlement in the Delaware Valley.* New York: Oxford University Press, 1988. Levy examines the Quaker family in the settlement of Pennsylvania, Delaware, and New Jersey.

Nash, Gary B. *Quakers and Politics: Pennsylvania, 1681–1726.* Boston: Northeastern University Press, 1993. Nash examines the dominant role that Quakers played in Pennsylvania politics, particularly that of William Penn, conflicts with the Penn family, and tensions between Quakers and new settlers who settled the frontier regions.

Schwartz, Sally. *"A Mixed Multitude": The Struggle for Toleration in Colonial Pennsylvania.* New York: New York University Press, 1988. Pennsylvania was the first colony that did not have an established church and welcomed peoples of all denominations.

World Wide Web

"Penn's Holy Experiment: The Seed of a Nation." http://www.pym.org/exhibit/p078.html. Web site that emphasizes Penn's achievements as a city planner (he planned Philadelphia) and his fairly liberal approach (for the time) to criminal justice.

"William Penn." http://www.phmc.state.pa.us/ppet/penn/page1.asp. Biography of Penn by the Pennsylvania Historical and Museum Commission.

"William Penn, Visionary Proprietor." http://xroads.virginia.edu/~CAP/PENN/pnhome.html. Includes chapters on Penn's dealings with Native Americans and his plan for the city of Philadelphia.

"William Penn's Welcome Week." http://www.ushistory.org/Penn/. Links to various exhibits about Penn, his writings, and other individuals who were important in the Quaker movement and the founding of Pennsylvania.

Multimedia Source

Saints & Strangers. Vision Video, 2002. 1 DVD. 59 minutes. Uses live action to emphasize the role of the Congregationalist, Quaker, Baptist, and Anglican denominations in early America.

38. Robert La Salle Explores the Mississippi and Names the Region "Louisiana" (1682)

Nothing encouraged European exploration of the North American interior like the fur trade. Comparatively lightweight, easy to transport, and very valuable, fur trading companies and the *Coeur de Bois* (woods runners) probed deep into the continent, seeking new sources of animal pelts. For the French, the trade depended on stable relations with Native American peoples. In 1682, Robert La Salle led an expedition south down the Mississippi. The purpose of the expedition was to establish relations with native peoples, trade with them, and most importantly, to ascertain the extent of the Mississippi River. Hernando de Soto became the first explorer to see and cross the river in 1543, but no European had attempted to traverse its length. On his journey south, La Salle took note of the Indians and the alluvial soil deposits along the river and realized that it emptied into the Gulf of Mexico.

La Salle recognized that the European power that occupied the lands around the mouth of the Mississippi also controlled access to the heart of the continent. With the English settling the Atlantic seaboard, La Salle realized that the French had to control the interior in order to confine them to the coast. La Salle claimed the mouth of the Mississippi and lands surrounding it, naming the region "Louisiana" in honor of King Louis XIV. La Salle encouraged the French government to quickly occupy and take control of the mouth of the Mississippi, lest another European power do so.

TERM PAPER SUGGESTIONS

1. Earlier missionaries and explorers traversed the Mississippi, but did not travel all the way to its mouth. Why not? What held them back?
2. During his journey south, La Salle noted that there were intermittent Native American communities. La Salle's observations are at odds with those of Spaniards who accompanied the de Soto expedition 130 years earlier. What had changed in the American Southeast?
3. A recurring theme in La Salle's explorations of the Great Lakes and the Mississippi is that many of his followers seemed to eventually mutiny against him. Investigate why this seems to happen to La Salle. Is there something in La Salle's leadership style that causes resentment? Or can the mutinies be attributed to hardships beyond La Salle's control?
4. Discuss the North American fur trade in the context of providing the impetus for the exploration of the North American interior.

ALTERNATIVE TERM PAPER SUGGESTIONS

1. It is 1682 and you are accompanying La Salle as his secretary. La Salle asks you to prepare a PowerPoint presentation for him to use when he meets with French King Louis XIV. The presentation must include maps and must make the point that colonizing the interior of the continent is the best strategy for the French to pursue.
2. As La Salle's secretary, you are also tasked with keeping a record of the expedition's day-to-day affairs. Using Henri de Tonti and Louis Hennepin as sources, prepare an oral report, to be given via podcast, that summarizes the expedition's discoveries.

SUGGESTED SOURCES

Primary Sources

Hennepin, Louis. *A New Discovery of a Vast Country in America, by Father Louis Hennepin. Reprinted from the Second London Issue of 1698, with Facsimiles of Original Title-Pages, Maps, and Illustrations, and the Addition of Introduction, Notes, and Index by Reuben Gold Thwaites.* 2 vols. Chicago: A. C. McClurg & Co., 1903. http://www.americanjourneys.org/aj-124/index.asp. Louis Hennepin was a Recollect missionary who accompanied La Salle on his explorations. When Hennepin published his narrative, he was accused of trying to take credit for La Salle's discoveries.

Kellogg, Louise P., ed. *Early Narratives of the Northwest, 1634–1699.* New York: Scribner's, 1917. Available at Google Books. Contains a narrative by Henri de Tonti, a member of La Salle's expeditions.

Relation of the Discoveries and Voyages of Cavelier de La Salle from 1679 to 1681: The Official Narrative. Trans. Melville B. Anderson. Chicago: The Caxton Club, 1901. http://www.americanjourneys.org/aj-122/index.asp. There is some question as to the identity of this work's author, but most historians believe individuals who accompanied La Salle on his explorations compiled it, working from his notes.

Secondary Source

Galloway, Patricia K., ed. *La Salle and his Legacy: Frenchmen and Indians in the Lower Mississippi Valley.* Jackson: University Press of Mississippi, 1982. This work traces La Salle and the early settlement of French Louisiana.

World Wide Web

"Historical Narratives of Early Canada: La Salle." http://www.uppercanadahistory.ca/finna/finna3a.html. Good biography of La Salle and his explorations.

Multimedia Source

Voyage of Doom. PBS, 1999. VHS. 60 minutes. NOVA presentation that looks at the archaeological discovery and excavation of La Salle's flagship, *The Belle.*

39. Robert La Salle Leads an Expedition by Ship That Attempts to Find the Mouth of the Mississippi River (1684)

Two years after leading an expedition down the Mississippi River, Robert La Salle returned with a seaborne expedition from France. La Salle planned to land near the mouth of the Mississippi River and establish a post that would control the mouth of the river and begin French colonization of the North American interior. By controlling the center of the continent, the French could not only establish colonies but also attempt to keep the English confined to the Atlantic seaboard. The expedition began with four ships and 300 colonists, but met misfortune after misfortune. Pirates captured one of the vessels, another ran aground, and the expedition's flagship, *The Belle,* sank in Texas's Matagorda Bay. Although La Salle had traversed the Mississippi just a few years before, he had never approached the river from the seaward side and did not recognize its mouth. La Salle landed 200 miles west of the Mississippi on the Gulf Coast in what is now eastern Texas and established a post named Fort St. Louis (near present-day Houston). The colony quickly ran short of food and other provisions. Additionally, the local Karawanka Indians killed many of the colonists. La Salle led several expeditions on foot eastward, attempting to find the Mississippi. By 1687, only 36 colonists were still alive, and they rebelled and murdered La Salle. A year later, the Karawanka Indians attacked Fort St. Louis, capturing or killing its 25 remaining inhabitants.

TERM PAPER SUGGESTIONS

1. It seems incredible that La Salle somehow missed the mouth of the Mississippi River. However, the river and its mouth were very different in the seventeenth century. Discuss how La Salle could have missed the mouth of the river. To be fair, do you think that most other navigators would have missed it as well?
2. The would-be colonists had plenty of reasons to be upset with La Salle—after all, they ended up nowhere near the Mississippi—but why did the French post at Fort St. Louis fail? What caused the colonists to revolt against and murder La Salle?
3. Discuss the motivations behind the French decision to gain control of the Mississippi River. Keep in mind the French intended to do this with relatively few colonists in North America. How did they plan to control the entire length of the Mississippi?
4. Discuss the Louisiana colony that the French eventually founded. The colony, while under French control, was never more than a backwater and never really became a commercial success. Analyze why Louisiana never met French expectations and why they kept it.
5. Louisiana did become something of a melting pot, with French colonists, Indians, and African slaves all making up part of the population. Discuss how French colonial authorities governed the colony and made sure that neither the Indians or the Africans ever gained the upper hand.

ALTERNATIVE TERM PAPER SUGGESTIONS

1. You are one of the French colonists who mutinied against and murdered La Salle. You have been apprehended by French authorities and charged with murder. Your only chance is to write a convincing statement, arguing that due to extenuating circumstances, the killing of La Salle by you and your cohorts should be ruled justifiable homicide. Use your imagination and make it good. Otherwise, you have a date with the hangman!
2. You are La Salle's public relations person. Despite his missing the mouth of the Mississippi, landing in the wrong place, and losing three of his four ships, he orders you to prepare a podcast that will be broadcast back home in France. He also orders you to put a positive spin on things, yet he also states that you cannot lie. At the same time, you must appeal for help from France. Good luck.

SUGGESTED SOURCES

Primary Sources

Joutel, Henri. *A Journal of the Last Voyage Perform'd by Monsr. de la Sale, to the Gulph of Mexico, to Find Out the Mouth of the Missisipi River; Containing An Account of the Settlements He Endeavour'd to Make on the Coast of the Aforesaid Bay, His Unfortunate Death, and the Travels of His Companions for the Space of Eight Hundred Leagues across That Inland Country of America, Now Call'd Louisiana, (and Given by the King of France to M. Crozat,) till They Came into Canada.* London: Printed for A. Bell, B. Lintott, and F. Baker, 1714. http://www.americanjourneys.org/aj-121/index.asp. Joutel is an interesting character in his own right. He escaped being assassinated by La Salle's murderers and a later massacre at Fort St. Louis. Over a year and a half, he led six other Frenchmen north up the Mississippi, reaching Quebec in 1688.

Joutel, Henri. *The La Salle Expedition to Texas: The Journal of Henri Joutel, 1684–1687.* Ed. William C. Foster. Austin: Texas State Historical Association, 1998. Much like the previous book, but it includes material that eighteenth-century English publishers omitted.

Kellogg, Louise P., ed. *Early Narratives of the Northwest, 1634–1699.* New York: Scribner's, 1917. Available at Google Books. Contains a narrative by Henri de Tonti, a member of La Salle's expeditions.

Relation of the Discoveries and Voyages of Cavelier de La Salle from 1679 to 1681: The Official Narrative. Trans. Melville B. Anderson. Chicago: The

Caxton Club, 1901. http://www.americanjourneys.org/aj-122/index.asp. There is some question as to the identity of this work's author, but most historians believe it was compiled by individuals who accompanied La Salle on his explorations.

Talon, Pierre, and Jean-Baptiste Talon. *Voyage to the Mississippi through the Gulf of Mexico, 1687.* Ed. Robert S. Weddle. http://www.americanjourneys.org/aj-114/index.asp. This is an English translation of a 1698 interview with the Talon brothers. Make sure you read the background information on the two brothers. They have quite a story!

Secondary Sources

Bruseth, James E., and Toni S. Turner. *From A Watery Grave: The Discovery And Excavation of La Salle's Shipwreck,* La Belle. College Station: Texas A&M University Press, 2007. Contains an account of how *La Belle* ran aground and was wrecked plus an account of the excavation of the wreck and what researchers have found on the remains of the ship.

Weddle, Robert S. *The Wreck of the* Belle, *the Ruin of La Salle.* College Station: Texas A&M University Press, 2001. Deals with the discovery and excavation of La Salle's flagship, *La Belle.*

World Wide Web

"The Belle." http://www.texasbeyondhistory.net/belle/. University of Texas Web site that offers an overview of La Salle and his men in Texas and the fate of their ship.

"Nova Online: Voyage of Doom." http://www.pbs.org/wgbh/nova/lasalle/. Companion Web site that explores the excavation of La Salle's flagship, *The Belle.*

"Texas State Historical Commission: Archeology." http://www.thc.state.tx.us/archeology/aadefault.shtml. Click on "La Salle Projects" in the left column. Texas is conducting ongoing excavations of La Salle's ship, *The Belle,* and Fort St. Louis.

Multimedia Source

Voyage of Doom. PBS, 1999. 1 VHS tape. 60 minutes. NOVA presentation that looks at the archaeological discovery and excavation of La Salle's flagship, *The Belle.*

40. James II Establishes the Dominion of New England in an Attempt to Tighten Royal Control of the Colonies (1685)

Massachusetts long resisted royal control, even going so far as to assert that the colony could decide which English laws applied to it. Charles I considered revoking the colony's charter, but the English Civil War interfered. When Charles II came to the throne in 1660, Massachusetts initially refused to recognize him as king. Suspecting that Massachusetts flouted the Navigation Acts, in the 1670s the British government sent investigators who confirmed that the colony failed to observe English law. In 1685, James II ascended to the throne and placed in motion the plan for the Dominion of New England. In short, the Dominion would be a supercolony that included all of New England, New York, and much of present-day New Jersey.

James appointed New York Governor Edmund Andros to govern the Dominion. Andros moved quickly, revoking the charters of the New England colonies, dispensing with elected assemblies, and making the Anglican Church the state church of the region. In addition, he forbade New England towns from having more than one town meeting a year. He also removed Puritan judges and sheriffs, replacing them with men loyal to him. Andros also enforced the Navigation Acts and levied additional taxes on New England. The Dominion cost more to operate than the former colonial governments. Andros's salary was more than the old Massachusetts legislature combined, and he had two companies of soldiers, who had to be paid and provisioned by the colonists. Things looked bleak for the New Englanders, until some good news came from England in 1689.

TERM PAPER SUGGESTIONS

1. Examine the actions of Edmund Andros in instituting the Dominion of New England. Could Andros have done this in a way that would have provoked less opposition?
2. Discuss the tensions that existed between the Crown and the New England colonies in the years before James II instituted the Dominion of

New England. If the New England colonies had been more cooperative with the Crown, would there have even been a Dominion of New England?

3. Discuss the impact of the governmental changes that Andros instituted in New England. Why did Andros limit New England communities to one town meeting per year? How did his policies affect taxation and commerce in New England?

ALTERNATIVE TERM PAPER SUGGESTIONS

1. It is 1685 and Massachusetts Bay Colony has hired you as their public relations representative. You are given the task of trying to convince King James II that the Dominion of New England is an unnecessary move and that the Crown will collect more taxes without it. James II has agreed to attend an informational session. Prepare a PowerPoint presentation designed to sway the king to the colony's point of view.
2. You are an advisor to Edmund Andros. Andros anticipates a great deal of resistance from the New England colonies. Andros asks you to prepare an advertising campaign, consisting of podcasts and newspaper ads that will "soften up" the colonists.

SUGGESTED SOURCES

Primary Sources

Andrews, Charles M., ed. *Narratives of the Insurrections, 1675–1690.* New York: Scribner's, 1915. Available on Google Books and at the Internet Archive at www.archive.org. Collection of excerpts from primary source documents.

"Commission of Sir Edmund Andros for the Dominion of New England. April 7, 1688." http://www.yale.edu/lawweb/avalon/states/mass06.htm. Text of Edmund Andros's commission as governor of the Dominion of New England. As you read this document, note that the Crown gave Andros almost total power over the colonies.

Secondary Sources

Breen, T. H. *The Character of the Good Ruler: A Study of Puritan Political Ideas in New England, 1630–1670.* New Haven, CT: Yale University Press, 1970. While this book deals primarily with colonial politics, it also addresses the Dominion of New England.

Hall, Michael G. *Edward Randolph and the American Colonies, 1676–1703.* Chapel Hill: University of North Carolina Press, 1960. Biography of an English official who spent much of his career in the colonies attempting to regulate trade.

Hall, Michael G. *The Last American Puritan: The Life of Increase Mather, 1639–1723.* Middletown, CT: Wesleyan University Press, 1988. One of the key leaders of Massachusetts Bay Colony, Mather objected voraciously to the Dominion of New England.

Johnson, Richard R. *Adjustment to Empire: The New England Colonies, 1675–1715.* New Brunswick, NJ: Rutgers University Press, 1981. The New England colonies in a period of tightening royal control.

Lovejoy, David S. *The Glorious Revolution in America.* New York: Harper & Row, 1972. Good overview of the Dominion of New England and the responses of the various colonies to it.

Sosin, Jack M. *English America and the Revolution of 1688.* Lincoln: University of Nebraska Press, 1982. Offers the American side of England's Glorious Revolution.

World Wide Web

"The Glorious Revolution of 1688." http://www.thegloriousrevolution.org/. Offers a chronology of events and a very useful encyclopedia that includes incidents, documents, and brief biographies of key people.

41. Massachusetts Colonists Revolt Against the Dominion of New England (1688)

In 1685, James II ascended to the British throne upon the death of his brother Charles II. James, a believer in the divine right of kings, ruled arbitrarily, ignoring Parliament. As king, James was also the titular head of the Anglican Church, yet he was also a practicing Catholic and pushed for religious toleration in the realm, something that was abhorrent to Anglicans, and especially to Puritans in British North America. In the spring of 1688, James's wife gave birth to a son, raising fears that James had started a Catholic dynasty that would rule England for years to come.

Anglican clergymen and English aristocrats conspired with William of Orange (who had a claim to the English throne through his wife, Mary, James's daughter) to launch what was essentially an unopposed invasion of England. The conspirators hoped that the threat of invasion would force James to heed Parliament and appoint a Protestant successor. Instead, James fled to France, seeking the protection of King Louis XIV. William, seeking an ally against Louis, assumed the throne. For their part, the English proclaimed William's invasion a "Glorious Revolution" that spared the realm Catholic rule. Rumors of the Revolution reached the colonies. Edmund Andros attempted to suppress news of the rebellion, but Massachusetts Puritans, spreading the rumor that Andros was a closet Catholic who planned to surrender New England to the French, rebelled, placing him and other administrators in jail. The Massachusetts Puritans hoped to return to their former form of government. William, however, refused to restore their old charter. Henceforth, Massachusetts would be governed by a governor appointed by the Crown, and a popularly elected assembly.

TERM PAPER SUGGESTIONS

1. In the twenty-first century, most of us would regard the concept of religious toleration favorably. Why would the push for religious toleration by James II have been so upsetting to English Protestants?
2. Discuss the role of Anglican clergy in James's ouster as king. Would this have been considered treasonous? Why or why not?
3. William the Conqueror is usually regarded as the last successful invader on England in 1066. William of Orange, however, landed in England in 1688 at the head of a Dutch army, but it is usually not described as an invasion. Could it accurately be described as an invasion? Discuss the politics behind this.
4. James II wished to be an absolute ruler much in the vein of Louis XIV of France. Why did this put him at loggerheads with Parliament?
5. The colonists in Massachusetts began their revolt against Governor Andros in an era where the news from England was rather sketchy. What do you think made them certain they were right in rebelling against Andros?

ALTERNATIVE TERM PAPER SUGGESTIONS

1. It is 1688 and Edmund Andros has hired you to censor the news from England. What steps would you take in an effort to keep New England colonists from learning about the Glorious Revolution in England?
2. It is 1688 and your job is to spread the word through the colonies that the Glorious Revolution has taken place in England. Make a podcast that accurately explains to the colonists what has transpired in England.

SUGGESTED SOURCES

Primary Source

Andrews, Charles M., ed. *Narratives of the Insurrections, 1675–1690.* New York: Scribner's, 1915. Contains accounts regarding the revolt in Boston and the arrest and imprisonment of Edmund Andros. Available on Google Books and at the Internet Archive at www.archive.org.

Secondary Sources

Breen, T. H. *The Character of the Good Ruler: A Study of Puritan Political Ideas in New England, 1630–1670.* New Haven: Yale University Press, 1970. While this book deals primarily with colonial politics, it also addresses the Dominion of New England.

Hall, Michael G. *Edward Randolph and the American Colonies, 1676–1703.* Chapel Hill: University of North Carolina Press, 1960. Biography of an English official who spent much of his career in the colonies attempting to regulate trade and includes his role in the Glorious Revolution in America.

Hall, Michael G. *The Last American Puritan: The Life of Increase Mather, 1639–1723.* Middletown, CT: Wesleyan University Press, 1988. One of the key leaders of Massachusetts Bay Colony, Mather objected voraciously to the Dominion of New England.

Johnson, Richard R. *Adjustment to Empire: The New England Colonies, 1675–1715.* New Brunswick, NJ: Rutgers University Press, 1981. The New England colonies in a period of tightening royal control.

Lovejoy, David S. *The Glorious Revolution in America.* New York: Harper & Row, 1972. Good overview of the Dominion of New England and the responses of the various colonies to it.

Sosin, Jack M. *English America and the Revolution of 1688.* Lincoln: University of Nebraska Press, 1982. Offers the American side of England's Glorious Revolution.

World Wide Web

"Declaration of the Prince of Orange, October 10, 1688." http://www.jacobite.ca/documents/16881010.htm. Proclamation by William of Orange justifying his invasion of England.

"The Glorious Revolution of 1688." http://www.thegloriousrevolution.org/. Offers a chronology of events and a very useful encyclopedia that includes incidents, documents, and brief biographies of key people.

42. King William's War (1689–1697)

The English nobility and Anglican clergy who conspired to make William of Orange the new king of England did not foresee that he would bring his war with him. William was already engaged in a conflict with France's Louis XIV in what came to be known as the War of the League of Augsburg in Europe. William's new subjects in North America began their own offshoot of the conflict, which they called King William's War (English colonists usually named their wars after their current monarch). English and French colonists did little actual fighting, mainly because of the difficulties involved in getting the two sides into contact with one another so that they could fight in the North American wilderness. To his credit, Edmund Andros, whom the colonists cast in jail during the revolt against the dominion of New England, had done a good job of readying the colonies for the coming conflict.

The attempts of the New England colonies to invade French Canada ended in disaster. New England produced one unusual war hero during the conflict, a woman named Hannah Dustin. A captive of the Abenakis for six weeks, Dustin convinced her fellow captives to help her attack and kill their sleeping captors. They killed the Abenakis and scalped them (Massachusetts offered a bounty for the scalps of enemy Indians). Upon her return to Massachusetts, Dustin was lauded from Puritan pulpits as a hero.

TERM PAPER SUGGESTIONS

1. North American offshoots of European wars generally involved little real combat. What were some of the problems that prevented American colonies from pursuing these wars more aggressively?
2. Examine the efforts of the New England colonies to launch an invasion of French Canada. Why did they fail?
3. Compare the stories of Hannah Dustin and Mary Rowlandson (found in entry 34. King Philip's War). Why did these two women react differently to captivity?

ALTERNATIVE TERM PAPER SUGGESTIONS

1. It is 1689 and the leaders of Massachusetts have asked you to come up with a workable plan to invade Canada. Using contemporary maps, create a PowerPoint presentation demonstrating how you plan to conquer French Canada.
2. It is 1689 and the governor of Canada has asked you to come up with a workable plan to invade New England. Using contemporary maps, create a PowerPoint presentation demonstrating how you plan to conquer New England.

SUGGESTED SOURCES

Primary Sources

Lincoln, Charles Henry, ed. *Narratives of the Indian Wars, 1675–1699.* New York: Scribner's, 1913. Available at Google Books. Contains an account by Cotton Mather regarding the war.

"Mather, Cotton, Magnalia Christi Americana." http://www.geocities.com/Heartland/Plains/2559/dustin2.html. Selection from Cotton Mather's (who interviewed Dustin) book about her exploits.

Secondary Sources

Chet, Guy. *Conquering the American Wilderness: The Triumph of European Warfare in the Colonial Northeast.* Amherst: University of Massachusetts Press, 2003. Chet argues that contrary to popular conceptions, European military tactics prevailed in North America.

Eccles, W. J. *The Canadian Frontier, 1534–1760.* Albuquerque: University of New Mexico Press, 1983. Eccles offers the reader the French perspective of the conflict.

Leach, Douglas Edward. *Arms for Empire: A Military History of the British Colonies in North America, 1607–1763.* New York: Macmillan, 1973. Good synthesis of the colonial military establishment, the operation of the colonial militia, and an overview of the four wars between the English and the French in North America.

Leach, Douglas Edward. *Roots of Conflict: British Armed Forces and Colonial Americans, 1677–1763.* Chapel Hill: University of North Carolina Press, 1986. Examines the role of British forces in North America.

Peckham, Howard H. *The Colonial Wars: 1689–1762.* Chicago: University of Chicago Press, 1964. Offers an overview of colonial participation in the colonial wars.

Steele, Ian K. *Warpaths: Invasions of North America.* New York: Oxford University Press, 1994. Steele's *Warpaths* is one of the best compact histories of the colonial wars.

World Wide Web

"The Hannah Dustin Story—March 15, 1697." http://kingsley.locke.net/gen/dustin/hannah.htm. Presents the story of Hannah Dustin and photographs of her statue in Haverhill, Massachusetts.

"The Story of Thomas and Hannah Dustin/Duston of Haverhill, Massachusetts." http://www.hannahdustin.com/index2.html. Genealogical information, an account of Dustin's captivity and escape, and many photos (some from old postcards) of her statues in Haverhill and Penacook, Massachusetts.

43. Leisler's Insurrection in New York (1689)

The results of England's Glorious Revolution varied from one colony to the next. Several colonies, upset with their royal governors appointed by James II, acted quickly on the sometimes vague rumors about the revolt in England. Believing the new monarchs, William and Mary, would restore local self-government, many of these rebels deposed the royal governors and transferred power to their local assemblies. New York, however, did not have a representative assembly. Governor Francis

Nicholson of New York, perhaps waiting to sort out rumor from fact, hesitated in proclaiming William and Mary the new rulers of England. As in New England, rumors circulated that the governor was a closet Catholic, who planned to surrender the colony to the French. Emboldened by Massachusetts's arrest and imprisonment of Edmund Andros, the New York City militia, led by Jacob Leisler, seized control of the city and drove Governor Nicholson from the colony.

Leisler deposed the royal governor and appointed himself the leader of the colony. Leisler exploited divisions within the colony, gaining much of his support from the Dutch population, who resented English rule. However, the merchants opposed Leisler and convinced the king that he was a rebel. Leisler reinforced this impression when he initially refused to turn over control of New York City to the first royal troops to arrive in 1691. When the new governor, appointed by the king, arrived, he was placed on trial and hanged.

TERM PAPER SUGGESTIONS

1. There were a number of groups who vied for control of New York in the wake of England's Glorious Revolution. Identify and discuss these factions and why they competed for control of the colony.
2. Investigate the administration of Jacob Leisler. How was he able to successfully gain control of New York City? What sort of internal opposition did he face while he governed the colony?
3. Why did Jacob Leisler refuse to turn over control of the colony to the first British troops who arrived after the revolution?

ALTERNATIVE TERM PAPER SUGGESTIONS

1. It is 1689 and Jacob Leisler has hired you as his minister of propaganda. Your job is put together podcasts that will be broadcast throughout the New York colony. You have to make several different variations of the podcast, each targeting specific factions within the colony.
2. It is 1691 and Jacob Leisler has hired you as his defense attorney. Prepare a PowerPoint presentation that you will show to the jury in an effort to save his life. Good luck!

SUGGESTED SOURCES

Primary Source

Andrews, Charles M., ed. *Narratives of the Insurrections, 1675–1690.* New York: Scribner's, 1915. Contains excerpts from primary documents regarding Leisler's administration, arrest for treason, and execution. Available at Google Books and at the Internet Archive at www.archive.org.

Secondary Sources

Leder, Lawrence H. *Robert Livingston, 1654–1728, and the Politics of Colonial New York.* Chapel Hill: University of North Carolina Press, 1961. Looks at colonial politics in New York, including the period of Leisler's Rebellion.

Lovejoy, David S. *The Glorious Revolution in America.* New York: Harper & Row, 1972. Good overview of the Dominion of New England and the responses of the various colonies to it.

Reich, Jerome R. *Leisler's Rebellion: A Study of Democracy in New York, 1664–1720.* Chicago: University of Chicago Press, 1953. Examines Leisler's role as a merchant in New York, his rebellion, and its aftermath.

Sosin, Jack M. *English America and the Revolution of 1688.* Lincoln: University of Nebraska Press, 1982. Offers the American side of England's Glorious Revolution.

World Wide Web

"The Jacob Leisler Papers Homepage." http://www.nyu.edu/leisler/. Still under construction as of March 2009, this archive contains a biography of Jacob Leisler and will make documents relating to his governance of New York available.

44. Coode's Rebellion in Maryland (1689)

The colony of Maryland experienced a rebellion of its own as word began to filter into British North America about England's Glorious Revolution. Lord Baltimore, the colony's proprietor, had increased taxes and quitrents, despite the fact that most of Maryland's colonists were actually losing money thanks to the depressed market for their tobacco. Baltimore also provoked resentment by awarding the colony's top political offices to his friends, relatives, and fellow Catholics.

Lord Baltimore did take steps to proclaim William and Mary the new rulers of England, but his courier to Maryland died en route. When rumors of the revolution in England reached planter John Coode, he organized a militia named the Protestant Association and quickly raised a force estimated to be between 700 and 800 men. Coode and other Protestants accused the colony's largely Catholic government of conspiring to surrender Maryland to the French, and they seized control of the colony without bloodshed. Coode and the Protestant Association remained in control of Maryland until a royal governor arrived in 1692. Maryland became a royal colony for a time, and the Anglican Church became the established church. Lord Baltimore still retained ownership of the colony, but lost political control of it until another Lord Baltimore became an Anglican in 1716 and the colony was awarded to him.

TERM PAPER SUGGESTIONS

1. Investigate the life of John Coode. This was not the first time that Coode challenged the government of the colony. Why was Coode frequently at odds with Maryland's government?
2. How did Coode's Rebellion change the governing structure in Maryland?
3. Discuss the social and religious changes that took place in Maryland in the wake of Coode's Rebellion.

ALTERNATIVE TERM PAPER SUGGESTIONS

1. It is 1689 and the governor of Maryland has appointed you to be the colony's minister of propaganda. Your job is to launch a public relations campaign designed to dissuade the colony's protestant majority from joining John Coode and overthrowing the government.
2. It is 1689 and you have been ordered to assume command of the militia that has remained loyal to the governor. You are greatly outnumbered by Coode and his men. How do you intend to defend the colonial government?

SUGGESTED SOURCES

Primary Source

Andrews, Charles M., ed. *Narratives of the Insurrections, 1675–1690.* New York: Scribner's, 1915. Contains excerpts from primary documents dealing with Coode's Rebellion. Available at Google Books and at the Internet Archive at www.archive.org.

Secondary Sources

Carr, Lois Green, and David William Jordan. *Maryland's Revolution of Government, 1689–1692.* Ithaca, NY: Cornell University Press, 1974. Good, thorough history of Maryland during the Glorious Revolution.

Land, Aubrey C. *Colonial Maryland: A History.* Millwood, NY: KTO Press, 1981. A good history of Maryland from settlement to the American Revolution.

Main, Gloria L. *Tobacco Colony: Life in Early Maryland, 1650–1720.* Princeton, NJ: Princeton University Press, 1982. Main's book is primarily an economic history of Maryland and its dependence on tobacco.

World Wide Web

"Exploring Maryland's Roots: Library, John Coode (c. 1648–1708/9)." http://mdroots.thinkport.org/library/johncoode.asp. Biography of John Coode.

45. Salem Witchcraft Trials (1692)

In 1692, teenage girls in Salem Village began experiencing strange fits. Questioned by adults, the girls accused other residents of the village of being witches and wizards, who tormented them by spectral means. The girls began by accusing a slave, Tibuta, who supposedly instructed them in divining the future and making urine cakes (supposedly used in love spells). Encouraged by the Reverend Samuel Parrish, the girls widened the circle of the accused, leveling charges at approximately 185 people ranging from a four-year-old girl to the very elderly. Most of the accused were older, widowed women, who usually lacked anyone to speak up on their behalf.

Willing to believe the charges, the court allowed the introduction of "spectral evidence." The accusers often shrieked and writhed on the floor in court, all the while claiming the accused were "pinching" or otherwise tormenting them. Perhaps fearing the loss of property, or of harsher punishment, many of the accused confessed to having interactions with the Devil and, in turn, accused others of witchcraft. In all, 19 people were executed by the Massachusetts authorities. When the young women widened the circle of the accused to include the wife of the governor and other prominent people, authorities finally moved to end the trials.

The Salem witchcraft trials have attracted attention from many historians, and there is wide disagreement as to what prompted the outbreak. Some historians claim the restrictiveness of Puritan society was to blame, while others place the blame on the ministers and judges who uncritically accepted the accusations. Since the Salem witchcraft trials, the phrase "witch hunt" has come to signify harassing of others for no good reason.

TERM PAPER SUGGESTIONS

1. The causes behind the witchcraft hysteria in Salem are still being debated by historians today. Choose one of the many competing theories (which can be found in any of the secondary sources listed) and evaluate it.
2. Using some of the Web sites listed, choose and examine some of the confessions of Salem residents accused of witchcraft. Think about why people would confess to such acts. What prompted many people to confess?
3. Discuss the introduction of "spectral evidence" at the Salem witchcraft trials. How did the accusers exploit this? Why were the jurists so willing to believe it?
4. Women, particularly older women, were far more likely to be accused than anyone else in Salem. Examine the reasons for this.
5. What may have prompted the accusers to target certain individuals?

ALTERNATIVE TERM PAPER SUGGESTIONS

1. It is 1692 and you are a defense attorney in Salem, Massachusetts. As you might expect, you are very busy! Select a case from one of the Web sites given here and prepare a defense for your client. Prepare a PowerPoint presentation in an effort to demonstrate to the jury that your client is innocent.
2. It is 1692 and you have been accused of witchcraft. Go to the "Famous American Trials: Salem Witchcraft Trials, 1692" site and click on the button that says "You are accused!" You will be given six options as to what you can do to extradite yourself from this predicament. Explain which option you would choose, and why you think it is the best one.

SUGGESTED SOURCES

Primary Sources

Burr, George Lincoln, ed. *Narratives of the Witchcraft Cases.* New York: Scribner's, 1914. Contains excerpts from the Salem witchcraft trials. However, the Web sites given here contain the most complete set of primary documents. You can find this book at both Google Books and the Internet Archive at www.archive.org.

"Salem Witch Trials Documentary Archive." http://etext.virginia.edu/salem/witchcraft/. Web site with court documents, letters, maps, and contemporaneous books covering the witchcraft trials.

Secondary Sources

Boyer, Paul, and Steve Nissenbaum. *Salem Possessed: The Social Origins of Witchcraft.* Cambridge, MA: Harvard University Press, 1974. Perhaps the best survey of the Salem witchcraft outbreak, Boyer and Nissenbaum see the social and economic conflicts between Salem Village and Salem Town as the genesis of the witchcraft hysteria.

Demos, John P. *Entertaining Satan: Witchcraft and the Culture of Early New England.* New York: Oxford University Press, 1982. Not really about the Salem witchcraft trials, but case studies of individuals accused of witchcraft.

Godbeer, Richard. *The Devil's Dominion: Magic and Religion in Early New England.* Cambridge: Cambridge University Press, 1992. Highlights the use of "folk magic" by ordinary people in New England and how easily one could find oneself accused of witchcraft.

Karlsen, Carol F. *The Devil in the Shape of a Woman: Witchcraft in Colonial New England.* New York: Norton, 1987. Karlsen looks mainly at the gender-based circle of accusations in and around Salem in 1692, but also looks at the economics of witchcraft.

Norton, Mary Beth. *In the Devil's Snare: The Salem Witchcraft Crisis of 1692.* New York: Vintage, 2002. Norton argues that the trauma caused by Indian attacks on New England's northern frontier may have been the catalyst for the witchcraft hysteria.

World Wide Web

"Famous American Trials: Salem Witchcraft Trials, 1692." http://www.law.umkc.edu/faculty/projects/ftrials/salem/salem.htm. Contains documents, images, a map of Salem, and a "witchcraft jeopardy" game.

"Salem: Witchcraft Hysteria." http://www.nationalgeographic.com/salem/. Very well done National Geographic Web site that allows students to follow a narrative of a traveler and see how the belief in witchcraft pervaded New England.

Multimedia Sources

In Search of History—Salem Witch Trials. History Channel, 2005. 1 DVD. 50 minutes. This presentation uses a combination of reenactments and still images. It also includes interviews with scholars who have studied and written about the trials.

Witchcraft in America: Behind the Crucible. Educational Video Network, Inc., 2004. 1 DVD. 21 minutes. Offers a comparison between history and its reinterpretation in Arthur Miller's play, *The Crucible.*

46. Spain Reestablishes Control over the Pueblos (1692–1696)

After driving the Spaniards out of New Mexico in 1680, Popé, the Tewa medicine man who masterminded the revolt, began a campaign to do away with all Spanish and Christian influences, including clothing, crops, tools, and livestock. However, while Pueblo peoples had little use for Spaniards or Christianity, they did have uses for metal tools, European crops, and sheep. In 1692, nobleman Diego de Vargas assumed the governorship of New Mexico and led an expedition to bring it under Spanish control. Through diplomacy, Vargas seemed to have won the allegiance of 23 Pueblo villages. In light of Vargas's apparent success, and concerned about French colonization initiatives, the viceroy of Mexico authorized him to recolonize New Mexico. In 1693, Vargas returned with 100 soldiers and 700 colonists and demanded that the Pueblo people evacuate Santa Fe. Vargas and his men stormed Santa Fe and acquired a foothold in New Mexico. Vargas was forced to wage military campaigns against the Pueblos throughout 1694 before he could firmly regain control of the region. Vargas accomplished the reconquest mainly by destroying Pueblo food supplies. Many Pueblos refused to submit and fled west, joining the Hopis, who remained beyond the reach of the Spanish.

However, when Franciscan missionaries reentered Pueblo communities to resume their missionary work, they discovered that native peoples remained hostile. In 1696, the Pueblos revolted, but this rebellion was not as well planned as the 1680 revolt, and the Spanish suppressed it very quickly. However, some Franciscans were killed during the uprising and their missions burned. In the aftermath of the 1696 revolt, the Franciscans were less heavy-handed in their conversion efforts.

TERM PAPER SUGGESTIONS

1. Why did the Pueblos seemingly welcome Vargas in 1693, but resist him the next year? What were their motivations?
2. Examine the strategy that Vargas employed to reconquer New Mexico. Was it sound? Did his strategy permit the Spanish to achieve all of their objectives?
3. Many Spanish officials were opposed to the reconquest of New Mexico on the grounds that the region had little of value. Why did they change their minds?
4. Examine the changes in Franciscan efforts to convert native peoples to Christianity. What were the major differences in the Franciscans' approach prior to the 1680 revolt and after the abortive 1696 revolt?

ALTERNATIVE TERM PAPER SUGGESTIONS

1. It is 1692 and Diego de Vargas has given you the task of attempting to win over Pueblo Indians. Prepare a podcast that emphasizes the good things (crops, metal tools, and sheep) that the Spanish brought to the Southwest.
2. It is 1693 and you are a Pueblo Indian. You have been asked to prepare a series of podcasts outlining reasons that native people should resist the return of the Spaniards.

SUGGESTED SOURCES

Primary Sources

Espinosa, J. Manuel, ed. *The Pueblo Indian Revolt of 1696 and Franciscan Missions in New Mexico: Letters of the Missionaries and Related Documents.* Norman: University of Oklahoma Press, 1988. Primary source letters from missionaries caught up in the aborted second Pueblo Revolt of 1696.

Hackett, Charles Wilson, ed. *Revolt of the Pueblo Indians of New Mexico and Otermín's Attempted Reconquest, 1680–1682 [volume 9—excerpt].* Trans. Clair Shelby Charmion. Albuquerque: The University of New Mexico Press, 1942. http://www.americanjourneys.org/aj-009b/summary/index.asp. Excerpts from primary documents pertaining to the revolt.

Secondary Sources

Gutiérrez, Ramón A. *When Jesus Came, the Corn Mothers Went Away: Marriage, Sexuality, and Power in New Mexico, 1500–1846.* Stanford, CA: Stanford University Press, 1991. Gutiérrez's history of the Southwest includes chapters on the Pueblo Revolt and the Spanish reconquest in 1692.

Knaut, Andrew L. *The Pueblo Revolt of 1680: Conquest and Resistance in Seventeenth Century New Mexico.* Norman: University of Oklahoma Press, 1997. Account of the planning, execution, and aftermath of the Pueblo Revolt.

Roberts, David. *The Pueblo Revolt: The Secret Rebellion That Drove the Spaniards Out of the Southwest.* New York: Simon & Schuster, 2004. Interesting look at the Pueblo Revolt that includes assessments of its impact on native peoples today.

Weber, David J. *The Spanish Frontier in North America.* New Haven, CT: Yale University Press, 1992. Perhaps the best history of Spain in North America.

Weber, David J., ed. *What Caused the Pueblo Revolt of 1680?* New York: Bedford/St. Martin's, 1999. Essays by five historians that examine the hows and whys of the 1680 Pueblo revolt.

World Wide Web

"Archives of the West to 1806." http://www.pbs.org/weta/thewest/resources/archives/one/pueblo.htm. Companion Web site for the PBS series *The West.* It contains letters from Franciscan missionaries who survived the revolt.

"The Pueblo Revolt of 1680." http://www.nativepeoples.com/article/articles/121/1/The-Pueblo-Revolt-of-1680/Page1.html. Article about the Pueblo Revolt.

"Trouble for the Spanish: The Pueblo Revolt of 1680." http://www.neh.gov/news/humanities/2002-11/pueblorevolt.html. Essay about the Pueblo Revolt.

Multimedia Source

The Pueblo. Schlessinger Media, 1994. 1 DVD. 30 minutes. Explores Pueblo history and culture.

47. The Iroquois Great Peace with New France and New York (1701)

A half century after initiating the "Beaver Wars," the Iroquois failed to gain control of the fur trading routes of the Great Lakes and Ohio country. Moreover, they suffered significant casualties, so many that some European observers noted that there were more "naturalized Iroquois" (adopted war captives) than native-born Iroquois. In addition, the French had invaded Iroquois lands with impunity in the 1690s. By the late 1690s, the Iroquois were regularly losing battles to their Algonquin enemies and realized that they could not count on their new English allies (who replaced the Dutch in 1664). Lacking a military means out of their difficulties, the Iroquois instead embarked on a two-pronged diplomatic strategy that required them to engage the English colony of New York, and New France.

In negotiating with the French, the Iroquois promised not to involve themselves in future conflicts between the French and the English. The French needed the Iroquois to remain intact so that their allies could not trade with the English at Albany. The French agreed to the truce with the Iroquois, but their native allies were not part of the agreement, so the Iroquois could still make war on them. At almost the same time that an Iroquois delegation negotiated with the French, another contingent of Iroquois diplomats treated with the New York colony. The Iroquois agreement with New York stipulated that they would assist in future conflicts against the French, but they encumbered the colony with impossible-to-fill conditions, requiring them to first secure hunting territories in Ontario for the Iroquois.

TERM PAPER SUGGESTIONS

1. Examine the failure of the Iroquois to win the Beaver Wars. Why were they not able to bring these conflicts to successful conclusion?

2. Examine the role of the Hudson's Bay Company in prolonging the Beaver Wars.
3. What were the real goals of Iroquois diplomats as they set out to negotiate the "Great Peace?"
4. Why were the French, who had been at odds with the Iroquois for so long, so willing to agree to terms with them? How did the Great Peace help protect French trade?
5. Assess the long-term impact of the Great Peace on Iroquois relations with the French and the English. Which party to these agreements benefited the most?

ALTERNATIVE TERM PAPER SUGGESTIONS

1. It is 1701 and you are an Iroquois diplomat. You have been authorized to devise a diplomatic strategy that will buy peace and stability for the Iroquois League. Before you set out for Quebec or Albany, you are to brief other Iroquois diplomats. Prepare a PowerPoint presentation that will outline the diplomatic initiative for them.
2. It is 1701 and you are a native person who is opposed to the Iroquois. You have acquired intelligence that the Iroquois have launched a diplomatic initiative, designed to make peace with the French and their native allies. Your job is to keep this from happening.

SUGGESTED SOURCES

Primary Sources

"The Great Peace of 1701." http://staff.imsa.edu/socsci/skinner/The%20Great%20Peace%20of%201701.html. English translation of the treaty between New France and the Iroquois in 1701.

O'Callaghan, Edmund Bailey, and Berthold Fernow, eds. *Documents Relative to the Colonial History of the State of New York.* 15 vols. Albany: Weed, Parsons & Co., 1853–1887. New York colony's side of the negotiations can be found in volume 4 of this set; the French documents are in volume 9. This entire set is available online at the Internet Archive at www.archive.org.

Secondary Sources

Aquila, Richard. *The Iroquois Restoration: Iroquois Diplomacy on the Colonial Frontier, 1701–1754.* Detroit: Wayne State University Press, 1983.

Aquila examines the Iroquois negotiations in 1700 and 1701 and how they shaped the next half century of Iroquois diplomacy.

Fenton, William N. *The Great Law and the Longhouse: A Political History of the Iroquois Confederacy.* Norman: University of Oklahoma Press, 1998. Fenton, in one of his last works, offers perhaps one of the best histories of the Iroquois League.

Havard, Gilles. *The Great Peace of Montreal of 1701: French-Native Diplomacy in the Seventeenth Century.* Trans. Phyllis Arnoff and Howard Scott. Montreal: McGill-Queen's University Press, 2001. One of the few works that focus on the Great Peace.

Richter, Daniel K. *The Ordeal of the Longhouse: The Peoples of the Iroquois League in the Era of European Colonization.* Chapel Hill: University of North Carolina Press, 1992. Includes a section on the Great Peace, while examining tensions within the Iroquois League.

Richter, Daniel K., and James Merrell. *Beyond the Covenant Chain: The Iroquois and Their Neighbors in Indian North America.* Syracuse, NY: Syracuse University Press, 1987. Collection of essays on Iroquois influence in sixteenth- and seventeenth-century North America.

World Wide Web

"Rediscovering 'The Great Peace': The Landmark Peace Treaty of Montréal Turns 300 Years Old." http://www.npr.org/programs/wesat/features/2001/treatyofmontreal/010804.treatyofmontreal.html. Discusses the Great Peace and includes images of the treaty.

Multimedia Source

1701, The Great Peace of Montreal. Outremont, Quebec, Canada: Telefilm Canada, 2002. Betacam SP. 52 minutes. Tells the story of the Great Peace of 1701 and how it still affects native people today.

48. Queen Anne's War (1702–1713)

Queen Anne's War, like the other colonial conflicts, was named by English colonists for their reigning monarch. In Europe, the conflict became known as the War of the Spanish Succession, because one of the issues revolved over who would sit on the Spanish throne. Queen Anne's war pitted England, the Netherlands, and Austria against France and Spain. King William's War (1689–1697) left some issues regarding North America undecided, most notably control of the fur trade and fishing rights on the Grand Banks. While there were far fewer Frenchmen than Englishmen in North America, the French had improved their position by adding forts on the Great Lakes such as at Detroit, as well as along the Mississippi and Gulf Coast at Mobile and Biloxi. Despite their superior numbers, the English colonies were disorganized and did not work together during the conflict. The French and their native allies carried off over 100 captives after their raid on Deerfield, Massachusetts, in 1704. The English managed to seize the French trading post at Port Royal in 1710. For the most part, however, the actions of both sides in North America were indecisive. The English, for example, attacked St. Augustine in Spanish Florida but were unable to seize control of the fortress there. Likewise, a joint French and Spanish expedition attacked the English port of Charleston, South Carolina, but with little success. The peace settlement (Treaty of Utrecht) resulted in a minimal redrawing of colonial boundaries. England acquired control of Newfoundland and Rupert's Land (Hudson's Bay Company territory). Most importantly, however, England and France would remain at peace for 25 years.

TERM PAPER SUGGESTIONS

1. Why were most European military efforts in the Americas unsuccessful? Does there seem to be a central reason that attacks on ports such as St. Augustine and Charleston usually failed?
2. Examine the reasons why the English succeeded in seizing Port Royal from the French.
3. Between the end of King William's War and the beginning of Queen Anne's War, the French strengthened their defenses in North America, while the British appear to have done very little. Examine the reasons for this.
4. The Treaty of Utrecht resulted in France and England being at peace with each other for 25 years, the longest such period in the eighteenth century. What factors contributed to this relatively long period of peace between the two rival nations?

ALTERNATIVE TERM PAPER SUGGESTIONS

1. It is 1702 and you have been given the job of defending England's North American colonies from French attack. Prepare a PowerPoint presentation for the Queen, outlining how you plan to protect her colonies.
2. It is 1702 and the French Crown has given you the job of conquering all of the English colonies in North America. King Louis XIV has summoned you to Versailles. Using Powerpoint, give him an overview of your plan to beat the English.

SUGGESTED SOURCES

Primary Source

O'Callaghan, Edmund Bailey, and Berthold Fernow, eds. *Documents Relative to the Colonial History of the State of New York.* 15 vols. Albany: Weed, Parsons & Co., 1853–1887. Relevant English documents may be found in volumes 4 and 5 of this set; the French documents are in volume 9. This entire set of documents is available online at the Internet Archive at www.archive.org.

Secondary Sources

Chet, Guy. *Conquering the American Wilderness: The Triumph of European Warfare in the Colonial Northeast.* Amherst: University of Massachusetts Press, 2003. Chet argues that, contrary to popular conceptions, European military tactics prevailed in North America.

Leach, Douglas Edward. *Arms for Empire: A Military History of the British Colonies in North America, 1607–1763.* New York: Macmillan, 1973.

Leach, Douglas Edward. *Roots of Conflict: British Armed Forces and Colonial Americans, 1677–1763.* Chapel Hill: University of North Carolina Press, 1986.

Peckham, Howard H. *The Colonial Wars: 1689–1762.* Chicago: University of Chicago Press, 1964. Both Leach and Peckham offer overviews of colonial participation in the colonial wars.

Steele, Ian K. *Warpaths: Invasions of North America.* New York: Oxford University Press, 1994. Steele's *Warpaths* is one of the best compact histories of the colonial wars.

World Wide Web

"Queen Anne's War: War of the Spanish Succession, 1702–1713." http://www.u-s-history.com/pages/h846.html. Provides a brief synopsis of the conflict.

49. Deerfield Massacre (1704)

On February 29, 1704, a force composed of approximately 300 Native Americans, mostly Abenakis, Hurons, and Mohawks from the French mission at Kahnawake, and four dozen French Canadians, launched a surprise attack against the western Massachusetts town of Deerfield. With the guards of the town asleep, the Indians made their way inside the palisade at night, quickly overpowered the defenders, and quickly seized the town's most important citizens as prisoners. The most important prisoner of all was the town's minister, John Williams, and his family. A little over 30 townspeople died in the raid, and over 100 were seized as captives. The French and the Indians then looted the houses and began to burn the town. By daybreak, English reinforcements arrived from the nearby village of Hatfield and put the French and Indians to flight. However, with the snow three feet deep, the English could not pursue the French and Indians, who were on snowshoes. The Indians, fearful of being pursued, hurried their captives along on the 300 mile journey to Canada, killing those who could not keep up, including the Reverend Williams's wife, who had given birth just a few days earlier.

Once in Canada, the English captives were adopted by native families or held by the French. Puritan parents were horrified to learn that the French Jesuits attempted to convert their children to Catholicism. Massachusetts authorities negotiated ransoms with the French and managed to repatriate most of the captives, with some exception, the most notable being Williams's daughter Eunice.

TERM PAPER SUGGESTIONS

1. Examine the defenses of the town of Deerfield. Could Deerfield have possibly thwarted the Indian-French attack?
2. Discuss the attackers' emphasis on securing prisoners. What did the French propose to do with the captives? What did the Native Americans propose to do with them?
3. Discuss the preparations that the Native Americans made to conduct their captives over the 300 mile trek to Canada. Discuss their treatment of the captives during the journey.

4. Discuss the process of ransoming the captives. What pressures—personal and economic—were the captives subject to in Canada?

ALTERNATIVE TERM PAPER SUGGESTIONS

1. You are a French official in Quebec in 1705. The English have paid the ransom for a particular captive, a child. However, the child is in the custody of a Native American family that refuses to surrender her. What inducements can you give the family to convince them to surrender the child?
2. You are a captive who likes your life in Canada very much, and you do not wish to return to Massachusetts. You know this will be a blow to your surviving relatives in New England, and that they will not understand. Compose a letter and try to explain your decision to them.

SUGGESTED SOURCES

Primary Source

Williams, John. *The Redeemed Captive Returning to Zion.* Carlisle, MA: Applewood Books, 1987. John Williams's narrative of his captivity in Canada. Williams was the minister for the village of Deerfield, and his narrative has heavy religious overtones.

Secondary Sources

Demos, John Putnam. *The Unredeemed Captive: A Family Story from Early America.* New York: Vintage, 1995. The story and the aftermath of the Deerfield Massacre as related through the life of Eunice Williams (the daughter of John Williams) who married a Native American and remained in Canada, never returning to her biological family.

Haefeli, Evan, and Kevin Sweeney. *Captors and Captives: The 1704 French and Indian Raid on Deerfield.* Amherst: University of Massachusetts Press, 2003. Haefeli and Sweeney provide stories from both sides of the attack on Deerfield.

World Wide Web

"The Deerfield Massacre." http://www.americanheritage.com/articles/magazine/ah/1993/1/1993_1_82.shtml. Article by John Demos regarding the attack on Deerfield.

"The Lessons of 1704." http://www.memorialhall.mass.edu/classroom/curriculum_5th/unit.html. Offers lesson plans.

"Raid on Deerfield: The Many Stories of 1704." http://1704.deerfield.history.museum/. The best Web site for learning about the Deerfield Massacre. This site has maps, lists of artifacts, and explanations of the hostility between the England and the French. It also provides the French, English, and Native American perspectives of the attack.

50. First Successful Colonial Newspaper Established in Boston (1704)

The first colonial newspaper, *Publick Occurrences,* appeared in Boston in 1690 and lasted for only one issue, as the authorities quickly shut it down. Many newspapers appeared during the colonial period, but most did not survive any length of time, some printing only one or two issues before going out of business. The survival of local papers depended on two factors. One was the tolerance of the local authorities and the other was the region's literacy rate. For example, the South, the region with the lowest literacy rate, had the fewest newspapers. *The Boston News-Letter,* the first successful colonial newspaper, debuted in 1704. As the colony with perhaps the highest literacy rate, other newspapers followed in Massachusetts, and some remained in publication for years. *The Boston Gazette* began publication in 1719 and continued until nearly the end of the eighteenth century. *The New York Weekly Journal* was established in 1733 and did not cease publication for 60 years. Philadelphia, the largest city in British North America, boasted *The American Weekly Mercury,* which began in 1719 and ended its print run in 1746. Perhaps the best-known paper in the city (and perhaps all of the colonies) was Benjamin Franklin's *Pennsylvania Gazette,* which began publication in December 1736 and ended almost exactly 39 years later. Most colonial newspapers did not employ their own reporters and tended to reprint stories from other newspapers. For the most part, early newspapers consisted of advertisements for goods and notices of rewards for the apprehension of runaway slaves. Usually a newspaper printer also doubled as the local postmaster and would be permitted to freely distribute his paper through the mail.

TERM PAPER SUGGESTIONS

1. Why would authorities in 1690 Boston shut down *Publick Occurrences* so quickly? What about the paper did they find objectionable?
2. Most colonial newspapers had very short publication runs, often lasting for only a few issues. What circumstances prevented most colonial newspapers from being more successful?
3. Examine the history of some of the more successful colonial newspapers. Why did they succeed where other papers failed?
4. Later in the colonial period, there would be a boom in printing during the Great Awakening (see entries 62 and 64 for information on the Great Awakening). What accounted for this boom? Did it last?

ALTERNATIVE TERM PAPER SUGGESTIONS

1. It is 1705 and you live in Boston. You have decided to start a newspaper. However, you do not have the money to do it all by yourself, so you are looking for investors. Put together a PowerPoint presentation that you will show to a meeting of potential investors. Be sure to include what you will need in order to start your paper and how you plan to profit.
2. You are a printer for a Philadelphia newspaper in 1735. Your employer has directed you to lay out the format for this week's issue. Make a newspaper with the headlines and advertisements.

SUGGESTED SOURCES

Primary Source

Copeland, David A. *Debating the Issues in Colonial Newspapers: Primary Documents on Events of the Period.* Westport, CT: Greenwood Press, 2000. Contains excerpts from colonial newspapers regarding the most important events of the period.

Secondary Sources

Clark, Charles E. *The Public Prints: The Newspaper in Anglo-American Culture, 1665–1740.* New York: Oxford University Press, 1994. Argues that because colonial newspapers reprinted so much from the English Press they extended the culture of the mother country into America.

Copeland, David A. *Colonial American Newspapers: Character and Content.* Newark: University of Delaware Press, 1997. Argues that colonial publishers did more than merely copy English newspapers.

Levy, Leonard. *Emergence of a Free Press.* New York: Oxford University Press, 1985. Levy argues that a free press truly did not exist in America until after the Revolution.

Richardson, Lyon N. *A History of Early American Magazines, 1741–1789.* New York: Thomas Nelson & Sons, 1931. One of the few books that examines the history of American magazines in the eighteenth century (most of which had a short publication life) and the rivalries between their publishers.

Sloan, William David, and Julie Hedgepeth Williams. *The Early American Press, 1690–1783.* Westport, CT: Greenwood Press, 1994. This is part of a six volume set that looks at the history of American journalism. This volume goes up to the American Revolution.

Smith, Jeffery A. *Printers and Press Freedom: The Ideology of Early American Journalism.* New York: Oxford University Press, 1988. Argues that the Founding Fathers saw freedom of the press as essential to the new republic.

World Wide Web

"All American: Colonial Journalism: Journalism by Mark Canada." http://www.uncp.edu/home/canada/work/allam/16071783/news/. Brief article that has links to the *Pennsylvania Gazette* and *Maryland Gazette.*

"Archiving Early America: Pages from the Past." http://www.earlyamerica.com/earlyamerica/past/. Contains sample pages from the *Pennsylvania Gazette, Boston Gazette,* and *Massachusetts Centinel.*

"Early American Newspapering by James Breig." http://www.colonialwilliamsburg.com/Foundation/journal/spring03/journalism.cfm. Article about the press in early America.

"Historybuff.com." http://www.historybuff.com/library/refseventeen.html. Contains information on the first ten newspapers printed in British North America.

"Scholars in Action: Analyze a Colonial Newspaper." http://historymatters.gmu.edu/mse/sia/newspaper.htm#. Offers advice on reading and interpreting colonial newspapers

51. Tuscarora War (1711)

English colonists in the Carolinas discovered that Indian slaves were one of the most valuable commodities they could exchange with Caribbean planters. English traders offered native warriors muskets, powder, and shot in exchange for slaves. European arms and ammunition gave native peoples a formidable advantage over their enemies. Other native peoples went into the slave trade in order to acquire the weapons they now needed to protect themselves from being enslaved themselves. Indian slaves were shipped to the Caribbean because remaining in the colony presented them with too many opportunities to escape. The Iroquoian-speaking Tuscaroras enjoyed a period of peace with English colonists, participating in the deerskin and Indian slave trades. In 1711, however, pressured by the arrival of more English colonists and by a large group of newly arrived Swiss and German Palatines who were part of Baron Christoph von Graffenreid's attempts to start a colony, the Tuscaroras went to war against North Carolina. North Carolina appealed for help from other colonies, and South Carolina responded, sending a militia and a number of Indian allies. The South Carolinians and their native allies defeated the Tuscaroras, destroyed the principal town, and seized many as captives who were sold into slavery. The defeat of the Tuscaroras had long-term consequences, as the survivors of the tribe fled north and joined the Iroquois League as its sixth nation. Tuscarora warriors would guide other Iroquois warriors in future attacks against native peoples on the Virginia and Carolina frontiers.

TERM PAPER SUGGESTIONS

1. Discuss Tuscarora participation in the Indian slave trade. Why did they turn away from the slave trade and oppose the Carolinians? What were the drawbacks of participating in the slave trade?
2. Discuss the role of the Iroquois League in the Tuscarora War. Did they do anything to encourage or discourage the Tuscarora in pursuing hostilities with the Carolinians? Did their decision to shelter the Tuscaroras after the war affect British Indian policy?
3. In which ways did the Tuscarora War presage the later Yamasee War? How were the causes of the two conflicts similar and different?

ALTERNATIVE TERM PAPER SUGGESTIONS

1. It is 1711 and you are a Tuscarora Indian. Write a blog that seeks to justify the actions of the Tuscarora toward the Carolinians and the other Europeans in the region.
2. It is 1711 and you are a representative of the government of North Carolina. Your government intends to pursue and punish the Tuscaroras. However, the Tuscaroras have applied for, and received, the protection of the powerful Iroquois League. Iroquois representatives have agreed to meet with you to hear your arguments as to why they should not protect the Tuscaroras. Prepare a PowerPoint presentation that you hope will bring them around to your point of view.

SUGGESTED SOURCES

Primary Sources

"Documenting the American South: Colonial and State Records of North Carolina." http://docsouth.unc.edu/csr/index.html/volumes. Volumes one and two contain primary source documents regarding the Tuscarora War.

O'Callaghan, Edmund Bailey, and Berthold Fernow, eds. *Documents Relative to the Colonial History of the State of New York.* 15 volumes. Albany: Weed, Parsons & Co., 1853–1887. Many of the Tuscaroras sought refuge among the Iroquois in New York. Documents pertaining to them and the war with the Carolinas can be found in volume five. This entire set of documents is available online at the Internet Archive at www.archive.org.

Secondary Sources

Corkran, David H. *The Carolina Indian Frontier.* Columbia: University of South Carolina Press, 1970. Corkran discusses some of the long-term effects of the Tuscarora War.

Crane, Verner W. *The Southern Frontier, 1670–1732.* New York: Norton, 1981. Discusses the Tuscarora War and British expansion in the Southeast.

Gallay, Alan. *The Indian Slave Trade: The Rise of the English Empire in the American South, 1670–1717.* New Haven: Yale University Press, 2002. Gallay points out that European settlement on Tuscarora lands prompted the conflict.

Merrell, James H. *The Indians' New World: Catawbas and Their Neighbors from European Contact through the Era of Removal.* Chapel Hill: University of

North Carolina Press, 1989. Discusses the long-term effects of the Tuscarora War, the Iroquois attacks on the Catawbas, and other peoples in the Southeast.

World Wide Web

"The M-Files: The Tuscarora War." http://www.tuscaroras.com/pages/history/1711_the_tuscarora_war.html. Reproduction of a series that appeared in the *Charlotte Observer.* This one has a short narrative of the war plus maps.

"The Way We Lived in North Carolina." http://www.waywelivednc.com/before-1770/tuscarora-war.htm. Short narrative about the Tuscarora War with illustrations and a link to a map.

52. New York Slave Uprising (1712)

Slavery in the northern colonies differed significantly from slavery in the other colonies. Whereas slavery, like the colonies themselves, was mostly rural, northern cities such as New York and Boston accounted for roughly 15 to 20 percent of their colonies' slave population. For the most part, these urban slaves labored as domestic servants, often in the homes of upper-class merchants, although at times their owners hired them out as labor.

Northern urban blacks were often frustrated in attempting to find mates. For one thing, most African women sold into slavery would have already been sold in the South. Unlike most slaves in the South, slaves in the North lived in their masters' house, eating and sleeping in close proximity to whites. Because slaves composed a smaller percentage of the population, slave codes in the northern colonies were not as draconian as in the South. Unlike the South, slaves in New York City could move about freely, making it easier to meet with other slaves and plan a revolt.

In 1712, 24 desperate slaves revolted, setting fires to buildings in New York City and killing whites as they fled. All of them were sentenced to death, with six of them cheating the hangman by committing suicide.

As a result of the 1712 uprising, New York adopted slave codes that strongly mirrored those of the South. Blacks could not meet in groups larger than three people and could not bear firearms. Owners were permitted to punish their slaves in any way they saw fit, provided the slave did not lose life or limb.

TERM PAPER SUGGESTIONS

1. Discuss the differences in slavery between New York City and other colonies in British North America prior to 1712. What accounted for these differences?
2. On average, conditions for slaves in the North were better than for slaves in the South. What prompted slaves in New York City to revolt?
3. Discuss how a slave's labor and relations with their owners differed in New York from other colonies in British North America.
4. In the wake of the 1712 revolt, New York put a much stricter slave code into effect. How effective was the code in deterring future slave revolts?

ALTERNATIVE TERM PAPER SUGGESTIONS

1. You are a slave in 1712 New York. You were not involved in the revolt, but you sympathize with the slaves who did revolt. Prepare a blog that explains the slaves' position to the general public.
2. You are a slaveholder in 1712 New York. You are shocked that your slaves have participated in the revolt. Prepare a blog arguing for stricter supervision of slaves.

SUGGESTED SOURCES

Primary Source

O'Callaghan, Edmund Bailey, and Berthold Fernow, eds. *Documents Relative to the Colonial History of the State of New York.* 15 volumes. Albany: Weed, Parsons & Co., 1853–1887. Documents relative to the 1712 slave uprising may be found in volume five. This entire set of documents is available online at the Internet Archive at www.archive.org.

Secondary Source

Berlin, Ira. *Many Thousands Gone: The First Two Centuries of Slavery in North America.* Cambridge, MA: Harvard University Press, 1998. One of the best histories of colonial slavery.

World Wide Web

"New York: The Revolt of 1712." http://www.pbs.org/wgbh/aia/part1/1p285.html. Page from the PBS companion Web site for their *Africans in America* presentation.

"New York Slave Law Summary and Record." http://www.slaveryinamerica.org/geography/slave_laws_NY.htm. Good overview of slavery in New York.

"Slavery in New York." http://www.slavenorth.com/newyork.htm. Includes a good summary of the history of slavery in New York.

Multimedia Sources

"Africans in America." http://www.pbs.org/wgbh/aia/home.html. This is another PBS Web site, which also contains many of the features found in "Slavery and the Making of America." However, it contains more detail regarding slavery in the colonial period.

"Slavery and the Making of America." http://www.pbs.org/wnet/slavery/. This is the companion Web site for the 2004 PBS program of the same name. Contains an overview of the history of slavery in British North America and the United States.

53. Yamasee War in the Carolinas (1715–1716)

One of the key suppliers of Indian slaves to British traders in the Carolinas, the Yamasee allied themselves with North and South Carolina during the 1711 war against the Tuscarora. However, like other native peoples who engaged in the slave trade, they found themselves inadequately paid for their captives and heavily in debt to English slave traders.

When Yamasee warriors could not pay their debts, colonial slave traders seized their wives and children and sold them into slavery. The Yamasee responded by first killing traders and then destroying farms and plantations.

What made the Yamasee War different from other Indian wars in the South was that the English were not able to use different groups of native peoples against one another. The Yamasee obtained assistance from Creek and Catawba peoples who had also been victimized by English slave traders. Faced with united Indian peoples and unable to find native allies at first, the Carolinians obtained help from Virginia. Virginia also assisted by cutting off the Yamasee's supplies of powder and shot. In 1716, the Tuscarora, seeking revenge, allied themselves with the English and led other members of the Iroquois League in attacks on Catawba villages. The Cherokees, initially neutral, also came to the aid of the Carolinians. Traditional enemies of the Yamasee, the Cherokees had become increasingly dependent on European trade goods that Carolina traders provided them with. Many Yamasee were captured and sold into slavery, while others fled south to Florida, allied themselves with the Spanish, and engaged in attacks on the Carolina frontier.

TERM PAPER SUGGESTIONS

1. Discuss the Indian slave trade in the American Southeast. Why were native peoples willing to participate in the trade? What were the drawbacks of participating in the slave trade?
2. Examine the slave trade between the Carolinas and the British sugar islands in the Caribbean. What commodities were traded? Why was there a demand for Native American slaves?
3. Why did the Carolinians make it a point to ship Native Americans out of the colony? What did they fear would happen if they remained within the colony?
4. In the years after the Yamasee War, the colonists decided that they did need to have Indians on their frontiers. In light of the Yamasee War, this seems surprising. Why did the colonial governments want Indians on their frontiers?
5. Discuss the willingness of other colonies to assist the Carolinas and the decision of the Cherokees to help the colonists. Given what had happened to other native people, why did the Cherokees seem unconcerned about becoming the targets of slave hunters?

ALTERNATIVE TERM PAPER SUGGESTIONS

1. It is 1715 and you are a Yamasee person. The leader of your band, knowing that you have considerable technological expertise, has asked you to start a

blog. The purpose of the blog is to dissuade other colonies and the Cherokees from assisting the Carolinians in their war against the Yamasee.

2. It is 1715 and the governor of Carolina has given you the mission of going to the Creek Indians. Your job is to convince them to stay out of the war. Prepare a PowerPoint presentation that outlines why it is to their advantage to stay neutral or, better yet, to join the Carolinians. Good luck.

SUGGESTED SOURCES

Primary Source

"Dear Skins, Furrs and Younge Indian Slaves." http://appalachiansummit.tripod.com/chapt4.htm. Contains excerpts from primary sources regarding the war.

Secondary Sources

Axtell, James. *The Indians' New South: Cultural Change in the Colonial Southeast.* Baton Rouge: Louisiana State University Press, 1997. Axtell examines the changes that took place in the Southeast with the arrival of Europeans, including the slave trade.

Corkran, David H. *The Carolina Indian Frontier.* Columbia, SC: University of South Carolina Press, 1970. A history of native peoples and colonists in Carolina.

Crane, Verner W. *The Southern Frontier, 1670–1732.* New York: Norton, 1981. Deals with native peoples in the colonial period and the Indian slave trade.

Gallay, Alan. *The Indian Slave Trade: The Rise of the English Empire in the American South, 1670–1717.* New Haven, CT: Yale University Press, 2002. Gallay's book is the best account of the Indian slave trade in the colonial south.

Merrell, James H. *The Indians' New World: Catawbas and Their Neighbors from European Contact through the Era of Removal.* Chapel Hill: University of North Carolina Press, 1989. Merrell's history of the Catawba people includes how they made a place for themselves in the colonial world as slave catchers.

Oatis, Steven J. *A Colonial Complex: South Carolina's Frontiers in the Era of the Yamasee War, 1680–1730.* Lincoln: University of Nebraska Press, 2004. One of the few histories of the Yamasee War.

World Wide Web

"Dear Skins, Furrs and Younge Indian Slaves." http://appalachiansummit.tripod.com/chapt4.htm. Excerpts from the journal of James Moore, a trader who traded with the Indians for slaves.

"Yamassee War of 1715." http://ourgeorgiahistory.com/wars/Georgia_Wars/yamasee_war.html. Brief informative article about the Yamasee War.

54. French Establish New Orleans, Gaining Control of the Mississippi River (1718)

In the years following Robert La Salle's exploration of the Mississippi and his subsequent failure to create a colony near its mouth, the French reestablished their presence in the region by building a fur trading post among the Quapaw Indians in present-day Arkansas in the 1680s. In the next decade, French explorer and soldier Pierre Le Moyne d'Iberville established small seaports on the Gulf Coast at Mobile and Biloxi, and in 1699, he rediscovered the mouth of the Mississippi. Concerned that an ongoing war between the Choctaws and Chickasaws could affect the nascent colony—and fearful that English colonists may employ the Chickasaws as military proxies—the French negotiated a peace between them. The French envisioned a chain of forts, stretching from the Gulf of Mexico to the mouth of the St. Lawrence River, that would keep the English confined to the region between the Atlantic seaboard and the Appalachians. French Louisiana grew slowly, however. In 1702, the population consisted of a few slaves and 122 soldiers. More concerned with the War of Spanish Succession, the French Crown ignored the colony. After the war, the French turned over management of the colony to the Company of the Indies. The company imported colonists—oftentimes convicts—and encouraged them to raise tobacco and indigo for export. In 1718, the company established New Orleans, 125 miles up the Mississippi, located among rich alluvial soils, rather than the loose sands at the mouth of the river. New Orleans quickly became the capital, major seaport, and population center of Louisiana.

TERM PAPER SUGGESTIONS

1. French attempts to establish a colony in Louisiana proceeded at a very slow pace. Examine the reasons why.
2. In establishing New Orleans as their primary seaport in Louisiana, the French faced a number of challenges regarding the terrain and topography of the area. Discuss these challenges.
3. The location of New Orleans had a number of built-in drawbacks for a seaport. Examine and discuss why the French chose to construct New Orleans in spite of these drawbacks.
4. Discuss the French relations with native peoples in Louisiana. What lessons did they draw from their experiences in Canada? How did they treat peoples in the Southeast differently?
5. Discuss the strategic plan of the French to keep the English confined to the region east of the Appalachian Mountains. Was it feasible? If so, why? If not, what would the French have had to do to make it work?

ALTERNATIVE TERM PAPER SUGGESTIONS

1. It is 1718 and the Company of the Indies has hired you as their chief engineer. Your first assignment is to make a city plan for New Orleans and to plan the port. Prepare a PowerPoint presentation for your brand new employers to show how you plan to do this.
2. It is 1720 and you have been appointed the assistant to the governor of Louisiana. The governor has directed you to prepare plans for the defense of New Orleans from a naval attack.

SUGGESTED SOURCES

Primary Source

Historical Collections of Louisiana: Embracing Translations of Many Rare and Valuable Documents Relating to the Natural, Civil and Political History of That State. Compiled and translated by B. F. French. 5 volumes. New York: D. Appleton & Company, 1846–1853. This five-volume set contains documents relating to the early history of Louisiana and much of the Gulf Coast and Southeast, and is available at both the Internet Archive at www.archive.org and Google Books. Volume two contains documents pertaining to the founding of New Orleans.

Secondary Sources

Eccles, W. J. *The French in North America, 1500–1783.* East Lansing: Michigan State University Press, 1998. Eccles links the history of New Orleans with that of the other French possessions in North America.

Usner, Daniel H. *Indians, Settlers, & Slaves in a Frontier Exchange Economy: The Lower Mississippi Valley before 1783.* Chapel Hill: University of North Carolina Press, 1992. Unser discusses French Louisiana and the founding of New Orleans.

World Wide Web

"A History of New Orleans." http://www.madere.com/history.html. This historical account of New Orleans includes a good analysis of the problems the French faced in establishing the city.

55. Beginnings of the Plains Indian Horse and Gun Culture (1720s–1750)

The most common stereotype of Native Americans involves horses, tepees, and buffalo. This image, however, while it has a basis in fact, was part of the horse and gun culture complex of the Great Plains and did not exist for more than a couple hundred years. The elements needed to make this culture a reality came with Europeans, first the horse, and then the gun.

For millennia, native peoples lived on the Great Plains, but most were sedentary farmers who lived in river valleys and hunted bison to supplement their diet. Native peoples from other regions came to the plains to hunt buffalo, and a few peoples relied heavily on hunting. Buffalo hunting on foot was difficult and dangerous. Hunters sometimes dressed themselves in a wolf skin, approached a herd, and attempted to kill buffalo with bows and arrows. Other times an entire village would go on a hunt and attempt to stampede bison over a cliff.

Horses arrived with Europeans. More than likely, the first horses on the plains were traded to native peoples by Pueblo peoples who learned to ride while serving the Spanish. Horses changed native people's concepts of distance and of wealth. Horses became the measure of a man's wealth, and tepees, formerly small enough to be transported by a dog pulling a travois, now became much larger.

The arrival of the horse resulted in native peoples of the plains becoming nomadic hunters. The plains also became a magnet for native peoples who left the eastern woodlands and became plains bison hunters.

TERM PAPER SUGGESTIONS

1. Compare and contrast life for people on the Great Plains before and after the horse. Examine the ways the horse altered day-to-day life for native people.
2. How did the advent of the horse and gun culture alter family life for native peoples? How did the roles of men and women change?
3. Examine the peoples of the eastern woodlands (such as Santee Dakotas and Cheyenne) who migrated to the Great Plains. What cultural changes did they experience?
4. The horse and gun culture also had negative consequences for native people and the environment of the Great Plains. Examine some of these consequences.

ALTERNATIVE TERM PAPER SUGGESTIONS

1. You are a woodland native in 1650 and you have just learned about the horse and how peoples on the plains are using this new animal to improve their lives. Make a podcast designed to encourage other native peoples to leave the woodlands and begin new lives on the plains.
2. You are a plains native in 1650, and recently, life has been pretty good for you and your people. Hunting, for example, is a lot easier now that you have the horse. Unfortunately, peoples from the eastern woodlands are starting to migrate to the plains and sometimes they kill "your" buffalo. Make a podcast that attempts to make eastern woodlands people think that the plains is not the place to be.

SUGGESTED SOURCES

Primary Source

Calloway, Colin G., ed. *Our Hearts Fell to the Ground.* Boston: Bedford/St. Martin's, 1996. Calloway includes native views of the arrival of horses and European diseases to the Great Plains.

Secondary Sources

Calloway, Colin G. *One Vast Winter Count: The Native American West before Lewis and Clark.* Lincoln: University of Nebraska Press, 2003. One of the best and most thorough accounts regarding the development of the horse and gun culture of the Great Plains.

Holder, Preston. *The Hoe and the Horse on the Plains: A Study in Cultural Development Among North American Indians.* Lincoln: University of Nebraska Press, 1970. One of the few books that examines the process of Native American peoples making the transition from woodland farmers to plains hunters.

Webb, Walter Prescott. *The Great Plains.* Lincoln: University of Nebraska Press, 1981. A history of the interaction between the environment of the Great Plains and the peoples who have lived there.

White, Richard. *The Roots of Dependency: Subsistence, Environmental, and Social Change Among the Choctaws, Pawnees, and Navajos.* Lincoln: University of Nebraska Press, 1983. Addresses many of the changes that took place on the Great Plains before 1800. White's work is more comparative in nature.

World Wide Web

"American Notes: Travels in America, 1750–1920." http://memory.loc.gov/ammem/lhtnhtml/lhtnhome.html. This Library of Congress Web site includes accounts from explorers and traders on the Great Plains.

Multimedia Sources

500 Nations. Warner Home Video, 1995. 5 DVDs. 372 minutes. Narrated by Kevin Costner, this series is divided into eight episodes on five DVDs. Episode seven deals with the Great Plains.

The West. PBS, 1996. 5 DVDs. 707 minutes. One of the best presentations about the West and includes lots of information about the Great Plains.

56. Sieur de la Vérendrye Explores the Northern Plains (1727)

In the 1720s, France feared that the English Hudson's Bay Company (HBC) would expand southward, gaining control of the Northern Plains fur trade and the alliance of the region's native peoples. Should this occur, New France's westward expansion would be blocked. The HBC, it turned out, did not attempt to expand southward, but the fear that they could, and the French belief that an "interior sea" located on the western plains could provide a shortcut to Asia, prompted them to send an expedition. Leadership of the expedition was entrusted to Sieur de la Vérendrye, a military officer. The government of New France had little funding for the project, obliging Vérendrye to establish trading posts as he sojourned across the plains to pay the expeditions' expenses. Vérendrye established trade relations with the Cree, but, like other native peoples, the Cree linked trade relations to military alliances, requiring Vérendrye to give them military assistance. He supplied a Cree war party that sold him a number of Lakota captives who were transported east and sold into slavery in Montreal. Just as Samuel de Champlain made the Iroquois into French enemies in 1609, Vérendrye now made the Lakotas into foes who frustrated French expansion on the western plains. Assiniboine peoples informed Vérendrye that the Mandan peoples of the upper Missouri River knew the route to the Pacific Ocean, and in 1738 he met the Mandans and learned this was not true. In 1742, two of his sons led another westward expedition that possibly reached South Dakota's Black Hills, but turned back, having found nothing of value.

TERM PAPER SUGGESTIONS

1. What fueled French fears that the Hudson's Bay Company would expand southward? What would have been the consequences for New France?
2. Where did the French (and other Europeans) get the idea that there may be some sort of inland sea or a shortcut to the Pacific Ocean?
3. Vérendrye's westward expedition proceeded very slowly, mainly because of a lack of financing. Examine the strategy of establishing fur trading posts to finance Vérendrye's explorations. What were the advantages? What were the drawbacks?
4. Allying himself with various Native American groups during his explorations offered advantages and disadvantages to Vérendrye. Discuss what some of these advantages and disadvantages would have been.
5. Vérendrye placed a lot of stock in native informants. What were his informants correct about? What did they mislead him about?

ALTERNATIVE TERM PAPER SUGGESTIONS

1. It is 1727 and you have been appointed as an assistant to Sieur de la Vérendrye. He has asked you to find investors for his exploration since the government of New France will not fund it. Prepare a PowerPoint about the expected riches that the expedition will find and how this will benefit those who invest in the expedition.
2. It is the 1730s and Sieur de la Vérendrye has appointed you to be his advisor regarding his interactions with Native Americans. The chief issue is that Vérendrye wants to trade with native peoples, but he does not want to be dragged into military alliances with them. Native people, however, see trade and alliances as inextricably entwined. Using a PowerPoint presentation, your job is to explain to them that the French do not have the same view, and that they should accept this.

SUGGESTED SOURCES

Primary Sources

La Vérendrye, Pierre Gaultier de Varennes et de. *Journals and Letters of La Vérendrye and His Sons.* Ed. Lawrence J. Burpee. Toronto: The Champlain Society, 1927. These are the edited journals of La Vérendrye and his sons. Available at The Champlain Society Digital Collection, http://link.library.utoronto.ca/champlain/search.cfm?lang=eng.

Woods, Raymond W., and Thomas Thiessen, eds. *Early Fur Trade on the Northern Plains: Canadian Traders among the Mandan and Hidatsa Indians, 1738–1818.* Norman: University of Oklahoma Press, 1985. Contains excerpts from fur traders who came after the La Vérendryes.

Secondary Sources

DeVoto, Bernard. *The Course of Empire.* Boston: Houghton Mifflin, 1952. Good overall history of the exploration of the North American West.

Smith, G. Hubert. *The Explorations of the La Vérendyres in the Northern Plains, 1738–1743.* Ed. W. Raymond Woods. Lincoln: University of Nebraska Press, 1980. Smith originally wrote much of this book in 1951. It was edited and published by Wood with much more attention on the native peoples of the region.

World Wide Web

"The La Vérendryes: Family of Explorers." http://www.collectionscanada.gc.ca/explorers/h24-1530-e.html. Gives a brief overview of the La Vérendryes and their explorations of the Northern Plains.

Multimedia Source

The Pathfinders. CBC Television, 2000. 1 DVD. 120 minutes. This is episode six of the 32-hour *Canada: A People's History* produced by CBC from 2000 to 2001. Includes the La Vérendryes and other explorers.

57. Natchez Wars (1729)

The last vestige of the Mississippian Indian culture, the Natchez differed significantly from other native peoples of the Southeast, maintaining large earthen ceremonial mounds, topped by temples in which lived the "suns," the chiefs who held the power of life and death over their subjects. In the 1720s, the French built Fort Rosalie near present-day Natchez, Mississippi, the site of the Natchez's grand village. Because of their dependence on French trade goods, the Natchez tolerated the French presence. However, friction developed between the French and the Natchez when unfenced livestock destroyed the Indians' cornfields. The Indians usually killed and ate the offending animals, and the French retaliated by requiring the Natchez to pay tribute. In 1729, the French ordered one of the Natchez villages to move so that it could be transformed into a tobacco plantation. Finally pushed too far, the Natchez executed a well-planned attack, killing the garrison at Fort Rosalie, and seizing French women and children as captives whom they then adopted. Most disconcerting for the French was that large numbers of African slaves joined the Natchez. Fearing they faced both an Indian war and a slave rebellion, and lacking manpower in Louisiana, the French enlisted the Choctaw to fight the Natchez on their behalf. The Choctaw destroyed Natchez villages in 1730, and by 1732 had absorbed Natchez captives or had given them to the French, who sold them into slavery in the Caribbean.

TERM PAPER SUGGESTIONS

1. Nearly 200 years before the French-Natchez War, Spanish explorer Hernando de Soto decimated most of the Mississippian Indian culture. What factors enabled the Natchez to remain as the last representatives of this vanished culture?
2. Examine the relationship between the French and native peoples. The French engaged in hostile situations with the Natchez and other peoples in the Southeast, yet they secured the Choctaws as allies. What were the French motivations for befriending the Choctaws but not other native peoples? What were the Choctaw motivations for allying themselves with the French?
3. The French appropriation of a Natchez village was the last straw in a long string of incidents between the two peoples. Trace the events that led to the Natchez War.
4. When the Natchez massacred the French garrison at Fort Rosalie, they wiped out one-third of all the Frenchmen then in Louisiana. Examine the demographics of French Louisiana. The French were outnumbered by Indians and African slaves. How did they control or try to control the colony?
5. Compare and contrast French treatment of the Natchez and other peoples in the American Southeast with the French treatment of native peoples in Canada. What accounts for the difference in relations between the French and Native Americans in these two regions?

ALTERNATIVE TERM PAPER SUGGESTIONS

1. You are a French official in Louisiana in the 1720s. Your job is to devise a plan that will allow the French to rule a colony where they are greatly outnumbered by native people and Africans. The governor of Louisiana wants you to brief him on your plan. Prepare a PowerPoint presentation as to how you will do this.
2. It is 1729 and you are a Natchez diplomat. The Natchez and the French are already at war, and you are pretty sure that the French will seek military assistance from the Choctaw. Your task is to convince the Choctaw that

they should not side with the French. Prepare a podcast that argues that the Choctaw should not help the French, but should instead assist other native people.

SUGGESTED SOURCES

Primary Source

Le Page du Pratz, Antoine-Simon. *History of Louisisana, Or of the Western Parts of Virginia and Carolina.* Du Pratz lived among the Natchez and the French for 16 years in Louisiana, and he includes an account of the war with the Natchez. His *History* is available at www.Gutenberg.org and at Google Books.

Secondary Sources

Barnett, James F., Jr. *The Natchez Indians: A History to 1735.* Jackson: University Press of Mississippi, 2007. The newest and one of the best histories of the Natchez people.

Eccles, W. J. *The French in North America, 1500–1783.* East Lansing: Michigan State University Press, 1998. Eccles includes a brief account of the Natchez War.

Usner, Daniel J. *Indians, Settlers, and Slaves in a Frontier Exchange Economy: The Lower Mississippi Valley before 1783.* Chapel Hill: University of North Carolina Press, 1992. Usner looks at relations between native people and the French in Louisiana.

Woods, Patricia Dillon. *French-Indian Relations on the Southern Frontier, 1699–1762.* Ann Arbor, MI: UMI Research Press, 1980. Unpublished dissertation that nonetheless has a good account of the Natchez War.

World Wide Web

"The Grand Village of the Natchez Indians." http://mdah.state.ms.us/hprop/gvni.html. Deals with Natchez history and culture.

"Grand Village of the Natchez Indians." http://www.nps.gov/nr/travel/mounds/gra.htm. National Park Service Web site about the Natchez villages and construction and preservation of the mounds.

58. James Oglethorpe Establishes the Colony of Georgia as a Buffer between Spanish Florida and English Colonies (1732)

In the late 1720s, Carolina officials founded a new colony south of the Savannah River and named it Georgia in honor of George II. In 1732, British investors and social reformers obtained a royal charter for the colony. The key member of the Georgia Trustees was James Oglethorpe, who came to Georgia as the governor in 1733.

The Georgia Trustees hoped the colony would be an outlet for England's urban poor. By granting the poor their own farms, the Trustees hoped they would learn the value of hard work. The first colony largely subsidized by the Crown, the British government bore more than 90 percent of the cost of transporting and setting up on farms more than 1,800 colonists during the colony's first decade.

The Carolinians hoped Georgia would provide a buffer between Spanish Florida and themselves. From time to time, native allies of the Spanish raided the Carolinas. By keeping land grants to Georgia colonists small (about 50 acres), the trustees hoped to develop a fairly densely populated colony, capable of turning out a large militia in times of emergency.

The colony forbade slavery, on the grounds that it compromised military security and that poor Englishmen transported to Georgia had to learn hard work.

The restriction on slavery provoked protests from colonists who wished to establish larger plantations. Would-be large planters pressured Parliament, who rescinded the prohibition on slavery in 1751, and Georgia, in a relatively small amount of time, became a slave society similar to the Carolinas.

TERM PAPER SUGGESTIONS

1. Research and discuss James Oglethorpe's motivations for backing the establishment of the Georgia colony.
2. Discuss the views of the Trustees regarding the poor who would be shipped to Georgia.

3. Perhaps the primary reason that the Carolinas so strongly backed the establishment of Georgia was that it would create a buffer between them and Spanish Florida. Analyze the threat that Florida posed to the Carolinas in the early eighteenth century.
4. Georgia, despite the intentions of the Trustees, became a slave society much like the Carolinas. How and why did this happen?

ALTERNATIVE TERM PAPER SUGGESTIONS

1. It is 1732 and James Oglethorpe has hired you as his public relations specialist. Your job is to create interest in settling the colony of Georgia. Oglethorpe orders you to prepare a public relations campaign and wants you to brief him on how it will succeed. Prepare PowerPoint presentations and podcasts and be ready to impress your boss.
2. It is 1732 and you are a Spanish commander in Florida. Prepare a PowerPoint presentation that you will give to the Spanish colonial authorities. Your objective is to impress upon them the threat the new colony of Georgia would present to Florida.

SUGGESTED SOURCES

Primary Source

Montgomery, Sir Robert. *A discourse concerning the design'd establishment of a new colony to the south of Carolina, in the most delightful country in the universe.* London: n.p., 1717. This is a promotional tract that extolls and, as one can tell from the title, greatly exaggerates Georgia's potential. Available from the Internet Archive at www.archive.org.

Secondary Sources

Jackson, Harvey H., and Phinizy Spalding, eds. *Forty Years of Diversity: Essays on Colonial Georgia.* Athens: University of Georgia Press, 1984. Essays by scholars about colonial Georgia.

Jackson, Harvey H., and Phinizy Spalding, eds. *Oglethorpe in Perspective: Georgia's Founder After Two Centuries,* Tuscaloosa: University of Alabama Press, 1989. A collection of essays that reevaluate the role of Georgia's founder.

Rees, Trevor Richard. *Colonial Georgia: A Study in British Imperial Policy in the Eighteenth Century.* Athens: University of Georgia Press, 1963. Since most of England's North American colonies were established in the seventeenth century, this book examines changes in colonial policy during the period when Georgia, the last of the 13 colonies was established.

Wood, Betty. *Slavery in Colonial Georgia, 1730–1775.* Athens: University of Georgia Press, 1984. Examines the development of slavery in Georgia, which was originally supposed to be a free colony.

World Wide Web

"Colonial Georgia." http://ourgeorgiahistory.com/history101/gahistory03.html. Overview of Georgia's colonial history.

"Colonial Settlement, 1600s–1763." http://lcweb2.loc.gov/learn/features/timeline/colonial/georgia/georgia.html. Library of Congress Web site that provides an overview of the colony's founding and links to primary source documents.

59. Printer John Peter Zenger Stands Trial for "Seditious Libel" (1734–1735)

In 1734, New York Governor William Cosby suspended the colony's chief justice for ruling against him in a court case. Frustrated that New York's only newspaper, the *New York Gazette,* would not publish their criticisms of the governor, the governor's opponents funded the establishment of the *New-York Weekly Journal,* published by German immigrant John Peter Zenger. After publishing articles critical of Governor Cosby throughout most of 1734, New York authorities arrested and jailed Zenger in November 1734, charging him with "seditious libel"—in other words, the prosecution claimed that Zenger printed untrue statements in an effort to provoke resistance to the government. The government attempted to limit what evidence could be presented at the trial. When Zenger's trial begin in late July 1735, he found himself represented by Philadelphia's Andrew Hamilton (no relation to Alexander Hamilton), widely considered the best trial lawyer in the colonies. The judges instructed the jury not to consider the truth or falseness of the articles; the only issue was whether Zenger printed them. Hamilton argued to the jury that Zenger could not be guilty of libel because the criticisms that he published of the governor were true. After a short deliberation, the jury found Zenger not guilty. The Zenger trial is important in that it is the first example of jury nullification. It is also one of the first decisions in American history upholding the freedom of the press, and it established that truth is a defense against a charge of libel.

TERM PAPER SUGGESTIONS

1. Examine the concept of jury nullification. How does it work?
2. Discuss the charge of "seditious libel." Could such a charge be made today? Could the truth always be a perfect defense against such a charge?
3. Discuss the influence of the Zenger trial on the American concept of freedom of the press.
4. Andrew Hamilton is not very well known today, but in the eighteenth century he was one of the best-known attorneys in British North America and also something of an architect, designing Independence Hall. Examine and trace Hamilton's career.

ALTERNATIVE TERM PAPER SUGGESTIONS

1. It is 1734 and you work for New York Governor William Cosby. Governor Cosby has had quite enough of Zenger and his newspaper. He orders you to draw up the order that will shut down the paper and put Zenger in jail. However, the governor complicates matters when he tells you to do it in such a way that it will not rouse the public. Good luck.
2. It is 1735 and you are Andrew Hamilton's legal clerk. Hamilton wants you to prepare a PowerPoint presentation for when he makes his argument to the jury.

SUGGESTED SOURCES

Primary Sources

"Peter Zenger and Freedom of the Press." http://www.earlyamerica.com/earlyamerica/bookmarks/zenger/. Contains a narrative of the trial and pages from Zenger's *New-York Weekly Journal.*

Rutherford, Livingston. *John Peter Zenger; His Press, His Trial, and a Bibliography of Zenger Imprints.* New York: Dodd, Mead, and Company, 1904.

Contains an account of Zenger's trial. Available at the Internet Archive at www.archive.org and Google Books.

"The Trial of John Peter Zenger." http://www.courts.state.ny.us/history/Zenger.htm. Contains primary sources and images of John Peter Zenger's trial.

World Wide Web

"Famous American Trials: John Peter Zenger Trial, 1735." http://www.law.umkc.edu/faculty/projects/Ftrials/zenger/zenger.html. This very useful Web site contains the trial transcript, chronology events, letters, images, links, and a bibliography.

Multimedia Source

Studio One: The Trial of John Peter Zenger. 1953. 59 minutes. Available at the Internet Archive at www.archive.org. This is a somewhat hokey 1950s TV drama about Zenger's trial, but it does get most of the essential facts correct.

60. "Walking Purchase" (1737)

Pennsylvania, under its founder, William Penn, developed a reputation for treating native peoples fairly. By the 1730s, Penn's heirs needed more land to sell to would-be colonists. James Logan, the colony's chief justice and head of Indian affairs, met with Lenni-Lenape (Delaware) chiefs in 1732 and presented them with a purported copy of a 1686 treaty that required them to surrender land west of the Delaware River to the extent that a man could traverse in a day and half. The Lenni-Lenape protested that they had no recollection of such a treaty, but Logan convinced them to have the area traversed on foot, in accordance with the document. The Lenni-Lenape thought that the "walk" would be done at a normal pace. Logan, however, had other ideas. He ordered a trail cleared through the woods, hired three athletes to execute the walk, and arranged for them to be followed by men on horseback to carry food and water for them. On the day of the walk, the frustrated Lenni-Lenape protested as the walkers ran, rather than walked. To Logan's chagrin, the Lenni-Lenape refused to leave their lands. Unable to convince the colony's Quaker-dominated legislature to use force against the Lenni-Lenape, Logan enlisted the help of the Iroquois League. During a conference at Philadelphia in 1742, the Iroquois bluntly ordered the Lenni-Lenape to leave eastern Pennsylvania. The removal of the Lenni-Lenape had far-reaching consequences. The Lenni-Lenape would move to the Ohio River Valley, a move that would contribute to a war between England and France for the control of the North American continent.

TERM PAPER SUGGESTIONS

1. The Iroquois and the Lenni-Lenape had a complicated relationship that involved the use of gender and kinship terms in diplomacy between the two peoples.
2. Trace the changing relationship between the Lenni-Lenape and the colony of Pennsylvania from William Penn to the Walking Purchase.
3. Why did James Logan have to turn to the Iroquois to force the Lenni-Lenape to move? Why could he not persuade Pennsylvania's own legislature to use force?
4. Discuss the Iroquois's instructions to the Lenni-Lenape to move. Many Lenni-Lenape did not go where the Iroquois specified. Why?

ALTERNATIVE TERM PAPER SUGGESTIONS

1. You are a Lenni-Lenape diplomat in 1732. You and other Lenni-Lenape have learned that James Logan is announcing that he has a treaty stating that you have promised to sell land to Pennsylvania. Even though you do not have a written copy of the treaty, you have the wampum belts (used as mnemonic devices) that record all of your agreements with Pennsylvania. Make a PowerPoint presentation showing how wampum belts were used to record treaties.
2. It is 1732 and James Logan has hired you to draft a "treaty" that the Lenni-Lenape purportedly signed with William Penn in 1686. To make it convincing, you will have to examine old treaties and try to forge the marks of Indian leaders. Good luck, and do not get caught.

SUGGESTED SOURCES

Primary Sources

Calloway, Colin G., ed. *The World Turned Upside Down.* Boston: Bedford/St. Martin's, 1994. Calloway includes native accounts of the Walking Purchase and its aftermath.

Kent, Donald H., ed. *Pennsylvania Indian Treaties, 1737–1756.* Frederick, MD: University Publications of America, 1984. Includes the agreements that forced the Lenni-Lenape to move.

Secondary Sources

Harper, Steven Craig. *Promised Land: Penn's Holy Experiment, the Walking Purchase, and the Dispossession of Delawares, 1600–1763.* Bethelem, PA: Lehigh University Press, 2006. Traces the history of Indian relations in colonial Pennsylvania from Penn's original dealings with the Lenni-Lenape, through the Walking Purchase, and the end of the French and Indian War.

Hinderaker, Eric. *Elusive Empires: Constructing Colonialism in the Ohio Valley, 1673–1800.* New York: Cambridge University Press, 1997. Many of the Lenni-Lenape ended up in the Ohio country and were involved in conflicts between Europeans and later the Americans for control of the Ohio River Valley.

Jennings, Francis. *The Ambiguous Iroquois Empire: The Covenant Chain Confederation or Indian Tribes with English Colonies from Its Beginnings to the Lancaster Treaty of 1744.* New York: Norton, 1984. The Iroquois colluded with Pennsylvania to divest the Lenni-Lenape of their lands, and Jennings touches on that.

Wallace, Anthony F. C. *King of the Delawares: Teedyuscung, 1700–1763.* Philadelphia: University of Pennsylvania Press, 1949. Reprinted, Syracuse University Press, 1990. Although Teedyuscung did not come to prominence until after the Walking Purchase, Wallace includes a good account of it and its effects to set up his biography of this Lenni-Lenape leader.

Weslager, C. A. *The Delaware Indians: A History.* New Brunswick, NJ: Rutgers University Press, 1972. A good, through history of the Lenni-Lenape people.

World Wide Web

"The Walking Purchase." http://www.phmc.state.pa.us/ppet/walking/page1.asp?secid=31. Offers a brief narrative of the Walking Purchase.

"The Walking Purchase, August 25, 1737." http://www.docheritage.state.pa.us/documents/walkingpurchase.asp. Contains a detailed description of the Walking Purchase, images of documents, and transcriptions of the documents.

Multimedia Source

Indians of North America: The Lenape. Schlessinger Media, 1994. VHS. 30 minutes. A compact history of the Lenni-Lenape that includes the Walking Purchase.

61. Stono Rebellion in South Carolina (1739)

The British Colony of South Carolina had long been in a precarious position. Beginning in the early eighteenth century, the colony had finally hit upon a sustainable economic enterprise, the growing of rice. However, Englishmen knew nothing about growing rice. African slaves, however, were familiar with the crop, and in the early eighteenth century South Carolina became the only colony in British North America where African slaves were in the majority. Fearful of slave revolts, the colony enacted strict laws regarding slaves and free blacks. At the same time, in an effort to cause unrest in the colony, Spanish authorities in Florida let it be known that slaves who fled South Carolina and reached their territory would be granted their freedom. The Stono Rebellion (named after the Stono River) began in September 1739 when slaves on a plantation rebelled, broke into a store, and took guns and ammunition. They began to march south toward Florida. Unlike most slaves who attempted not to attract attention, they had a flag, drums, and chanted "liberty" on their march. As they moved south, slaves from other plantations joined them as they burned seven plantations and killed about 20 whites. The next day, the 80 or so slaves found themselves facing a militia of 100 armed and mounted men who killed all but 30 of the slaves. The survivors fled into swamps, but all of them were captured or killed by Indian allies of South Carolina in the coming weeks. As a warning to other would-be rebels, the Carolinians placed the heads of the slaves on posts between the battlefield and the capitol of Charles Town.

TERM PAPER SUGGESTIONS

1. African slaves outnumbered English colonists in South Carolina since the early eighteenth century. Discuss the security measures the colony adopted

to thwart slave rebellions. Why did these measures not work during the Stono Rebellion?

2. Why did the slaves who participated in the Stono Rebellion make themselves conspicuous?
3. Discuss the role of the Spanish colony of Florida. How did the Spaniards make it known to slaves in South Carolina that they would find a safe haven there?
4. Discuss the role of South Carolina's Indian allies. Why did the Indians assist the Carolinians and not the slaves?
5. Examine the aftermath of the Stono Rebellion. South Carolina already had strict laws regarding the control of slaves at the time of the rebellion. How did Carolina further increase these restrictions?

ALTERNATIVE TERM PAPER SUGGESTIONS

1. It is 1739 and you are a participant in the Stono Rebellion. Many of the planners advocate attempting to flee south quickly, and to try and not attract attention on the way. You, however, are on the side of those who wish to proceed slowly, and with much fanfare. Prepare a PowerPoint presentation designed to sway the other side. Make sure you have a good argument for taking this position.
2. It is 1739 and you are a Spanish official in Florida. Your job is to try and foment unrest among slaves in South Carolina. Prepare a podcast that will be heard by slaves in South Carolina. Give them reasons to revolt and flee to Florida.

SUGGESTED SOURCES

Primary Source

Smith, Mark Michael. *Stono: Documenting and Interpreting a Southern Slave Revolt.* Columbia: University of South Carolina Press, 2005. This collection contains analysis and primary source documents from the Stono Rebellion.

Secondary Sources

Littlefield, Daniel C. *Rice and Slaves: Ethnicity and the Slave Trade in Colonial South Carolina.* Baton Rouge: Louisiana State University Press, 1981. Discusses the Stono Rebellion and its probable causes.

Weir, Robert M. *Colonial South Carolina: A History.* Milwood, NY: KTO Press, 1983. A history of colonial South Carolina.

Wood, Peter. *Black Majority: Negroes in Colonial South Carolina from 1670 through the Stono Rebellion.* New York: Knopf, 1974. Wood includes a good account of the Stono Rebellion and its results.

World Wide Web

"Africans in America: The Stono Rebellion." http://www.pbs.org/wgbh/aia/part1/1p284.html. A companion Web site for the PBS *Africans in America* presentation, this portion of the site offers a synopsis of the revolt, links to interviews with scholars, and primary source documents.

Multimedia Source

Africans in America. PBS, 1998. 2 DVDs. 180 minutes. Includes an account of the Stono Rebellion and its aftermath.

62. George Whitefield Begins His First Tour of the Colonies (1739)

Jonathan Edward's *A Faithful Narrative of the Surprising Work of God,* published in 1737, became one of the most influential pieces of literature produced during the Great Awakening, a transatlantic revival that lasted between the 1730s and 1760s. Many evangelicals consulted Edward's *Faithful Narrative* as a "how to" manual for conducting revivals. Among Edward's readers was a newly ordained Anglican minister, George Whitefield (pronounced "wit-field"). Using a portable pulpit, the short, slight, and cross-eyed Whitefield began preaching in fields and parks, reaching people who normally did not attend church. Whitefield's dramatic sermons, and his voice—which Benjamin Franklin estimated could easily be heard by an audience of 30,000 people—made him a sensation in England. In 1739, Whitefield began his first tour of the colonies. Using broadsides, newspapers, handbills, and advance men to announce his revivals, Whitefield became the first American celebrity. Most of the population of British North America had heard Whitefield preach, read something by or about him, or at least heard of him. Whitefield was very successful in the North where printing and a fairly dense settlement pattern attracted large numbers of people to his revivals. He was less successful in the South, which had little printing and a more diffused settlement pattern. Whitefield became a business partner and personal friend of Benjamin Franklin. News of Whitefield's revivals sold newspapers, and Franklin published his sermons as well. The two did not always agree on religious matters, but Franklin noted that Whitefield could be very persuasive. Franklin once attended a Whitefield sermon, determined to contribute nothing to the collection plate, but ended the evening by emptying his pockets. Whitefield conducted several revivals in British North America and died in West Newburyport, Massachusetts, in 1770.

TERM PAPER SUGGESTIONS

1. Discuss the influence of Jonathan Edwards's *A Faithful Narrative of the Surprising Work of God* on George Whitefield and other Great Awakening clergy.
2. Discuss Whitefield's appeal to eighteenth-century audiences. How did his physical appearance (small, slight, and cross-eyed) work to his advantage?
3. Not everyone in the colonies viewed George Whitefield favorably. Discuss the views of Whitefield's opponents.
4. Examine the relationship between George Whitefield and Benjamin Franklin. Discuss their friendship and their differing religious views.

ALTERNATIVE TERM PAPER SUGGESTIONS

1. It is 1739 and George Whitefield is about to embark on his first revival in British North America. Whitefield wants to take advantage of new technologies, so he has asked you to prepare podcasts to promote his revivals.
2. It is 1739 and, wanting to use new technologies, George Whitefield has asked you to select any one of his sermons and to make a PowerPoint presentation that will accompany it.

SUGGESTED SOURCES

Primary Sources

Franklin, Benjamin. *The Autobiography and Other Writings.* Ed. Kenneth Silverman. New York: Penguin, 1986. Franklin mentions Whitefield several times in the course of his autobiography.

Kidd, Thomas S., ed. *The Great Awakening: A Brief History with Documents.* Boston: Bedford/St.Martin's, 2008. Contains an informative narrative about the Great Awakening and extracts from sermons and documents, including those by and about George Whitefield.

Whitefield, George. *Memoirs of George Whitefield.* Ed. John Gilllies. New Haven, CT: Whitmore & Buckingham and H. Mansfield, 1834. Contains extracts from Whitefield's journals and many of his sermons. Available at Google Books and the Internet Archive at www.archive.org.

Secondary Sources

Bonomi, Patricia U. *Under the Cope of Heaven: Religion, Society, and Politics in Colonial America.* New York: Oxford University Press, 1989. Examines the place of religion in colonial public life.

Butler, John. *Awash in a Sea of Faith: Christianizing the American People.* Cambridge, MA: Harvard University Press, 1990. Examines the development of Christianity in America beginning with England and up to the mid-nineteenth century. It also includes a good chapter on George Whitefield's influence.

Lambert, Frank. *"Pedlar in Divinity": George Whitefield and the Transatlantic Revivals, 1737–1770.* Princeton, NJ: Princeton University Press, 1994. Scholarly biography of George Whitefield.

Lambert, Frank. *Inventing the Great Awakening.* Princeton, NJ: Princeton University Press, 1999. Lambert argues that Edwards and other Great Awakening ministers set out to "invent" the Awakening, that it was not spontaneous.

Stout, Harry S. *The Divine Dramatist: George Whitefield and the Rise of Modern Evangelicalism.* Grand Rapids, MI: Eerdmans, 1991. Examines Whitefield's role as a minister and his use of theatrics in his ministry.

World Wide Web

"The Anglican Library—George Whitefield." http://www.anglicanlibrary.org/whitefield/index.htm. Contains a short biography of Whitefield and most of his surviving sermons.

"The First Great Awakening." http://nationalhumanitiescenter.org/tserve/eighteen/ekeyinfo/grawaken.htm. Offers an overview of the Great Awakening and discusses the roles played by George Whitefield, Jonathan Edwards, and other prominent clergy.

"Religion and the Founding of the American Republic." http://www.loc.gov/exhibits/religion/religion.html. This Library of Congress Web site offers a superb history of religion in America.

Multimedia Source

The First Great Awakening. School Media Associates, DVD. 1994. 10 minutes. Brief introduction to the Great Awakening.

63. Russians Make Contact with Aleutian Peoples (1740s)

Beginning in the late sixteenth and into the seventeenth century, Russia began to expand eastward in Siberia. In the late seventeenth century, Russia occupied the Kamchatka Peninsula and used it as a base for their explorations of the northern Pacific. Just as colonizing nations of Western Europe searched for a passage through the Americas that would allow them to reach Asia, Russia hoped to find a passage that would allow them to reach Western Europe. In 1741 Russian explorers Vitus Bering and Alexeii Chirikov reached southern Alaska where they came under attack by Tlingit peoples. In the mid-1740s Russian fur traders made contact with Aleutian peoples. In most cases the traders would seize control of a village and, holding the women and children hostage, would demand that the men go hunting for furs. When each man brought back his quota of furs, his family would be released. While the Aleut men were hunting for furs, the Russians often sexually exploited their women. Being forced to hunt for furs prevented Aleut men from hunting sea mammals and animals, as well as from fishing for food that their people needed to survive. The Aleuts rebelled in 1763–1764, but the Russians responded so savagely that the Aleuts never attempted it again. In the 1780s Siberian merchants attempted to regulate hunting in Alaska, and established a base on Kodiak Island. The Russians reduced the sexual exploitation of native women, and the presence of Russian Orthodox missionaries also helped stabilize relations. The Russians continued to move south along the Pacific coast, establishing trading posts in northern California in the nineteenth century.

TERM PAPER SUGGESTIONS

1. Compare and contrast two major themes in American history: American westward expansion and Russian eastward expansion.
2. Discuss Russian objectives in exploring North America. How did they mirror those of other European nations?
3. Compare and contrast Russian treatment of Native Americans with the English, French, and Spanish.
4. Examine Russian exploration and establishment of trading posts as they move southward along North America's Pacific coast. How did this bring them into conflict with other colonizing powers?

ALTERNATIVE TERM PAPER SUGGESTIONS

1. The Russian American fur trading company has appointed you as their public relations person. Your first assignment is to convince the czar to give the company a charter. Put together a PowerPoint presentation that points out to the czar the economic and strategic advantages Russia will realize from having a presence in North America.
2. The Russian American fur trading company also wants to attract foreign investment. Prepare a series of full-page newspaper ads that will run abroad.

SUGGESTED SOURCES

Primary Source

Steller, Georg W. *Journal of a Voyage with Bering, 1741–1742.* Ed. O. W. Frost. Stanford, CA: Stanford University Press, 1988. Steller was a German naturalist who accompanied the Bering expeditions. He was the first to observe and record several kinds of birds (all of which he named after himself) and the Steller Sea Cow (now extinct).

Secondary Sources

Barratt, Glynn. *Russia in Pacific Waters, 1715–1825.* Vancouver: University of British Columbia Press, 1981. History of Russian explorations in the Pacific.

Fisher, Raymond H. *Bering's Voyages: Whiter and Why.* Seattle: University of Washington Press, 1977. Examines Bering's voyages and the motivations behind them.

Gibson, James R. *Imperial Russia in Frontier America: The Changing Geography of Supply of Russian America, 1784–1867.* New York: Oxford University Press, 1976. Good history of Russia in America.

Grinev, Andrei Val'terovich. *The Tlingit Indians in Russian America, 1741–1867.* Trans. Richard L. Bland and Katerina G. Solovjova. Lincoln: University of Nebraska Press, 2005. Examines contacts between the Tlingit peoples and Russians, as well as the British and the Americans.

Hunt, William R. *Artic Passage: The Turbulent History of the Land and People of the Bering Sea, 1697–1975.* New York: Scribner's, 1975. History of the native peoples of the Bering Sea and their encounters with the Russians and later European traders.

Smith, Barbara Sweetland, and Redmond J. Barnett, eds. *Russian America: The Forgotten Frontier.* Tacoma: Washington State Historical Society, 1990. Collection of essays about Russian America.

World Wide Web

"The Russian Colonization of Alaska." http://lcweb2.loc.gov/intldl/mtfhtml/mfak/mfakrcol.html. This Library of Congress Web site offers a brief history, timelines, and links to translations of primary source documents.

"Russian Exploration of the Northwest Coast of North America." http://pages.quicksilver.net.nz/jcr/~vrussian1.html. Offers a brief history of Russian exploration of Alaska and the Pacific Northwest.

64. Jonathan Edwards Delivers Sermon Entitled "Sinners in the Hands of an Angry God" (1741)

The son and grandson of Puritan ministers, Jonathan Edwards entered Yale University at age 13 and graduated four years later as his class valedictorian. Like most Yale students in the early eighteenth century, Edwards trained to become a minister, and he aimed to replace his grandfather, Samuel Stoddard, as the minister of the Congregational Church in Northampton, Massachusetts, in 1729. Edwards believed that a minister must touch not only the intellect of his congregation but their emotions as well. Perhaps the best known of the American ministers during the transatlantic revival known as the Great Awakening, Jonathan Edwards conducted several revivals in the Connecticut River Valley. Edwards believed that it was necessary to terrify his listeners with graphic descriptions of what awaited the nonconverted in the afterlife, and then to offer them the hope of salvation. During his tenure in Northampton, Edwards wrote accounts of his efforts such as *A Faithful Narrative of the Surprising Work of God* (1737). This account was widely read on both sides of the Atlantic, and many novice ministers and pastors copied Edwards's techniques in hopes of replicating his success. Edwards's most famous piece of work, however, would be his sermon, *Sinners in the Hands of an Angry God* (1741), in which he compared the unconverted to spiders "or some loathsome insect" who were being held over the fiery pits of hell by a God who "is dreadfully provoked." After a dispute over the qualifications for church membership, the Northampton Congregational Church dismissed Edwards in 1750. He became a pastor in Stockbridge, Massachusetts, before assuming the presidency of the College of New Jersey shortly before his death in 1758.

TERM PAPER SUGGESTIONS

1. Why did Edwards and other Great Awakening evangelicals emphasize emotion during the conversion process?
2. Revivals had a long history in New England before Edwards; in fact, Edwards's grandfather Samuel Stoddard led a few revivals. Examine this history of revivals.
3. The enlightenment coincided with the Great Awakening. Why did evangelicals dislike the enlightenment or see it as a threat?
4. *Sinners in the Hands of an Angry God* is Edwards's best-known sermon, but his *Faithful Narrative of the Surprising Work of God* may have been more influential in the eighteenth century. Account for this work's influence.

ALTERNATIVE TERM PAPER SUGGESTIONS

1. It is 1741 and you are a member of Jonathan Edwards's congregation in Northampton, Massachusetts. Write a newspaper article describing the effect that his *Sinners in the Hands of an Angry God* has on you.

2. Of course, not everyone would have been thrilled with Edwards's sermons. Imagine that you heard Edwards's *Sinners in the Hands of an Angry God* and are less than impressed. Compose a newspaper editorial that argues with the points that Edwards made in his sermon.

SUGGESTED SOURCES

Primary Sources

Edwards, Jonathan. *Basic Writings.* Ed. Ola Elizabeth Winslow. New York: Signet Books, 1966. Good selection of Edward's writings.

Edwards, Jonathan. *The Jonathan Edwards Reader.* Ed. John E. Smith, Harry S. Stout, and Kenneth P. Minkema. New Haven, CT: Yale University Press, 2003. Another good selection that is a bit more thorough than the book edited by Winslow.

"The Jonathan Edwards Center at Yale University." http://edwards.yale.edu/. Possibly the most complete site about Edwards. Contains Edwards's writings and sermons, as well as articles about him.

"The Sermons of Jonathan Edwards." http://www.reformedsermonarchives.com/EdwardsTitle.htm. Collection of Jonathan Edwards's sermons.

Secondary Sources

Lambert, Frank. *Inventing the Great Awakening.* Princeton, NJ: Princeton University Press, 1999. Lambert argues that Edwards and other Great Awakening ministers set out to "invent" the Awakening and that it was not spontaneous.

Marsden, George M. *Jonathan Edwards: A Life.* New Haven, CT: Yale University Press, 2004. Latest and best biography of Edwards.

World Wide Web

"Christian Classics Ethereal Library." http://www.ccel.org/e/edwards/. This Calvin College Web site features a biography of Edwards and his writings.

Multimedia Source

Life and Theology of Jonathan Edwards. Enjoying God Ministry, 2006. 5 DVDs. 300 minutes. This DVD collection offers a detailed examination of Jonathan Edward's life and theology.

65. New York Slave Conspiracy (1741)

In the eighteenth century, New York City had the greatest concentration of African slaves in British North America outside of the South. Totaling approximately 20 percent of the city's population, the large number of slaves—while an integral part of the city's economy—roused much suspicion. The New York Slave Conspiracy—if that is what it truly was—began with burglary in February 1741 when three slaves robbed a shop, taking with them jewelry and luxury goods. The authorities soon traced the stolen goods to a waterfront tavern. An indentured servant at the tavern, Mary Burton, accused the owners of the tavern (who held her indenture) of buying and selling the stolen goods. Shortly thereafter, a rash of fires broke out in New York City, including one that destroyed most of Fort George, the post that defended the city. Over the next few days there were other fires, including four in one day. Rumors flew that slaves were seen fleeing from buildings after setting them afire. Burton was the chief witness during the trial for the tavern owners, but now her story included a complicated plot that slaves and Catholics (England was then at war with Spain) were conspiring to burn most of the city and turn it over to the Spanish. Mainly on the strength of Burton's (who received a reward) testimony, more than 30 people were executed by hanging and burning. More than 70 slaves were transported to the British sugar colonies in the Caribbean.

TERM PAPER SUGGESTIONS

1. Why were the authorities in New York City so willing to believe Mary Burton?
2. Discuss the tension that existed in New York City in the early 1740s. Why were people so willing to believe tales about a conspiracy?
3. Research and discuss the people that Mary Burton accused. Is there some sort of pattern to her accusations?
4. Discuss the place of religion in this conspiracy. What made New Yorkers so willing to believe that slaves and Catholics would be working together to destroy the city?

ALTERNATIVE TERM PAPER SUGGESTIONS

1. It is 1741 and you have been appointed as the defense attorney for one of the accused slaves. You decide that the best way to defend your client is to discredit the prosecution's star witness, Mary Burton. Draft a paper to show how you plan to do this.
2. It is 1741 and Mary Burton has accused you of being in on the plot to burn the city and hand it over to the Spanish. Write out the pleas you will give to court in your effort to get out of this mess.

SUGGESTED SOURCES

Primary Sources

" 'Fire, Fire, Scorch, Scorch!': Testimony from the Negro Plot Trials in New York, 1741." http://historymatters.gmu.edu/d/6528/. Excerpts from testimony given at the New York slave trials in 1741.

Horsmanden, Daniel. *The New York Conspiracy.* Boston: Beacon Press, 1971. This is a reprint of Horsmanden's 1744 account of the slave conspiracy. Horsmanden was one of the judges and his biases are apparent in this work.

Zabin, Serena R., ed. *The New York Conspiracy Trials of 1741: Daniel Horsmanden's Journal of the Proceedings with Related Documents.* Boston: Bedford/St. Martin's, 2004. Contains excerpts of Horsmanden's journal and other contemporaneous documents.

Secondary Sources

Hoffer, Charles Peter. *The Great New York Conspiracy of 1741: Slavery, Crime, and Colonial Law.* Lawrence: University of Kansas Press, 2003. This history of the New York Slave Conspiracy focuses on the legal aspects of the cases.

Lepore, Jill. *New York Burning: Liberty, Slavery, and Conspiracy in Eighteenth-Century Manhattan.* New York: Knopf, 2005. Lepore's book is perhaps the most readable account of the New York Slave Conspiracy.

World Wide Web

"Africans in America: A List of White Persons Taken into Custody on Account of the 1741 Conspiracy." http://www.pbs.org/wgbh/aia/part1/1h302.html. Links to primary source documents from the trial.

"Terror in New York—1741, by Edwin Hoey." http://www.americanheritage.com/articles/magazine/ah/1974/4/1974_4_72.shtml. *American Heritage* article about the New York Slave Conspiracy.

Multimedia Source

Africans in America. PBS, 1998. 2 DVDs. 180 minutes. Includes an account of the New York Slave Conspiracy.

66. Treaty of Lancaster (1744)

The Treaty of Lancaster came about over the need to resolve territorial disputes between the Iroquois League and the English colonies of Pennsylvania, Virginia, and New York. In a 1736 agreement with Pennsylvania, the Iroquois claimed that Maryland and Virginia had taken land that was theirs, having defeated native peoples in those regions. The Pennsylvanians promised they would help the Iroquois secure payment from the other two colonies. In return for payment, the Iroquois surrendered all of their land claims in Maryland and Virginia. However, when the Iroquois diplomat Canasatego signed over the Shenandoah Valley to Virginia, he included a clause that the natives acknowledged the right of Great Britain to all lands within the colony of Virginia. Virginia's original charter stated from sea to sea. In other words, Canasatego had theoretically signed over all of North America to the British. The Virginia colony soon after began granting charters to land companies with the rights to sell land in the Ohio Country. A decade later, Virginia attempted to assert their rights to the Ohio River Valley under the terms of the Treaty of Lancaster, helping to provoke the French and Indian War.

The Treaty of Lancaster is also notable for Canasatego's suggesting to the colonies that they unite, like the Iroquois League. Some scholars have taken this as evidence that the Iroquois influenced the U.S. Constitution. The Treaty of Lancaster has also been cited as an excellent example of the process of diplomacy between Native Americans and English colonists and offers insights into the role of the "go betweens," the natives and colonists who did the translating and actually conducted diplomacy.

TERM PAPER SUGGESTIONS

1. Examine the issues that brought Iroquois and English representatives together at Lancaster. Were all of these issues resolved?
2. Scholars debate if the treaty minutes such as those of the Lancaster treaty are an accurate representation of what really occurred. Many of them argue that due to linguistic and cultural differences the treaty minutes cannot be accurate. Address this question.
3. Discuss the role of the "go betweens" such as Canasatego and Conrad Weiser. Why were these men critical to the success of the treaty? What did they have to do to ensure success?
4. During the July 4 meeting, Canasatego suggested that the colonists form a union much like the Iroquois. Some scholars trace the beginnings of the U.S. Constitution to this suggestion, while others believe that too much has been made of Canasatego's speech. Evaluate this idea. Could Canasatego's remarks be taken as the impetus of the Constitution? Why or why not?
5. Examine the long-term consequences of the Treaty of Lancaster. Did Canasatego really sell all of North America to the English, or is this an exaggeration?

ALTERNATIVE TERM PAPER SUGGESTIONS

1. It is 1744, and you are an Iroquois diplomat. Virginia and Maryland are reluctant to pay the Iroquois for their land claims in their colonies. You have been given the task of convincing the two colonies that Iroquois land claims in their colonies are legitimate. Prepare a PowerPoint presentation, complete with maps, and make an argument that the colonies should pay.
2. It is 1744 and you are a Virginia representative to the Treaty of Lancaster. You have just returned to Virginia. Draw up plans of how Virginia will begin settling the Ohio Country.

SUGGESTED SOURCES

Primary Source

Merrell, James H., ed. *The Lancaster Treaty of 1744 with Related Documents.* Boston: Bedford/St. Martin's, 2008. Contains the text of the treaty, plus Merrell's analysis of diplomacy between native people and English colonists, and the importance of "go betweens."

Secondary Sources

Anderson, Fred. *Crucible of War: The Seven Years' War and the Fate of Empire in British North America.* New York: Knopf, 2001. In this dense (but very interesting) book, Anderson argues that the waning of Iroquois influence had its beginnings at Lancaster.

Jennings, Francis. *The Ambiguous Iroquois Empire: The Covenant Chain Confederation of Indian Tribes with English Colonies from Its Beginnings to the Lancaster Treaty of 1744.* New York: Norton, 1984. Jennings argues that Iroquois never really had an empire and that their influence began to wane after the Lancaster Treaty.

Merrell, James H. *Into the American Woods: Negotiators on the Pennsylvania Frontier.* New York: Norton, 1999. Examines the process of Native American and colonial diplomacy and emphasizes the importance of the "go betweens."

Wallace, Anthony F. C. *King of the Delawares: Teedyuscung, 1700–1763.* Philadelphia: University of Pennsylvania Press, 1949. Reprinted, Syracuse, NY: Syracuse University Press, 1990. Wallace discusses the Treaty of Lancaster, Teedyuscung's nonparticipation, and its consequences for the Delaware people.

Wallace, Paul A. W. *Conrad Weiser, 1696–1760: Friend of Colonist and Mohawk.* Philadelphia: University of Pennsylvania Press, 1945. Biography of one of the "go betweens" involved with the Treaty of Lancaster. The German-born Weiser had a long career as a diplomat for the Pennsylvania colony.

World Wide Web

"Early Recognized Treaties with American Indian Nations." http://earlytreaties.unl.edu/treaty.00003.html. Contains page images and transcriptions from the Pennsylvania Historical Society's 1938 printing of Benjamin Franklin's Indian treaties.

67. King George's War Begins (1744)

The third conflict between the French and the English in North America was known to the colonists as King George's War (known as the War of the Austrian Succession in Europe). The war overlapped with a naval conflict fought between England and Spain that began in 1739, which is also known as the War of Jenkins's Ear. That conflict had it origins due to tensions over the establishment of Georgia, adjacent to Spanish Florida, and English flouting of Spanish trade laws, such as the case of Captain Jenkins, whose ear was removed by Spanish authorities as punishment for smuggling. Colonists were involved in ambitious, but failed, expeditions against the Spanish that attempted to seize the Caribbean ports of Cartagena and Porto Bello, as well as Saint Augustine in Florida. Poor British leadership and disease frustrated each of these attempts. In March 1744, France entered the war on the side of Spain. Most fighting in North America took place along the New York and New England frontier. There was also significant naval action in coastal waters, as French privateers attacked coastal towns and, in one instance, journeyed 60 miles up the Delaware River. British privateers bombarded Spanish ports in the Caribbean. However, the most spectacular—and surprising—result of the conflict in North America was the capture by New England forces of the formidable French fortress at Louisbourg. The British navy became a more important factor the longer the war lasted, severing communications and supply between Spain and France and their colonies. Lacking access to trade goods, many Native Americans abandoned the French and sided with the British who could supply their needs, and even many French colonists took part in an illegal trade with their English counterparts. The war ended in 1748 with the signing of the Treaty of Aix-la-Chapelle. All prewar colonial boundaries were restored, meaning, much to the dismay of New England colonists, that Louisbourg would be returned to the French.

TERM PAPER SUGGESTIONS

1. Examine the diplomatic background for King George's War. How did the French become involved in a conflict between England and France?
2. Examine the naval war between England and Spain in the Americas. What success did the English and Spanish have?
3. How did the end of King George's War contribute to the next North American conflict between France and England?
4. Discuss the role of Native Americans in King George's War.

ALTERNATIVE TERM PAPER SUGGESTIONS

1. It is 1739 and you are a British newspaper publisher. Compose an editorial advocating war with Spain, playing up the plight of Captain Jenkins as much as you can.
2. It is 1748 and you are an English trader living in Albany, New York. There are great profits to be made in smuggling. You realize there are great profits to be made by trading English manufactured goods to French colonists in Canada. Devise a map showing the route you would use to trade with the French in Montreal. Keep in mind that you will need to avoid the English military post, lest you be arrested for smuggling.

SUGGESTED SOURCES

Primary Source

Shirley, William, and Samuel Drake. *A Particular History of the Five Years French and Indian War in New England and Parts Adjacent: From Its Declaration by the King of France, March 15, 1744, to the Treaty with the Eastern Indians, Oct. 16, 1749, Sometimes Called Gov. Shirley's War; with a Memoir of Major-General Shirley.* Albany: Joel Munsell, 1870. Contains a historical narrative and Massachusetts Governor William Shirley's account of the war. It can be found at Google Books.

Secondary Sources

Chet, Guy. *Conquering the American Wilderness: The Triumph of European Warfare in the Colonial Northeast.* Amherst: University of Massachusetts Press, 2003. Chet argues that, contrary to popular conceptions, European military tactics prevailed in North America.

Leach, Douglas Edward. *Arms for Empire: A Military History of the British Colonies in North America, 1607–1763.* New York: Macmillan, 1973. Good synthesis of the colonial military establishment, the operation of the colonial militia, and an overview of the four wars between the English and the French in North America.

Leach, Douglas Edward. *Roots of Conflict: British Armed Forces and Colonial Americans, 1677–1763.* Chapel Hill: University of North Carolina Press, 1986. Examines the role of British forces in North America.

Peckham, Howard H. *The Colonial Wars: 1689–1762.* Chicago: University of Chicago Press, 1964. Offers an overview of colonial participation in the colonial wars.

Steele, Ian K. *Warpaths: Invasions of North America.* New York: Oxford University Press, 1994. Steele's *Warpaths* is one of the best compact histories of the colonial wars.

World Wide Web

"King George's War." http://www.ohiohistorycentral.org/entry.php?rec=510. Brief article about King George's War.

"Wars and Battles: King George's War, 1744–1748." http://www.u-s-history.com/pages/h847.html. Brief article about King George's War.

68. New Englanders Capture the French Post at Louisbourg (1745)

The French established a naval base at Louisbourg to guard the entrance to the St. Lawrence River, the lifeline to the key French settlements of Quebec and Montreal. Known as the "Gibraltar of the New World," Louisburg boasted massive stone walls and bristled with cannon. Despite its formidable defenses, the post did have its weaknesses. During the early phases of King George's War (1744–1748), French naval vessels from Louisbourg attacked New England merchant vessels. Alarmed, Massachusetts Governor William Shirley proposed that New England troops capture Louisbourg and neutralize it. Encouraged by intelligence reports that Louisbourg's garrison consisted of only 700 men who were short of provisions, Shirley raised a force of about 4,000 New England soldiers. Supported by the Royal Navy, New England troops landed in January 1745. They had a stroke of luck when the French abandoned outlying batteries, spiking their cannon as they retreated. Unfortunately for the French, the New England troops repaired the cannon and turned them on the fort. The most serious blow to the defenders came when the British navy captured a French resupply ship bound for the fortress. Louisbourg surrendered in June 1745, giving American colonists the greatest victory England would have in King George's War. Despite being reimbursed for their expenses by the British government, the colonists were dismayed when the Treaty of Aix-la-Chapelle (1748) returned the fortress to the French. For the first time, many colonists began to recognize some of the drawbacks of being part of a global empire.

TERM PAPER SUGGESTIONS

1. Louisbourg did seem impregnable, but it did have some weakness. Detail some of these weaknesses.
2. The success of British colonists at Louisbourg was one of the most surprising outcomes of King George's War. Should it have been so surprising? Did the British not give the colonists enough credit?
3. Why did the English give Fort Louisbourg back to the French after the war? Did they get something in return?
4. The terms of the Treaty of Aix-la-Chapelle were as unpopular in England as they were in British North America. Why was the treaty ill received by the British public?

ALTERNATIVE TERM PAPER SUGGESTIONS

1. It is 1745 and you are a French officer posted to Louisbourg. The fort's commander has summoned you and ordered you to plan defense of the post. Prepare a PowerPoint presentation that you will show at the next officers' meeting, outlining how you plan to defend the fort and keep it from falling into English hands.
2. It is 1745 and you are a member of the Massachusetts militia. Recognizing that you are an extraordinarily bright person, your commander has appointed you as the psychological warfare officer. Your job is to prepare podcasts that will be broadcast to the French defenders. Your goal is to convince the French to surrender or to diminish their will to fight.

SUGGESTED SOURCES

Primary Sources

Green, Samuel A., ed. *Three Military Diaries kept by Groton Soldiers in Different Wars.* Groton, MA: University Press, 1901. Includes a narrative of the Louisbourg campaign by Lieutenant Dudley Bradstreet. It is available from the Internet Archive at www.archive.org.

Shirley, William, and Samuel Drake. *A Particular History of the Five Years French and Indian War in New England and Parts Adjacent: From Its Declaration by the King of France, March 15, 1744, to the Treaty with the Eastern Indians, Oct. 16, 1749, Sometimes Called Gov. Shirley's War; with a Memoir of Major-General Shirley.* Albany: Joel Munsell, 1870. Contains a historical narrative and Massachusetts Governor William Shirley's account of the war. It can be found at Google Books.

Secondary Sources

Chet, Guy. *Conquering the American Wilderness: The Triumph of European Warfare in the Colonial Northeast.* Amherst: University of Massachusetts Press, 2003. Chet argues that, contrary to popular conceptions, European tactics prevailed in North America.

Downey, Fairfax. *Louisbourg: Key to a Continent.* Englewood Cliffs, NJ: Prentice-Hall, 1965. A good history about the fortress and its capture by New England troops.

Leach, Douglas Edward. *Arms for Empire: A Military History of the British Colonies in North America, 1607–1763.* New York: Macmillan, 1973.

Leach, Douglas Edward. *Roots of Conflict: British Armed Forces and Colonial Americans, 1677–1763.* Chapel Hill: University of North Carolina Press, 1986. Leach's two military histories chronicle Britain's military role in North America and their relations with American colonists.

McNeill, John Robert. *Atlantic Empires of France and Spain: Louisbourg and Havana, 1700–1763.* Chapel Hill: University of North Carolina Press, 1985. Examines the armies, navies, and major Atlantic outposts of the two other "great powers" of the colonial period, Spain and France.

Peckham, Howard H. *The Colonial Wars: 1689–1762.* Chicago: University of Chicago Press, 1964. Peckham offers an overview of the colonial wars.

Steele, Ian K. *Warpaths: Invasions of North America.* New York: Oxford University Press, 1994. One of the best compact histories of the colonial wars.

World Wide Web

"Fortress of Louisbourg: National Historic Site of Canada." http://www.pc.gc.ca/lhn-nhs/ns/louisbourg/index_e.asp. This Parks Canada Web site includes a brief history of the fort as well as details of its reconstruction.

"The Official Research Site for the Fortress of Louisbourg National Historic Site of Canada." http://fortress.uccb.ns.ca/. This Web site has photographs and a history of the Louisbourg fortress.

69. Benjamin Franklin Publishes Essay on Population (1751)

In 1751, Benjamin Franklin, perhaps the most famous man in British North America, published his essay *Observations Concerning the Increase of Mankind.* In this essay, Franklin for the first time challenged the then-traditional notion that England should rule America. Franklin was not advocating revolution, however. Franklin opened the possibility that one day there would be more English subjects in America than in England. Franklin claimed that Europe was already fully populated, that there was little land available, and that few could afford land so they could start their own farms. This forced Europeans to work for others and to postpone marriage and children. By contrast, America had plenty of land, and it was cheap, permitting colonists to marry and have children earlier. The population of America, Franklin calculated, doubled every two decades. Because of the vastness of the American continent, it would be ages before it could be fully populated. In his essay, however, Franklin made it clear that he envisioned an English North America. He rallied against Pennsylvania's German settlers who had not learned English or otherwise assimilated into the colony. In a backhanded sort of way, Franklin called for an end to the trans-Atlantic slave trade, stating that the only colors that should be present in America were "the lovely White and Red."

TERM PAPER SUGGESTIONS

1. In his essay *Observations Concerning the Increase of Mankind,* is Franklin advocating that America would one day be the center of the British Empire?
2. In the course of his essay Franklin makes the point that population growth in America benefits England. Examine this idea. Do you think that Franklin was correct?
3. Does Franklin favor or oppose slavery in the essay?

4. Why does Franklin not seem to care for German (he refers to them as "Palatines") immigrants? What is it about them that troubled him?

ALTERNATIVE TERM PAPER SUGGESTIONS

1. It is 1751 and Benjamin Franklin has hired you as his assistant. He thinks he is going to have to illustrate the ideas in his *Observations Concerning the Increase of Mankind* in order for people to more fully understand it. With that in mind, he has tasked you with preparing a PowerPoint presentation complete with maps and graphs.
2. It is 1751 and you are a radio talk show host. You have landed Benjamin Franklin as a guest. Prepare a list of questions you want to ask about his essay. Make sure you prepare a list of possible follow-up questions as well.

SUGGESTED SOURCES

Primary Sources

"The Papers of Benjamin Franklin." http://www.yale.edu/franklinpapers/. This is the official site for Benamin Franklin's papers.

"The Papers of Benjamin Franklin." http://franklinpapers.org/franklin/. This is the digital edition of Yale University's Benjamin Franklin papers project. It is affiliated with the preceding Web site.

Secondary Sources

Chaplin, Joyce E. *The First Scientific American: Benjamin Franklin and the Pursuit of Genius.* New York: Basic Books, 2006. Rather than the usual biography, Chaplin chooses to focus on Franklin as a scientist.

Morgan, Edmund S. *Benjamin Franklin.* New Haven, CT: Yale University Press, 2004. An excellent biography of Franklin.

Waldstreicher, David. *Runaway America: Benjamin Franklin, Slavery, and the American Revolution.* New York: Hill & Wang, 2004. Although this book is not about Franklin as the man of letters or science, it does include a good section regarding his *Observations Concerning the Increase of Mankind.*

Wood, Gordon S. *The Americanization of Benjamin Franklin.* New York: Penguin, 2004. Leading up to the tricentennial in 2006 of Franklin's birth, there was a spate of Franklin biographies. This is one of the best.

World Wide Web

"Population Politics: Benjamin Franklin and the Peopling of North America." http://www.ccis-ucsd.org/PUBLICATIONS/wrkg88.pdf. Essay by Alan Houston of the University of California at San Diego.

Multimedia Sources

Benjamin Franklin. History Channel, 2004. 1 DVD. 100 minutes. This program uses reenactments and interviews with Franklin biographers.

Benjamin Franklin. PBS, 2002. 1 DVD. 210 minutes. This program uses reenactments and narration to recreate Benjamin Franklin's life and contributions.

Biography: Benjamin Franklin—Citizen of the World. A&E Home Video, 2006. 1 DVD. 50 minutes. This program uses images, commentary, and Franklin's own writings to tell his story.

70. Benjamin Franklin Publishes Experiments with Electricity (1751)

Perhaps the most popular image Americans have of Benjamin Franklin involves his flying a kite in the midst of an electrical storm, trying to draw lightning from the sky. Eighteenth-century showmen used static electrical charges to create shocks and sparks, and Franklin witnessed such a performance in Boston in 1743. Franklin began experimenting with electricity, developing an early electrical battery by wiring several Leyden jars (an early storage device for electrical charges) together. Franklin kept attempting to find a practical use for electricity. One was to use an electric charge to kill chickens and turkeys, which Franklin argued rendered them very tender. Franklin argued against the prevailing erroneous notion that electricity consisted of two fluids, labeled as vitreous and resinous. Instead, Franklin noted it was a single element with positive and negative charges. The most immediate practical value of Franklin's experiments was his invention of the lightning rod, which protected houses, churches, barns, and all ships of the Royal Navy. Many of the members of the prestigious Royal Society cast doubt on the value of Franklin's experiments. However, most of the doubts were wiped away when his friend, Quaker merchant Peter Collinson, took Franklin's collected letters and had them published in a short book, *Experiments and Observations on Electricity, Made at Philadelphia in America.* The realization of what Franklin had done easily made him the most famous of the king's subjects in British North America.

TERM PAPER SUGGESTIONS

1. Examine the ideas that Franklin's contemporaries had regarding electricity. What did they get wrong? What did they get right?
2. Franklin's experiments with electricity made him perhaps the best-known colonist in British North America. Examine Franklin's fame, and how it spread, given the media of the eighteenth century.
3. Franklin's invention of the lightning rod was extremely important in the eighteenth century. Examine the congratulations that Franklin received from around the world for his invention.
4. The Royal Society expressed its doubts about Franklin's experiments. What bias did the members of the society possess? Were their biases directed at Franklin or colonials in general?

ALTERNATIVE TERM PAPER SUGGESTIONS

1. It is 1751 and Benjamin Franklin has hired you as his assistant. Franklin has found that it may be a good idea to illustrate his ideas. Your job is to make a series of diagrams to accompany his *Experiments and Observations on Electricity, Made at Philadelphia in America.*
2. It is 1751 and Benjamin Franklin has given you a franchise to sell his lightning rods. Design a full-page newspaper ad extolling the virtues of Franklin's lightning rods.

SUGGESTED SOURCES

Primary Source

http://franklinpapers.org/franklin/framedVolumes.jsp. Includes the full text of Franklin's *Experiments and Observations on Electricity, Made at*

Philadelphia in America. It also includes many other papers by Franklin concerning electricity as well as correspondence from scientists. In addition, this site includes Franklin's autobiography where Franklin refers to his experiments with electricity several times.

Secondary Sources

Chaplin, Joyce E. *The First Scientific American: Benjamin Franklin and the Pursuit of Genius.* New York: Basic Books, 2006. Rather than the usual biography, Chaplin chooses to focus on Franklin as a scientist.

Isaacson, Walter. *Benjamin Franklin: An American Life.* New York: Simon and Schuster, 2003. Isaacson includes a chapter about Franklin's career as a scientist and discusses his experiments with electricity.

Morgan, Edmund S. *Benjamin Franklin.* New Haven, CT: Yale University Press, 2004.

Wood, Gordon S. *The Americanization of Benjamin Franklin.* New York: Penguin, 2004. Leading up to the tricentennial in 2006 of Franklin's birth, there was a spate of Franklin biographies. Morgan's and Wood's are two of the best academic biographies.

World Wide Web

"Electrified Ben." http://sln.fi.edu/franklin/scientst/electric.html. This site discusses Franklin's theories about electricity and his experiments with lightning rods and lightning bells.

Multimedia Sources

Benjamin Franklin. History Channel, 2004. 1 DVD. 100 minutes. This program uses reenactments and interviews with Franklin biographers.

Benjamin Franklin. PBS, 2002. 1 DVD. 210 minutes. This program uses reenactments and narration to recreate Franklin's life and contributions.

Biography: Benjamin Franklin—Citizen of the World. A&E Home Video, 2006. 1 DVD. 50 minutes. This program uses images, commentary, and Franklin's own writings to tell his story.

71. George Washington Builds Fort Necessity (1754)

In the wake of King George's War (1744–1748), the French discovered that English fur traders from the colonies of Virginia and Pennsylvania were operating in the Ohio River Valley. The French quickly evicted the traders and began work on Fort Duquesne at the Forks of the Ohio in an effort to prevent further British incursions. The governor of Virginia commissioned 22-year-old George Washington, a lieutenant colonel of militia, and sent him to evict the French. Washington became lost and could not find the French Post when he and his men met Tanaghrisson (Half-King). A local Iroquois official and English partisan, Tanaghrisson offered to lead Washington to a nearby French encampment. Washington and his 47 men fought a brief engagement against 35 Frenchmen. However, Tanaghrisson and his warriors slew wounded French prisoners before Washington and his men could protect them. Knowing that the French would soon send an expedition against him, Washington and his men hastily constructed a small ramshackle affair that he christened Fort Necessity. Situated on low ground, and with most of their gunpowder ruined by a sudden rainstorm, Washington and his men were attacked by a superior force of French and Indians. Forced to surrender, Washington received lenient terms from the French that permitted him and his surviving men to leave. As part of the terms of surrender, Washington signed a confession (in French) that he murdered a French officer. Although Washington did not yet know it, he and his men had fired the opening salvos in a global conflict that would be known as the French and Indian War in America, and the Seven Years' War in Europe.

TERM PAPER SUGGESTIONS

1. Why would George Washington undertake such a hazardous mission as traveling to the Forks of the Ohio? What did he have to gain?
2. Examine Washington's interactions with Tanaghrisson (Half-King). Tanaghrisson seems to have had his own agenda, which differed from Washington's. What were Tanaghrisson's objectives?

3. Discuss Washington's selection of the site where he built Fort Necessity. By nearly every measure, it was a bad choice. Why did Washington choose such a site?
4. Discuss the surrender terms that Washington received from the French. Were they fair? Do you think they were lenient or harsh?
5. Washington's clash with the French is often cited as the opening of the French and Indian War. However, what factors led the governments of England and France to engage in a global conflict? What was the geopolitical situation at the time?

ALTERNATIVE TERM PAPER SUGGESTIONS

1. It is 1754 and you are George Washington's second in command. Washington has asked your advice as to where to place Fort Necessity. Draw a map of the area where the real Fort Necessity was, and change the site of the fort to where you think it should be. Attach a memo explaining your decision.
2. It is 1754 and you are a reporter for a colonial newspaper. You have arranged an interview with George Washington, who has just returned from his engagement with the French at Fort Necessity. Using Washington's journal as the basis for the interview, what do you think he would say?

SUGGESTED SOURCES

Primary Sources

Fitzpatrick, John C., ed. *The Writings of George Washington from the Original Manuscript Sources.* 39 volumes. Washington: GPO, 1931–1944. http://etext.virginia.edu/washington/fitzpatrick/. Fitzpatrick's edition of Washington's papers contains mainly documents that originated with Washington.

"The George Washington Papers at the Library of Congress, 1741–1799." http://lcweb2.loc.gov/ammem/gwhtml/gwhome.html. This Web site is home to the largest collection of George Washington's papers. This site features images of the original documents and transcriptions of them.

"The Maryland Gazette Featuring George Washington's Journal." http://www.earlyamerica.com/earlyamerica/milestones/journal/. Features PDF copies of the *Maryland Gazette* from 1754 and a transcript of the journal.

"The Papers of George Washington." http://gwpapers.virginia.edu/. The University of Virginia's George Washington Papers project, begun in 1969, will eventually include documents originating with Washington as well as correspondence to him. As of March 2009, this project has published Washington's papers up to 1793.

Secondary Sources

Anderson, Fred. *Crucible of War: The Seven Years' War and the Fate of Empire in British North America, 1754–1766.* New York: Knopf, 2000. As the 250th anniversary of the French and Indian War approached, a number of histories about the conflict appeared. This is undoubtedly the best and most complete.

Anderson, Fred. *The War That Made America.* New York: Viking, 2005. This is the companion book for the PBS presentation by the same name.

Ellis, Joseph J. *His Excellency: George Washington.* New York: Vintage, 2004. This is Joseph Ellis's take on George Washington, including his baptism by fire in 1754.

Hinderaker, Eric. *Elusive Empires: Constructing Colonialism in the Ohio Valley, 1673–1800.* New York: Cambridge University Press, 1997. Hinderaker examines the attempts of the French, the British, and later the Americans to gain control over the Ohio Country.

Leach, Douglas Edward. *Arms for Empire: A Military History of the British Colonies in North America, 1607–1763.* New York: Macmillan, 1973.

Leach, Douglas Edward. *Roots of Conflict: British Armed Forces and Colonial Americans, 1677–1763.* Chapel Hill: University of North Carolina Press, 1986. Leach's two military histories chronicle Britain's military role in North America and their relations with American colonists.

McConnell, Michael N. *A Country Between: The Upper Ohio Valley and Its Peoples, 1724–1774.* Lincoln: University of Nebraska Press, 1992. Includes an account of Washington's expedition to western Pennsylvania.

Peckham, Howard H. *The Colonial Wars: 1689–1762.* Chicago: University of Chicago Press, 1964. Peckham includes an account of George Washington at Fort Necessity.

Steele, Ian K. *Warpaths: Invasions of North America.* New York: Oxford University Press, 1994. Steele's *Warpaths* is one of the best compact histories of the colonial wars.

World Wide Web

"Fort Necessity." http://www.ohiohistorycentral.org/entry.php?rec=714. Contains a brief narrative, links, and a bibliography.

"Fort Necessity." http://www.statelibrary.state.pa.us/libraries/cwp/view.asp?a=11&Q=43270. Contains an interesting account of the archaeology of Fort Necessity.

"Fort Necessity: National Battlefield, Pennsylvania." http://www.nps.gov/fone/. National Park Service Web site contains an overview of the battle and its importance in American history.

Multimedia Sources

George Washington's First War: The Battles for Fort Duquesne. Paladin Communications, 2003. 1 DVD. 85 minutes. Uses reenactments, narration and interviews with historians to tell the stories of Fort Necessity and General Edward Braddock's defeat.

George Washington Remembers. PBS, 2004. 1 DVD. 24 minutes. This presentation is based on Washington's recollection later in his life of the French and Indian War.

The History Channel Presents Washington the Warrior. A&E Home Video, 2006. 1 DVD. 92 minutes. This presentation focuses on Washington's military service from the French and Indian War to the Revolution.

The History of Warfare: French & Indian War. Cromwell Productions, 2007. 1 DVD. 55 minutes. Uses reenactments, images, and commentary from historians in presenting the French and Indian War.

The War That Made America. PBS, 2005. 2 DVDs. 240 minutes. George Washington figures prominently in this PBS presentation, which uses documents, reenactments, and narration to tell the story of the French and Indian War.

When the Forest Ran Red. Paladin Communications, 2004. 1 DVD. 68 minutes. Uses reenactments, narration, and interviews with historians to reconstruct the French and Indian War.

72. Albany Congress (1754)

As the French moved to consolidate their hold on the Ohio River Valley, and the Iroquois League warned the British that their alliance to them was weakening, the Board of Trade, the British body responsible for the administration of the colonies, directed that the colonies meet at Albany, New York, to discuss a plan for a unified defense of the British North America. Only seven colonies sent representatives. The colonies presented the Iroquois with 30 wagonloads of goods but received only lukewarm promises of support in any future conflict with the French. However, some colonists had their own ideas as to how to unite the colonies. Benjamin Franklin of Pennsylvania and Thomas Hutchinson of Massachusetts proposed the Albany Plan of Union, which called for each colonial legislature to send representatives to a grand council that would be presided over by a president-general who would be appointed by the king. Each colony's level of representation would be proportional to its monetary contribution to this new way of governing the colonies, and the president-general would have the power to veto any acts of the council. Neither the Crown nor most of the colonies liked the plan. The English government did not care for the prospect of relinquishing some control over the colonies, and the colonies were not enthusiastic about the possibility that England would exert greater control over them in the person of the president-general. Some historians have regarded the Albany Plan of Union as a forerunner of the U.S. Constitution.

TERM PAPER SUGGESTIONS

1. Discuss the British colonies prior to the Albany Congress. Why was there a lack of unity among them?
2. Discuss the urgency on the part of the British to retain their ties to the Iroquois League. Why did the Iroquois not offer more assurances to the English colonies before departing Albany?
3. Examine the Albany Plan of Union. Which colony would have had the most say in the running of the Union? Which entity would have been more powerful: the Grand Council or the president-general?

4. What were some of the objections of the different colonies to the Albany Plan of Union? What were some the objections of the English government?
5. Many historians have argued that the Albany Plan of Union was something of a template for the later U.S. Constitution. Examine this idea.

ALTERNATIVE TERM PAPER SUGGESTIONS

1. It is 1754 and you have accompanied Benjamin Franklin to Albany as his assistant. Franklin is going to give the other colonial representatives a presentation regarding his proposed Plan of Union. He has asked you to prepare a PowerPoint presentation that covers each point.
2. It is 1754 and you are a representative from the English government. There are aspects of the Albany Plan of Union that you dislike. Prepare a PowerPoint presentation designed to rebut each aspect of the plan.

SUGGESTED SOURCES

Primary Sources

"Albany Plan of Union 1754." http://avalon.law.yale.edu/18th_century/albany.asp#1. Text of the Albany Plan of Union.

"The Papers of Benjamin Franklin." http://franklinpapers.org/franklin/framedVolumes.jsp. Franklin discusses the Albany Plan of Union in volume five of his papers and in his autobiography.

Secondary Sources

Anderson, Fred. *Crucible of War: The Seven Years' War and the Fate of Empire in British North America, 1754–1766.* New York: Knopf, 2000. One of the best in the recent spate of histories about the French and Indian War, and it includes a chapter on the Albany Congress.

Isaacson, Walter. *Benjamin Franklin: An American Life.* New York: Simon and Schuster, 2003. Isaacson discusses Franklin's formulation of the Albany Plan of Union in this biography.

Morgan, Edmund S. *Benjamin Franklin.* New Haven, CT: Yale University Press, 2004. Franklin's role in proposing the Albany Plan of Union is discussed in this biography.

Shannon, Timothy. *Indians and Colonists at the Crossroads of Empire: The Albany Congress of 1754.* Ithaca, NY: Cornell University Press, 2000. Discusses the Albany Congress and disputes the notion that the Albany Plan of Union was a template for the U.S. Constitution.

Wood, Gordon S. *The Americanization of Benjamin Franklin.* New York: Penguin, 2004. Discusses Franklin's role in the Albany Plan of Union.

World Wide Web

"The Albany Congress." http://www.nysm.nysed.gov/albany/albanycongress.html. Narrative about the Albany Congress.

"Albany Plan of Union, 1754." http://www.state.gov/r/pa/ho/time/cp/90611.htm. Discussion of the Albany Plan of Union.

Multimedia Sources

Benjamin Franklin. History Channel, 2004. 1 DVD. 100 minutes. This program uses reenactments and interviews with Franklin biographers and touches on Franklin's proposed Albany Plan of Union.

Benjamin Franklin. PBS, 2002. 1 DVD. 210 minutes. This program uses reenactments and narration to recreate Benjamin Franklin's life and contributions, including the Albany Plan.

Biography: Benjamin Franklin—Citizen of the World. A&E Home Video, 2006. 1 DVD. 50 minutes. This program uses images, commentary, and Franklin's own writings to tell his story and includes his efforts to persuade the colonies to accept the Albany Plan of Union.

The War That Made America. PBS, 2005. 2 DVDs. 240 minutes. This PBS presentation uses documents, reenactments, and narration to tell the story of the French and Indian War, including the Albany Plan of Union.

73. Braddock's Defeat (1755)

In the wake of Colonel George Washington's defeat at Fort Necessity in 1754, the English government decided to send a substantial force to North America, with the objective of seizing Forts Duquesne, Niagara, and Crown Point. General Edward Braddock and two regiments arrived in North America in March 1755. The various colonies reinforced Braddock's forces, giving him a total of about 2,200 men. Deciding to seize Fort Duquesne first, Braddock set out from Alexandria, Virginia.

His army was preceded by woodcutters who cut a road for his army, which moved slowly, trailed by a large baggage train. Braddock had a low opinion of the colonial troops assigned to him and an even lower opinion of Native Americans. Alarmed, the French at Fort Duquesne were aware of Braddock's steady advance. On July 9, 1755, with Braddock and his men only ten miles from the fort, the French commander dispatched a force of approximately 1,000 men—over 600 of them Native Americans—to slow Braddock while preparations were made to destroy the post to keep it from falling into enemy hands. Instead of merely slowing down Braddock, however, the few French regulars bottled up the road, while their Native American allies, used to fighting in the forest, poured fire onto the British, utilizing trees and rocks for cover. Braddock was killed, and George Washington, who accompanied the expedition as an aide to Braddock, took charge of covering the Army's retreat. Braddock's defeat encouraged the French and their native allies, and it made the British colonists wonder whether the British were up to the job of protecting the colonies.

TERM PAPER SUGGESTIONS

1. Examine the task that Braddock had been given (capturing Forts Duquesne, Niagara, and Crown Point). Given the resources that Braddock had at his disposal, were these obtainable objectives?
2. Braddock chose to attack Fort Duquesne, forcing him to hack a road through the wilderness. Were there better choices available in terms of military objectives?
3. Braddock had no experience fighting in North America. Did this contribute to his defeat?
4. Discuss the tactics employed by the French and Indians. Did they expect to defeat Braddock and his army?
5. Examine the reaction of American colonists to Braddock's defeat.

ALTERNATIVE TERM PAPER SUGGESTIONS

1. It is 1755 and you are an officer in the Virginia militia. Several other militia officers have expressed concern that General Braddock seems to know nothing about how to fight in the wilderness and he seems resistant to taking

advice. Your fellow officers have selected you to speak to the General. Using a great deal of tact, prepare a PowerPoint presentation that points out to General Braddock that fighting in America is different from fighting in Europe.

2. It is 1755 and you are a newspaper reporter in Pennsylvania. You have been asked to compose a report on Braddock's defeat. However, the government is concerned that the report may cause a panic. You are asked to be truthful in your report, yet play down how terrible Braddock's defeat was for the British.

SUGGESTED SOURCES

Primary Sources

"Braddock's Defeat, by George Washington, July 18, 1755." http://www.nationalcenter.org/Braddock%27sDefeat.html. Letter written by George Washington to his mother about Braddock's defeat.

Fitzpatrick, John C., ed. *The Writings of George Washington from the Original Manuscript Sources.* 39 volumes. Washington: GPO, 1931–1944. http://etext.lib.virginia.edu/washington/fitzpatrick/index.html. Fitzpatrick's edition of Washington's papers contains mainly documents that originated with Washington.

"A French Account of Braddock's Defeat in 1755." http://www.shsu.edu/~his_ncp/FrenBrad.html. A version of Braddock's defeat from the French point of view.

"French and Indian War Primary Sources." http://www.hsp.org/default.aspx?id=639. Contains the journal of William Trent, plans of Fort Duquesne, and a map of Braddock's route.

"The George Washington Papers at the Library of Congress, 1741–1799." http://lcweb2.loc.gov/ammem/gwhtml/gwhome.html. This Web site is home to the largest collection of George Washington papers. It features images of the original documents and transcriptions of them.

Hamilton, Charles, ed. *Braddock's Defeat: The Journal of Captain Robert Cholmley's Batman, the Journal of a British Officer, Halkett's Orderly Book.* Norman: University of Oklahoma Press, 1959. Contains three different firsthand accounts of Braddock's defeat.

"The Maryland Gazette featuring George Washington's Journal." http://www.earlyamerica.com/earlyamerica/milestones/journal/. Features PDF copies of the *Maryland Gazette* from 1754 and a transcript of the journal.

"The Papers of George Washington." http://gwpapers.virginia.edu/. The University of Virginia's George Washington Papers project, begun in 1969, will eventually include documents originating with Washington as well as correspondence to him. As of March 2009, this project has published Washington's papers up to 1793.

Secondary Sources

Anderson, Fred. *Crucible of War: The Seven Years' War and the Fate of Empire in British North America, 1754–1766.* New York: Knopf, 2000. One of the best in the recent spate of histories about the French and Indian War.

Anderson, Fred. *The War That Made America.* New York: Viking, 2005. This is the companion book for the PBS presentation by the same name. Both of these books contain chapters regarding Braddock's preparations for his expedition and his subsequent defeat.

Jennings, Francis. *Empire of Fortune: Crowns, Colonies, and Tribes in the Seven Years War in America.* New York: Norton, 1988. Discusses Braddock's defeat.

Leach, Douglas Edward. *Arms for Empire: A Military History of the British Colonies in North America, 1607–1763.* New York: Macmillan, 1973. A history of the British army in colonial America, including a section on Braddock's defeat.

Leach, Douglas Edward. *Roots of Conflict: British Armed Forces and Colonial Americans, 1677–1763.* Chapel Hill: University of North Carolina Press, 1986. Both of Leach's military histories discuss Braddock's defeat.

McConnell, Michael N. *A Country Between: The Upper Ohio Valley and Its Peoples, 1724–1774.* Lincoln: University of Nebraska Press, 1992. This work looks at the Ohio country through King George's War, the French and Indian War, and Pontiac's Rebellion.

Peckham, Howard H. *The Colonial Wars: 1689–1762.* Chicago: University of Chicago Press, 1964. A good history of the colonial wars that includes references to Braddock's defeat.

Steele, Ian K. *Warpaths: Invasions of North America.* New York: Oxford University Press, 1994. Steele's *Warpaths* is one of the best compact histories of the colonial wars.

Ward, Matthew C. *Breaking the Backcountry: The Seven Years' War in Virginia and Pennsylvania, 1754–1765.* Pittsburgh: University of Pittsburgh

Press, 2003. Ward addresses the expectations of Braddock's expedition and the results of his defeat.

World Wide Web

"The Battle of Monongahela 1755—Braddock's Defeat." http://www.britishbattles.com/braddock.htm. Very extensive Web site that features images, maps, and an analysis of the battle.

Multimedia Sources

George Washington's First War: The Battles for Fort Duquesne. Paladin Communications, 2003. 1 DVD. 85 minutes. This DVD uses reenactments, narration, and interviews with historians to tell the stories of Fort Necessity and Braddock's defeat.

George Washington Remembers. PBS, 2004. 1 DVD. 24 minutes. This presentation is based on Washington's recollection later in his life of the French and Indian War.

The History Channel Presents Washington the Warrior. A&E Home Video, 2006. 1 DVD. 92 minutes. This presentation focuses on Washington's military service from the French and Indian War to the Revolution.

The History of Warfare: French & Indian War. Cromwell Productions, 2007. 1 DVD. 55 minutes. Uses reenactments, images, and commentary from historians to present the French and Indian War.

The War That Made America. PBS, 2005. 2 DVDs. 240 minutes. This PBS presentation uses documents, reenactments, and narration to tell the story of the French and Indian War, including a good account of Braddock's defeat.

When the Forest Ran Red. Paladin Communications, 2004. 1 DVD. 68 minutes. Uses reenactments, narration, and interviews with historians to reconstruct the French and Indian War.

74. Battle of Fort William Henry (1757)

In 1757, France dispatched a new commander to North America, the Marquis de Montcalm. Montcalm had a long military career, but this was the first time that he served in North America. Word spread among

France's Native American allies that the king sent a great general to lead them to victory over the English, and Indians flocked to join Montcalm's army. Montcalm needed Native Americans to augment his army, but he also considered them a drain on his supplies, and thought them unreliable, as they often ignored orders. In his first battle Montcalm quickly forced the surrender of Fort Oswego (New York). However, he was shocked when his native allies killed wounded English prisoners and took personal captives. In his next battle, Montcalm assaulted Fort William Henry at the southern tip of Lake George, forcing its surrender in one week. Montcalm offered the British garrison safe passage, while the fort's military stores would become the property of the French. However, Montcalm did not consult his Native American allies who fought to obtain loot or captives. As the British column left the fort, Native Americans took personal possessions from the British and seized others as captives. The French assigned to guard the British were greatly outnumbered. Montcalm hurried to the scene, but when he attempted to liberate the Indians' captives, they killed and scalped them. Between 69 and 184 English perished, and Fort William Henry stoked anger toward the French among the British colonists. For their part, native warriors, upset that the French attempted to deprive them of captives and booty, did not provide a significant amount of support for the French for the remainder of the war.

TERM PAPER SUGGESTIONS

1. The Fort William Henry massacre appears in fictionalized form in the James Fenimore Cooper novel, *The Last of the Mohicans.* Compare Cooper's story with historical accounts. Which aspects of the massacre does Cooper portray accurately? Which portions are inaccurate?
2. Discuss Native American motivations for assisting the French war effort. Why did native people assist the French?
3. Examine Montcalm's assessment of his Native American allies. Were they more of an asset or a liability?
4. Examine the reactions of the colonists to news of the Fort William Henry Massacre. Did Fort William Henry stiffen colonial resistance to the French?

ALTERNATIVE TERM PAPER SUGGESTIONS

1. It is 1757 and you are the public relations officer for the Marquis de Montcalm. He has asked you to prepare a public relations campaign that will be aimed at British colonists. Your job is to play down reports of the massacre, and try to convince the colonists that rumors they are hearing are much exaggerated. To do this, you will prepare a podcast designed to soothe the fears of British colonists.
2. It is 1757 and you are the propaganda officer for the British army in North America. You have been given the task of exploiting the Fort William Henry massacre to the fullest. Prepare a podcast designed to provoke hatred and fear of the French.

SUGGESTED SOURCES

Primary Source

"An Account of Two Attacks on Fort William Henry, 1757." http://www.militaryheritage.com/wm_henry.htm. This site offers British accounts of two separate French attacks on Fort William Henry. One was a failed attack in March 1757, and the other was the successful siege in August 1757.

Secondary Sources

Anderson, Fred. *Crucible of War: The Seven Years' War and the Fate of Empire in British North America, 1754–1766.* New York: Knopf, 2000. One of the best in the recent spate of histories about the French and Indian War.

Anderson, Fred. *The War That Made America.* New York: Viking, 2005. This is the companion book for the PBS presentation by the same name.

Jennings, Francis. *Empire of Fortune: Crowns, Colonies, and Tribes in the Seven Years War in America.* New York: Norton, 1988. Jennings addresses the controversy regarding the massacre and its aftermath.

Leach, Douglas Edward. *Arms for Empire: A Military History of the British Colonies in North America, 1607–1763.* New York: Macmillan, 1973. A history of the British army in colonial America, including a section on Fort William Henry.

Leach, Douglas Edward. *Roots of Conflict: British Armed Forces and Colonial Americans, 1677–1763.* Chapel Hill: University of North Carolina Press, 1986. Leach discusses Fort William Henry in his two military histories.

Steele, Ian K. *Betrayals: Fort William Henry and the "Massacre."* New York: Oxford University Press, 1990. Offers an analysis of the incidents at Fort William Henry and the motivations of the participants.

Steele, Ian K. *Warpaths: Invasions of North America.* New York: Oxford University Press, 1994. Steele's *Warpaths* is one of the best compact histories of the colonial wars.

World Wide Web

"Fort William Henry." http://www.lakegeorgehistorical.org/site_1.htm. This Web site contains historical information about the Lake George area, including Fort William Henry.

Multimedia Sources

The History of Warfare: French & Indian War. Cromwell Productions, 2007. DVD. 55 minutes. This DVD uses reenactments, images, and commentary from historians in presenting the French and Indian War.

The War That Made America. PBS, 2005. 2 DVDs. 240 minutes. This PBS presentation uses documents, reenactments, and narration to tell the story of the French and Indian War, including a good account of Braddock's defeat.

When the Forest Ran Red. Paladin Communications, 2004. DVD. 68 minutes. This DVD uses reenactments, narration, and interviews with historians to reconstruct the French and Indian War.

75. William Pitt Becomes Prime Minister (1757)

By 1757, it was apparent that England was losing the Seven Years' War (the French and Indian War in America) on all fronts. A string of military disasters resulted in King George II appointing William Pitt the Elder (to distinguish him from his son, William Pitt the Younger, who would also be prime minister) prime minister. Never short on self-confidence, Pitt stated upon his appointment that "I can save this country, and no one else can." Pitt pursued a global strategy in the war, giving cash payments to England's Prussian allies to keep them in the war against France in Europe. In addition, Pitt sought cooperation from colonial governments in America and India by reimbursing them their costs in pursuing the war against the French. However, Pitt made the war in America his priority, seeking nothing less than the total expulsion of France from the North American continent. Pitt made winning the war against France the overriding purpose of his administration, and he did not care what it cost. By 1760, the war in North America was, for all practical purposes, over. However, England was greatly in debt, and the new king, George III, blamed Pitt for this state of affairs and forced him to resign. Pitt remained in Parliament and remained a thorn in the side of the king. While he briefly became prime minister again in the mid-1760s, he opposed many of England's attempts to tax the colonists and their attempts to put down the American Revolution.

TERM PAPER SUGGESTIONS

1. Discuss why the king opposed Pitt's elevation to prime minister.
2. How did Pitt secure the willing cooperation of colonial legislatures? He did reimburse their costs, but should they not have been willing to defend themselves without such incentives?
3. Pitt ran up an enormous national debt in winning the Seven Years' War, yet he later opposed efforts by the British government to tax colonists to help pay off the debts. Can these two positions be reconciled?

ALTERNATIVE TERM PAPER SUGGESTIONS

1. It is 1757 and you are an English news journalist. The war is not going well for England. Your editor has given you the job of composing an editorial that calls for Pitt to be named prime minister.
2. It is 1761 and you are an English news journalist. Your editor is aghast at the enormous national debt that Pitt has incurred in winning the war. Your editor wants you to write an editorial calling for Pitt's removal from office because he is fiscally irresponsible.

SUGGESTED SOURCES

Primary Source

Pitt, William. *Correspondence of William Pitt: When Secretary of State, with Colonial Governors and Military and Naval Commissioners in America.*

2 vols. Ed. Gertrude Selwyn Kimball. New York: Macmillan, 1906. Collection of primary source documents that include Pitt's correspondence with military commanders in North America.

Secondary Sources

Anderson, Fred. *Crucible of War: The Seven Years' War and the Fate of Empire in British North America, 1754–1766.* New York: Knopf, 2000. One of the best in the recent spate of histories about the French and Indian War.

Anderson, Fred. *The War That Made America.* New York: Viking, 2005. This is the companion book for the PBS presentation by the same name.

Black, Jeremy. *Pitt the Elder.* Cambridge, U.K.: Cambridge University Press, 1992. An academic biography of William Pitt and how he directed England to victory in the Seven Years' War (the French and Indian War in America).

Jennings, Francis. *Empire of Fortune: Crowns, Colonies, and Tribes in the Seven Years War in America.* New York: Norton, 1988. Jennings discusses the importance of Pitt to the eventual British victory in North America.

World Wide Web

"Foreign Affairs, William Pitt, the Elder, 1708–1778." http://www.u-s-history.com/pages/h1182.html. This Web site discusses William Pitt's views on foreign policy and on the conduct of the war.

"The Speeches of Lord Chatham." http://www.classicpersuasion.org/cbo/chatham/. Speeches of William Pitt.

76. Battle of Quebec (1759)

Quebec had enormous strategic importance for the French during the colonial period. The post was a choke point, preventing any other European foe from sailing down the St. Lawrence River and into the interior of the North American continent. It was also difficult to assault. On a plateau with steep cliffs, it commanded the St. Lawrence River. But it was also vulnerable. In the early eighteenth century, the French built Fort Louisbourg to guard the mouth of the St. Lawrence so that

Quebec could not be isolated, but in both King George's War (1744–1748) and the French and Indian War (1754–1763), the British captured it. This would have meant the English could sail down the St. Lawrence but not capture it. Under General James Wolfe, the British began their campaign to take Quebec in July 1759. They attempted to bombard the city, with little effect, and managed to slip a few ships past the fortress. In September Wolfe took a daring gamble. One night, his army scaled the cliffs and in the morning formed for battle on a field known as the Plains of Abraham. French commander the Marquis de Montcalm chose to lead his army out of the walled city of Quebec and engage the British. In the half-hour battle that followed, the English defeated the French. In the process both Wolfe and Montcalm were killed. Quebec was the decisive battle of the French and Indian War. Without Quebec, the French no longer controlled access to the interior of the continent.

TERM PAPER SUGGESTIONS

1. Examine the strategic importance of Quebec. Discuss how it helped the French control the interior of the North American continent.
2. Discuss the vulnerability of Quebec. What were some of the drawbacks the French had in attempting to defend the city?
3. Historians have debated the decision that the Marquis de Montcalm made in deciding to take his army outside the walls of Quebec and fight it out with Wolfe. What advantages would there have been had he chosen not to offer battle to Wolfe? What probable advantages could he have seen in deciding to fight?
4. By scaling the cliffs at night, Wolfe and his army took the French by surprise. However, there was much that could have gone wrong. Discuss the possible drawbacks of Wolfe's decision.

ALTERNATIVE TERM PAPER SUGGESTIONS

1. It is 1759 and you are an officer on General Wolfe's staff. General Wolfe is considering a plan that will have his army scale the cliffs outside Quebec. He has ordered you to prepare a PowerPoint presentation so he may go over the plan with his other officers. Your presentation must look at the possible advantages of the plan, as well as the potential disadvantages.

2. It is 1759 and you are an officer on the Marquis de Montcalm's staff. The Marquis is thinking about going outside the city and offering battle to Wolfe. He asks you for a PowerPoint presentation outlining the advantages and disadvantages of this course of action.

SUGGESTED SOURCES

Primary Source

Knox, John. *An Historical Journal of the Campaigns in North America: For the Years 1757, 1758, 1759, and 1760.* 3 volumes. Toronto: The Champlain Society, 1914–1916. This volume is also available online from the Champlain Society digital collection. http://link.library.utoronto.ca/champlain/search.cfm?lang=eng. Firsthand account by an English officer who served in North America.

Secondary Sources

Anderson, Fred. *Crucible of War: The Seven Years' War and the Fate of Empire in British North America, 1754–1766.* New York: Knopf, 2000. One of the best in the recent spate of histories about the French and Indian War.

Anderson, Fred. *The War That Made America.* New York: Viking, 2005. This is the companion book for the PBS presentation by the same name.

Jennings, Francis. *Empire of Fortune: Crowns, Colonies, and Tribes in the Seven Years War in America.* New York: Norton, 1988. Jennings offers a good account of the fall of Quebec.

Leach, Douglas Edward. *Arms for Empire: A Military History of the British Colonies in North America, 1607–1763.* New York: Macmillan, 1973. A history of the British army in colonial America, including a section on the battle at Quebec.

Leach, Douglas Edward. *Roots of Conflict: British Armed Forces and Colonial Americans, 1677–1763.* Chapel Hill: University of North Carolina Press, 1986. Both of Leach's military histories address the fall of Quebec.

Peckham, Howard H. *The Colonial Wars: 1689–1762.* Chicago: University of Chicago Press, 1964. Peckham discusses the fall of Quebec.

Steele, Ian K. *Warpaths: Invasions of North America.* New York: Oxford University Press, 1994. Steele's *Warpaths* is one of the best compact histories of the colonial wars.

World Wide Web

"The Battle of Quebec 1759." http://www.britishbattles.com/battle-of-quebec.htm. This very good site contains maps, images, and an overview of the battle.

"Seven Years War: The Siege of Quebec." http://faculty.marianopolis.edu/c.belanger/QuebecHistory/encyclopedia/SevenYearsWar-FrenchandIndianWar-TheSiegeofQuebec.htm. Contains an article about the siege of Quebec.

Multimedia Source

The War That Made America. PBS, 2005. 2 DVDs. 240 minutes. This PBS presentation uses documents, reenactments, and narration to tell the story of French and Indian War, including the Battle of Quebec.

77. Cherokee War (1759)

Numerous and powerful, the Cherokees had a population of approximately 12,000 in the 1750s. In colonial conflicts, they usually—but not always—sided with the British, partly because the proximity of English traders allowed them to satisfy their desire for European goods and partly because the French were allied with their Choctaw enemies. In 1759, Cherokees allied themselves with the British for a campaign against the French in Pennsylvania. On their way home, these same Cherokee warriors were attacked by Virginia colonists seeking bounties for Indian scalps. At almost the same time, Carolina frontiersmen invaded Cherokee hunting grounds. The Cherokees responded by killing approximately 30 colonists. South Carolina went to war against the Cherokees. Throughout 1759 and 1760 the Cherokees defeated the South Carolina militia and British regulars, even capturing Fort Loudon. However, Cherokee warriors were dependent on muskets, powder, and shot. As the war went on, ammunition became scare and the Cherokees could not defend themselves. The Cherokee turned to their Muscogee (Creek) neighbors for help. But the Muscogee, like the Cherokee, were now dependent on European goods and Carolina traders bribed them into remaining neutral. In 1761, British regulars and South Carolinians invaded the Cherokee country, destroying towns and cornfields. Forced to sue for peace, the Cherokee surrendered large tracts of their territory to the colonists. The peace agreement required the Cherokees to cut off all intercourse with the French.

TERM PAPER SUGGESTIONS

1. Examine Cherokee relations with the British. The British valued Cherokee assistance, so why did they go to war against them?
2. Examine Native American dependence on European trade goods. How did this come about? Did the Cherokees seek other trade partners? Why could they not shake their dependence?
3. During this conflict, Cherokee leaders often attempted to establish a peace with the colonists but were often thwarted by young warriors who responded to colonial provocations. How can this split between the warriors and their leaders be explained?

ALTERNATIVE TERM PAPER SUGGESTIONS

1. It is 1760 and you are a British negotiator. Your job is to try and end the Cherokee War, but you must satisfy both the young warriors and the old chiefs. Good luck.
2. It is 1761 and the colony of South Carolina has hired you as their minister of propaganda. Your job is to produce a podcast that will convince the Cherokees to surrender.

SUGGESTED SOURCES

Primary Sources

Adair, James. *The History of the American Indians.* London: Edward & Charles Dilly, 1775. James Adair was an English fur trader who lived and worked among the Cherokees and other peoples of the Southeast for more than 30 years. This copy of his *History* is available at the Internet Archive at www.archive.org.

Adair, James. *The History of the American Indians.* Ed. Kathleen Braund. Tuscaloosa: University of Alabama Press, 2005. A modern edited edition of Adair's *History.*

"Documenting the American South: Colonial and State Records of North Carolina." http://docsouth.unc.edu/csr/index.html/volumes. This site is still a work in progress, but as of March 2009, 24 of the 26 volumes of colonial records had been digitized, with the other two due soon. It has a search function.

Secondary Sources

Alden, John Richard. *John Stuart and the Southern Colonial Frontier.* New York: Gordian Press, 1966. One of the few biographies about John Stuart, the Superintendent of Indians Affairs for the South during the Cherokee War.

Anderson, Fred. *Crucible of War: The Seven Years' War and the Fate of Empire in British North America, 1754–1766.* New York: Knopf, 2000. One of the best histories of the French and Indian War.

Anderson, Fred. *The War That Made America.* New York: Viking, 2005. Both of Anderson's works contain accounts of the Cherokee War. This is a somewhat shortened version of Anderson's *Crucible of War.* It is also the companion volume to the PBS series by the same name.

Hatley, Tom. *The Dividing Paths: Cherokees and South Carolinians through the Revolutionary Era.* New York: Oxford University Press, 1995. A good, thorough history of the usually tense relations between the Cherokees and the Carolinians.

Jennings, Francis. *Empire of Fortune: Crowns, Colonies, and Tribes in the Seven Years War in America.* New York: Norton, 1988. Jennings includes the Cherokee War in his book about the French and Indian War.

Peckham, Howard H. *The Colonial Wars: 1689–1762.* Chicago: University of Chicago Press, 1964. Peckham counts the Cherokee War as one of the colonial wars.

Steele, Ian K. *Warpaths: Invasions of North America.* New York: Oxford University Press, 1994. Steele's *Warpaths* is one of the best compact histories of the colonial wars.

World Wide Web

"Cherokee War 1760–1762." http://www.ricehope.com/history/CherokeeWar 1760.htm. Gives a brief overview of the Cherokee War.

Multimedia Source

The Cherokee. Schlessinger Media, 1993. VHS. 30 minutes. Basic history of the Cherokee nation.

78. France Cedes All of Its North American Possessions in the Treaty of Paris (1763)

The French and Indian War (known as the Seven Years' War in Europe) was the fourth conflict that France and England waged in North America over an 80-year period. Whereas the earlier conflicts were inconclusive, insofar as North America was concerned, the outcome of this conflict was very different. France was forced to surrender all of its territories on the North American mainland. The British acquired all French territory in Canada and east of the Mississippi River, giving England the Ohio Country. In the European phase of the war, France had occupied the German principality of Hanover and now was forced to surrender it. Spain, while a largely ineffective ally of the French, largely benefited from the treaty. The Spanish had already acquired all French territory west of the Mississippi in a secret 1762 treaty, which was their price for entering the war against England. In the Treaty of Paris, Spain, in exchange for England returning Cuba to them (the British successfully invaded Cuba during the war), surrendered Florida to England. In many ways, the 1763 Treaty of Paris represented the high-water mark for the British Empire in the eighteenth century. On the one hand, England made vast territorial gains and became the dominant power in North America. However, the expansion of their Empire also meant that there was more territory to police and garrison, and the British were obliged to maintain a force of 10,000 men in North America. The end of the war provoked new conflicts with Native Americans, and tensions over England's efforts to pay its enormous war debts would cause a rift with the colonies.

TERM PAPER SUGGESTIONS

1. The end of the French and Indian War differed from previous conflicts in that the French were forced to surrender their American possessions. Why did France surrender their possessions this time, instead of in previous conflicts?

2. The terms of the 1763 Treaty of Paris greatly expanded the British Empire. However, expansion also brought some challenges as well. What were some of the difficulties the English faced now that their Empire had expanded?
3. Spain is often treated as an afterthought in the 1763 Treaty of Paris. Why did the British want to obtain Florida (which included the Gulf Coast to the Mississippi River)? Would it have been more advantageous for them to keep Cuba?
4. In 1763, many English subjects in North America hailed the Treaty of Paris as ushering in an era of peace, prosperity, and unfettered expansion. They also expressed enormous pride in being part of the British Empire.

ALTERNATIVE TERM PAPER SUGGESTIONS

1. It is 1763 and you are a French diplomat who has been assigned to negotiate with the British. You and your fellow diplomats will hold a strategy session before talking to the British. You have been asked to make a PowerPoint presentation to outline the Strategy. You have already decided among yourselves that North America is lost, but what areas of the French overseas empire do you want to retain?
2. It is 1763 and you are a reporter for a British newspaper. Your editor has asked you to write a story about England's new colonial possessions in North America. Keep in mind that most of your reading audience may not know much of the geography, nor would they know much about the flora, fauna, and native peoples of the new acquired regions.

SUGGESTED SOURCES

Primary Source

"Treaty of Paris 1763." http://avalon.law.yale.edu/18th_century/paris763.asp. This is the text of the Treaty of Paris.

Secondary Sources

Anderson, Fred. *Crucible of War: The Seven Years' War and the Fate of Empire in British North America, 1754–1766.* New York: Knopf, 2000. One of the best in the recent spate of histories about the French and Indian War.

Calloway, Colin. *The Scratch of a Pen: 1763 and the Transformation of North America.* New York: Oxford University Press, 2006. Addresses many of the effects of the 1763 Peace of Paris.

Jennings, Francis. *Empire of Fortune: Crowns, Colonies, and Tribes in the Seven Years War in America.* New York: Norton, 1988. Discusses the effects of the treaty.

World Wide Web

"The Treaty of Paris (1763) and Its Impact." http://www.ushistory.org/us/8d.asp. Offers an assessment of the effects of the treaty.

Multimedia Source

The War That Made America. PBS, 2005. 2 DVDs. 240 minutes. This very good PBS presentation uses documents, reenactments, narration, and interviews with prominent historians to tell the story of the French and Indian War and its aftermath, including the Treaty of Paris.

79. Pontiac's Rebellion (1763)

In 1763, a religious movement prompted by the visions of a Lenni-Lenape prophet, Neolin, swept the native peoples of the Ohio Country and Great Lakes region. Neolin maintained that the Master of Life was disappointed with native people, in large part because they had become dependent on European goods. Neolin argued that native people should forsake European-made goods and food, as well as avoid contact with Europeans. An Ottawa leader, Pontiac, tweaked Neolin's religious message, arguing that the French were different from other Europeans. Native people were also upset with the English because they—as part of an effort to cut costs—had discontinued the French practice of gift giving. Most of the gifts consisted of powder and shot, items that native people were now dependent on. Pontiac, with the goal of inducing the French to return, put together a wide-ranging conspiracy. In May 1763, native warriors captured every British post west of the Appalachians, except for the three most important: Forts Pitt, Niagara, and Detroit. Pontiac was in personal command at Detroit and subjected the post to a loose siege. Native warriors, however, had little experience in siege warfare. Moreover, the post could still be supplied by water and there was little the Indians could do about it. By fall, Pontiac's rebellion began to unravel. Needing to feed their families, his men deserted to go hunting, while at about the same time, British forces relieved Fort Pitt. The final blow came when French envoys informed Pontiac that the French were not returning to North America, and that they could not assist him. However, Pontiac's Rebellion was very costly for the British, and in an effort to prevent another conflict with the natives, the Crown announced the Proclamation of 1763, which closed settlements of the lands west of the Appalachian Mountains to the colonist.

TERM PAPER SUGGESTIONS

1. Examine the religious movement begun by Neolin. Some scholars have argued that it contains Christian elements. Discuss these elements. Where would Neolin have gotten them from?
2. Discuss the differences in the French and English approaches in dealing with Native Americans in the Ohio Country and Great Lakes region. Should the English have continued French policies?
3. During Pontiac's Rebellion, Native Americans were very successful in seizing most British posts in the West. However, they failed to take Forts Detroit, Pitt, and Niagara. Why did they succeed in most places but fail in others? Examine the tactics the natives used.
4. Native American warriors usually did not fare well when they had to conduct a siege of a European fort. Discuss the reasons for this.
5. What were some of the results of Pontiac's Rebellion? Did British policy toward Native Americans change?

ALTERNATIVE TERM PAPER SUGGESTIONS

1. It is 1763 and you are an assistant to Sir William Johnson, the British Superintendent of Indian Affairs. Jeffrey Amherst, the British military commander in North America, has ordered the end of the practice of gift giving to native people. Sir William thinks this is a mistake. He has ordered you to put together a PowerPoint presentation that will help him make his argument that it is actually cheaper to give the Indians gifts, rather than not give them.
2. It is 1763, you are a native person in the Ohio Country, and Pontiac has appointed you to be his minister of propaganda. Prepare a podcast designed to encourage other Native Americans to follow Pontiac in his war against the British.

SUGGESTED SOURCES

Primary Sources

Bradstreet, John, and Robert Rogers. *Diary of the Siege of Detroit in the War with Pontiac.* Ed. Franklin B. Hough. Albany: J. Munsell, 1860. Contains three separate firsthand accounts of Pontiac's Rebellion. Available at the Internet Archive at www.archive.org.

Burton, M. Agnes, ed. *Journal of Pontiac's Conspiracy, 1763.* Detroit: Michigan Society of the Colonial Wars, n.d. This is an English translation of a journal kept by an anonymous French habitant during the siege of Detroit. It is available from the Internet Archive at www.archive.org.

The Gladwin Manuscripts. Lansing, MI: Robert Smith Printing, 1897. This is the correspondence between Henry Gladwin, the British commander at Detroit, and other British officers, such as Jeffrey Amherst. Available at the Internet Archive at www.archive.org.

Morris, Thomas. "Journal of Captain Thomas Morris of His Majesty's XXVII Regiment of Infantry." *Early Western Travels, 1748–1846,* volume one. Ed. Reuben Gold Thwaites. 32 volumes. Cleveland, OH: A. H. Clark Co., 1904–1907. This is the journal of a British officer at Detroit. Thwaites's *Early Western Travels* are available at Google Books, the Internet Archive at www.archive.org, and the Library of Congress.

Secondary Sources

Anderson, Fred. *Crucible of War: The Seven Years' War and the Fate of Empire in British North America, 1754–1766.* New York: Knopf, 2000. One of the best in the recent spate of histories about the French and Indian War.

Calloway, Colin. *The Scratch of a Pen: 1763 and the Transformation of North America.* New York: Oxford University Press, 2006. Discusses Pontiac's Rebellion as one of the effects of the French and Indian War.

Dixon, David. *Never Come to Peace Again: Pontiac's Uprising and the Fate of the British Empire in North America.* Norman: University of Oklahoma Press, 2005. Attempts to argue that Pontiac's War was a precursor for the American Revolution.

Dowd, Gregory Evans. *A Spirited Resistance: The North American Indian Struggle for Unity, 1745–1815.* Baltimore, MD: Johns Hopkins University Press, 1992. Dowd discusses the role of Neolin and other Native American prophets in sparking Native American resistance movements, including Pontiac's.

Dowd, Gregory Evans. *War Under Heaven: Pontiac, The Indian Nations & the British Empire.* Baltimore, MD: Johns Hopkins University Press, 2002. Argues that Pontiac's Rebellion was sparked by Native American concerns over sovereignty.

Jennings, Francis. *Empire of Fortune: Crowns, Colonies, and Tribes in the Seven Years War in America.* New York: Norton, 1988. Discusses Pontiac's Rebellion.

Peckham, Howard H. *Pontiac and the Indian Uprising.* Princeton, NJ: Princeton University Press, 1947. Reprinted, Detroit: Wayne University Press, 1994. A straightforward, rather traditional history of Pontiac's Rebellion.

Steele, Ian K. *Warpaths: Invasions of North America.* New York: Oxford University Press, 1994. Steele's *Warpaths* is one of the best compact histories of the colonial wars.

Ward, Matthew C. *Breaking the Backcountry: The Seven Years' War in Virginia and Pennsylvania, 1754–1765.* Pittsburgh: University of Pittsburgh Press, 2003. Offers a good discussion of Pontiac's Rebellion.

White, Richard. *The Middle Ground: Indians, Empires, and Republics in the Great Lakes Region, 1650–1815.* New York: Cambridge University Press, 1991. White devotes an entire chapter to Pontiac and his rebellion, arguing that it restored matters to normal in the Old Northwest.

World Wide Web

"Wars and Battles: Pontiac's Rebellion, 1763–1766." http://www.u-s-history.com/pages/h598.html. Gives an overview of Pontiac's Rebellion.

Multimedia Sources

Frontier: Legends of Old Northwest. A&E Home Video, 1998. 4 DVDs. 240 minutes. The story of Pontiac's Rebellion is one of the four episodes that made up this series.

The War That Made America. PBS, 2005. 2 DVDs. 240 minutes. This PBS presentation is about the French and Indian War, but it also dwells on the aftermath, including Pontiac's Rebellion.

80. Paxton Boys Attack Native Americans in Pennsylvania (1763)

In the summer of 1763, reports of Native American attacks circulated in the Pennsylvania frontier. In July a small force of men from the town of Paxton, Pennsylvania, scouted along the Susquehanna River and came under attack by Native Americans. In the fall, another contingent of men from Paxton scouted a different section of the Susquehanna and discovered a destroyed camp of settlers from Connecticut. Fearful that hostile Native Americans were possibly about, residents of Paxton focused their suspicions on the nearby Conestoga Indians, who had long lived peacefully among the colonists, having signed treaties with Pennsylvania's founder, William Penn. In October, approximately 50 colonists, calling themselves the Paxton Boys, attacked the native village of Conestoga and killed most of the inhabitants. Alarmed by the actions of the Paxton Boys, the Quaker-dominated government of Pennsylvania placed the few surviving Conestoga people in protective custody in the town of Lancaster. However, local authorities did not post guards at the jail and the Paxton Boys slaughtered the surviving Conestogas. In January 1764, the Paxton Boys rode on Philadelphia, threatening to attack Lenni-Lenape (Delaware) Christian converts who had been sent there after the first Paxton attacks. The government of the colony formed a militia and with the backing of British troops already in the city forced the Paxton Boys to back down. However, in order to prevent bloodshed, Pennsylvania authorities promised not to prosecute the Paxton Boys if they returned home.

TERM PAPER SUGGESTIONS

1. Examine the history of the Conestoga Indians. Should they have had reason to fear their European neighbors?
2. The reaction of the Paxton Boys to Indian attacks and the response of the authorities in Philadelphia points to a split in Pennsylvania politics between colonists in the East and the West. Examine this idea.
3. Read Benjamin Franklin's *A Narrative of the Late Massacres.* What is the point that Franklin is attempting to make? What is his opinion of the Paxton Boys?

4. Discuss the differences between the Paxton Boys and other colonists. Many colonists could seem to differentiate between hostile and peaceful Indians, whereas the Paxton Boys seemed either unable or unwilling to do so.

ALTERNATIVE TERM PAPER SUGGESTIONS

1. It is 1763 and the governor of Pennsylvania has heard rumors about a planned attack on the Conestoga people. As the colony's public relations person, he has tasked you with preparing a podcast designed to quell any thought of attacking the Conestoga people.
2. It is January 1764, and the Paxton Boys are marching on Philadelphia. The colony's governor has asked you to make a podcast requesting the city's inhabitants to form a militia to repel them. Most of Philadelphia's population consists of Quakers, so this will be a tough sell. Good luck!

SUGGESTED SOURCES

Primary Sources

"Contact Primary Sources: Conflict." http://www.hsp.org/default.aspx?id=324#conflict. This site has an apology from the Paxton Boys (but no transcription) and a number of cartoons criticizing the Quakers and Benjamin Franklin for supporting the Conestoga.

Franklin, Benjamin. *A Narrative of the Late Massacres.* Philadelphia: n.p., 1764. http://franklinpapers.org/franklin/framedVolumes.jsp. This is Franklin's pamphlet, criticizing the Paxton Boys.

"Remonstrance of the Distressed and Bleeding Frontier Inhabitants of the Province." http://conspiracy.pasleybrothers.com/readings/paxton_boys.htm. This is the text of the Paxton Boy's justification for the massacre, which they sent to the colony's assembly.

Secondary Sources

Calloway, Colin. *The Scratch of a Pen: 1763 and the Transformation of North America.* New York: Oxford University Press, 2006. Calloway's account of the years after 1763 includes the Paxton Boys.

Dixon, David. *Never Come to Peace Again: Pontiac's Uprising and the Fate of the British Empire in North America.* Norman: University of Oklahoma Press, 2005. Discusses the Paxton Boys.

Dowd, Gregory Evans. *War Under Heaven: Pontiac, the Indian Nations & the British Empire.* Baltimore, MD: Johns Hopkins University Press, 2002. Discusses the belief among Paxton residents that the Conestogas were harboring hostile Indians among them.

Kenny, Kevin. *Peaceable Kingdom Lost: The Paxton Boys and the Destruction of William Penn's Holy Experiment.* New York: Oxford University Press, 2009. This new work is one of the few that focuses on the Paxton Boys and the aftermath of their actions.

Merrell, James H. *Into the American Woods: Negotiators on the Pennsylvania Frontier.* New York: Norton, 1999. Discusses unfounded rumors among Paxton residents that the Conestogas were allied with the French.

Merritt, Jane T. *At the Crossroads: Indians and Empires on a Mid-Atlantic Frontier, 1700–1763.* Chapel Hill: University of North Carolina Press, 2003. Examines the tensions between the Paxton Boys and the government of Pennsylvania.

World Wide Web

"Wars and Battles: Paxton Boys, 1763–1764." http://www.u-s-history.com/pages/h1188.html. Article about the Paxton Boys.

Multimedia Source

The War That Made America. PBS, 2005. 2 DVDs. 240 minutes. This PBS presentation is about the French and Indian War, but it also dwells on the aftermath, including the Paxton Boys.

81. Proclamation of 1763

In the wake of the British victory in the French and Indian War (1754–1763), American colonists celebrated, believing that now the lands west of the Appalachians would be open to settlement. Colonial land speculators invested heavily in companies that hoped to sell large tracts in the Ohio Country to colonists. However, the British government, facing a financial crisis, was determined to cut its costs in policing and garrisoning its new possessions in North America. Native American resistance, most notably Pontiac's Rebellion, forced the British to expend resources they could ill afford. Realizing that future wars against native people could be equally expensive, King George III issued the Proclamation of 1763 in October. The proclamation drew a line across the crest of the Appalachians, and required English colonists to remain east of the line. Colonial governments were forbidden to authorize land sales or surveys of land west of the proclamation line, and colonists living in what was now designated Indian Country were ordered to leave at once. The Proclamation also defined the boundaries of England's new acquisitions in Florida and Canada. Despite the proclamation, many colonists still settled west of the line. The British army evicted anyone caught, but the expanse of North America made it impossible for them to apprehend all but a few scofflaws. Many Americans in search of homesteads resented the proclamation. The Crown had intended that the proclamation would be a temporary measure, but it was never rescinded, and it still forms the basis of native land claims in Canada.

TERM PAPER SUGGESTIONS

1. What advantages did the Crown realize by establishing the Proclamation?
2. A few historians have asserted that another reason the British issued the Proclamation of 1763 was to keep the colonists confined to the region between the Eastern Seaboard and the Appalachians. Evaluate this argument.
3. Examine the stated rationale for the Proclamation of 1763. Could the Crown have found a way to open settlement west of the Appalachians, yet still keep the peace with Native Americans?
4. The Proclamation of 1763 was not meant to be permanent. What did the British plan to do after the proclamation was rescinded?

ALTERNATIVE TERM PAPER SUGGESTIONS

1. It is 1763 and you work for a company that has purchased land in the Ohio Country, hoping to sell it to would-be settlers. However, the Proclamation of 1763 means you cannot sell the land. Your boss has given you the job of putting together a PowerPoint presentation designed to make British officials reconsider the proclamation.
2. It is 1763 and you have been hired by Native Americans as their public relations person. As you might expect, they like the Proclamation of 1763.

They want you to put together a podcast that will tell the world they think King George is a great ruler.

SUGGESTED SOURCES

Primary Source

"The Royal Proclamation—October 7, 1763." http://avalon.law.yale.edu/18th_century/proc1763.asp. This is the text of the Proclamation of 1763.

Secondary Sources

Anderson, Fred. *Crucible of War: The Seven Years' War and the Fate of Empire in British North America, 1754–1766.* New York: Knopf, 2000. One of the best in the recent spate of histories about the French and Indian War.

Anderson, Fred. *The War That Made America.* New York: Viking, 2005. This is the companion book for the PBS presentation by the same name.

Calloway, Colin. *The Scratch of a Pen: 1763 and the Transformation of North America.* New York: Oxford University Press, 2006. Calloway's work dwells heavily on the Proclamation of 1763.

Dowd, Gregory Evans. *War Under Heaven: Pontiac, The Indian Nations & the British Empire.* Baltimore, MD: Johns Hopkins University Press, 2002. Discusses the Proclamation of 1763.

Jennings, Francis. *Empire of Fortune: Crowns, Colonies, and Tribes in the Seven Years War in America.* New York: Norton, 1988. Discusses the Proclamation of 1763 as repression of the colonists.

Steele, Ian K. *Warpaths: Invasions of North America.* New York: Oxford University Press, 1994. Steele's *Warpaths* is one of the best compact histories of the colonial wars.

World Wide Web

"Proclamation of 1763." http://www.ushistory.org/declaration/related/proc63.htm. Offers an analysis of the Proclamation and the text of the Proclamation itself.

Multimedia Source

The War That Made America. PBS, 2005. 2 DVDs. 240 minutes. This PBS presentation includes the Proclamation of 1763 and colonial reaction to it.

82. Beginnings of the Regulator Movement in the Carolina Backcountry (1760s)

In the 1760s, there were two separate regulator movements in the Carolina backcountry. In South Carolina, the movement arose out of a need to confront bandits and lawlessness. In North Carolina, the Regulators were formed in response to the excessive taxes placed on backcountry citizens by Royal Governor William Tyron. In the mid-1760s, there was a rash of crimes committed in the South Carolina backcountry by wandering bandits. Without sheriffs, courts, or jails, the South Carolina Regulators took the law into their own hands, whipping suspected criminals and sometimes burning their homes. They expanded their activities to include driving idlers and prostitutes out of their communities. As a result, the South Carolina legislature took action and, by the 1770s, the backcountry had lawmen, courts, and jails.

The North Carolina Regulators were composed of North Carolina frontiersmen. Less well off than many of the North Carolinians in the eastern part of the colony, they resented the taxes imposed on them by the colonial government. Their anger boiled over in 1767 when the colony instituted a liquor and poll tax in order to build a mansion for Governor Tyron. The Regulators invaded courtrooms, disrupted legal proceedings, and demanded the right to search court records in an effort to uncover corruption. As they became bolder, the regulators assaulted lawyers and judges. In 1771 Governor Tyron ended the Regulator Movement when he successfully led a force of 1,000 militia in a victory over 2,300 poorly led regulators at Alamance.

TERM PAPER SUGGESTIONS

1. Discuss the South Carolina Regulator Movement. Were they justified in their actions?
2. Discuss the results of the South Carolina Regulator Movement. They did get courts, jails, and law enforcement officers, but they obtained them by taking the law into their own hands. Could they have obtained the same results in a different way?

3. Discuss the grievances of the North Carolina Regulators. In a way, did their actions set an example for Shays' Rebellion in Massachusetts 15 years later?
4. Discuss the actions of North Carolina Governor William Tyron. Could he have ended the Regulator Movement without resorting to combat?

ALTERNATIVE TERM PAPER SUGGESTIONS

1. It is the mid-1760s and you are an agent for the government of South Carolina. You have just completed a tour of the backcountry. You file your report with the colonial government. You must impress on the government the need to establish law and order on the frontier. Prepare a PowerPoint presentation designed to make the governmental authorities appreciate the urgency of establishing a justice system on the frontier.
2. It is the early 1770s, and you are a reporter for a radio station in North Carolina. Using the primary source documents as a guide, prepare a podcast that will inform your listeners of what the Regulators are doing on the frontier.

SUGGESTED SOURCES

Primary Source

"Documenting the American South: Colonial and State Records of North Carolina." http://docsouth.unc.edu/csr/index.html/volumes. This set of primary sources has a number of documents relating to the Regulator Movement.

Secondary Sources

Brown, Maxfield. *South Carolina Regulators.* Cambridge, MA: Harvard University Press, 1963. A good basic history of the Regulator Movement in South Carolina.

Kars, Marjoleine. *Breaking Loose Together: The Regulator Rebellion in Pre-Revolutionary North Carolina.* Chapel Hill: University of North Carolina Press, 2002. The most recent work on the North Carolina Regulators.

Klein, Rachel N. *Unification of a Slave State: The Rise of the Planter Class in the South Carolina Backcountry, 1760–1808.* Chapel Hill: University of North Carolina Press, 1990. Klein includes a good section on the Regulator Movement.

World Wide Web

"Shew Yourselves to be Freemen": Herman Husband and the North Carolina Regulators, 1769." http://historymatters.gmu.edu/d/6233/. In this tract, North Carolina Regulators are urged to exercise their power at the ballot box and seize control of the colony.

83. Russians and Spaniards Explore and Settle the Pacific Coast (1760s)

In the 1760s, both Russia and Spain began the process of exploring and settling the North American Pacific coast. The Russians had established trading posts in Alaska and were very slowly beginning to move south along the Pacific coast. At almost the same time the Spanish had finally begun to colonize California, in large part because they feared a Russian incursion into what they considered their territories. In 1769, the Spanish sent two ships to San Diego Bay to begin the process of building a fort. The expedition was racked by disease, however, and not until the next year, when reinforcements arrived, did work start on a fort. In 1770, the Spanish moved farther north and established a post at Monterey Bay in central California. Many of these efforts went hand in hand with the expansion of the Spanish mission system. The Russians in Alaska followed a somewhat similar pattern. They began with a few trading posts, and, like the Spanish, their soldiers and traders had a difficult relationship with the natives. Russian relations with native people eased somewhat in the 1790s, with the introduction of Russian Orthodox missionaries. In the early nineteenth century, Russian traders extended their influence into northern California, their southernmost advance being halted at the aptly named Russian River, 200 miles north of present-day San Francisco.

TERM PAPER SUGGESTIONS

1. Compare and contrast Spanish and Russian relationships with Native Americans they encountered on the Pacific coast.
2. Discuss the economic resources of the Pacific coast region. What resources did the Spanish and Russians hope to gain control over?

3. Which country seems to have been more successful in their efforts to expand along the Pacific coast? Was either one truly successful?

ALTERNATIVE TERM PAPER SUGGESTIONS

1. It is 1769 and you have been chosen by Spanish colonial authorities to outline a plan for northward expansion along the Pacific coast. Prepare a PowerPoint presentation (complete with maps) showing how you think expansion should proceed.
2. It is the 1780s and Russian authorities ask you to outline a plan for southward expansion along the Pacific coast. Prepare a PowerPoint presentation (complete with maps) showing how you think expansion should proceed.

SUGGESTED SOURCES

Primary Source

"Meeting of Frontiers." http://frontiers.loc.gov/intldl/mtfhtml/mfhome.html. This Library of Congress Web site contains a host of primary source documents related to Russian colonization efforts in North America.

Secondary Sources

Barratt, Glynn. *Russia in Pacific Waters, 1715–1825.* Vancouver: University of British Columbia Press, 1981. A history of Russian exploration in the North Pacific Ocean.

Gibson, James R. *Imperial Russia in Frontier America: The Changing Geography of Supply of Russian America, 1784–1867.* New York: Oxford University Press, 1976. Gibson explores the difficulties Russia experienced in attempting to maintain their colonies in North America.

Smith, Barbara Sweetland, and Redmond J. Barnett, eds. *Russian America: The Forgotten Frontier.* Tacoma: Washington State Historical Society, 1990. A collection of essays about the Russian effort to establish a colony in North America.

Weber, David. *The Spanish Frontier in North America.* New Haven, CT: Yale University Press, 1992. The Spanish were among the first Europeans to explore the Pacific Northwest, and Weber has a good section on this.

World Wide Web

"Russian Exploration of the Northwest Coast of North America." http://pages.quicksilver.net.nz/jcr/~vrussian1.html. Offers a brief history of Russian exploration of Alaska and the Pacific Northwest.

"Spain and Russia in the West." http://lcweb2.loc.gov/intldl/mtfhtml/mfak/igspain.html. This Library of Congress Web site discusses Spanish-Russian competition on the Pacific coast.

84. Stamp Act (1765)

In the years after the French and Indian War, Great Britain sought out ways to pay the enormous debt they had accumulated during the war. With their own citizenry already heavily taxed, the English government sought to tax their colonies. Parliament took a minor step in 1764 with the Sugar Act, which evoked protest from only some colonists. The Stamp Act, however, passed in March 1765 and, set to go into effect on November 1, 1765, touched off widespread protest throughout the colonies. Designed to raise revenue to support the British army in America, the Stamp Act required that all printed material in the colonies, whether it be newspapers, almanacs, broadsides, contracts, insurance policies, ship's manifests, and even playing cards, had to use stamped paper or a separate stamp. The government appointed stamp tax agents as the exclusive sellers of the stamped paper or stamps. Colonialists protested almost immediately. Lacking representation in Parliament, the colonists argued that they could not be taxed without their consent. Mobs rioted in Boston, forcing stamp tax agents to resign. Nine colonies sent representatives to the Stamp Act Congress in New York City, which drafted the Declaration of Rights and Grievances. The Declaration stated the colonies owed their allegiance to England, but that they could only be taxed by their own elected assemblies. In March 1766, Parliament repealed the Stamp Act, but at the same time passed the Declaratory Act, which asserted that Parliament could legislate for the colonies "in all cases whatsoever." Colonists celebrated the repeal of the Stamp Act but ignored the implications of the Declaratory Act.

TERM PAPER SUGGESTIONS

1. British politicians often argued that the colonists were represented in Parliament by what they called "virtual representation." Examine this idea. Were the colonists truly represented?
2. Parliament was stunned by the violent reaction of the colonists to the Stamp Act. What accounted for their surprise? Why did they not anticipate that the Americans would be angry?
3. One feature of the riots in Boston was that mobs seemed to be acting under the direction of organizations such as the Sons of Liberty. Consider the use of mobs in eighteenth-century political protest.
4. Consider the colonists' argument that they lacked representation in Parliament. Could Parliament have arranged for a way for the colonies to have representation? Would such a step have averted future difficulties between England and the colonies?
5. The Declaratory Act provoked little comment in British North America in 1766. Discuss the implications of the Declaratory Act.

ALTERNATIVE TERM PAPER SUGGESTIONS

1. You are a radio talk show host in 1765 Boston, and you are really unhappy about the Stamp Act. Put together a podcast so that you can broadcast your opinion to your audience.
2. You are delegate to the Stamp Act Congress. You agree with the other delegates regarding the content of the Declaration of Rights and Grievances, but you want to go a step further and argue that the colonies should have a representative in Parliament. Put together a PowerPoint presentation to illustrate this argument.

SUGGESTED SOURCES

Primary Sources

"Connecticut Resolutions on the Stamp Act: December 10, 1765." http://avalon.law.yale.edu/18th_century/ct_resolutions_1765.asp. Connecticut's response to the Stamp Act.

"Great Britain: Parliament—An Act Repealing the Stamp Act; March 18, 1766." http://avalon.law.yale.edu/18th_century/repeal_stamp_act_1766.asp. This is Parliament's repeal of the Stamp Act.

"Great Britain: Parliament—The Declaratory Act; March 18, 1766." http://avalon.law.yale.edu/18th_century/declaratory_act_1766.asp. This is the Declaratory Act, passed the same day as the repeal of the Stamp Act.

"Great Britain: Parliament—The Stamp Act, March 22, 1765." http://avalon.law.yale.edu/18th_century/stamp_act_1765.asp. This is the text of the Stamp Act.

"Resolutions of the Continental Congress, October 19, 1765." http://avalon.law.yale.edu/18th_century/resolu65.asp. This is the text of the Declaration of Rights and Grievances.

"Resolves of the Pennsylvania Assembly on the Stamp Act, September 21, 1765." http://avalon.law.yale.edu/18th_century/penn_assembly_1765.asp. This is Pennsylvania's response, which asserts citizens can be taxed only if they consent to it.

Secondary Sources

Bullion, John L. *A Great and Necessary Measure: George Grenville and the Genesis of the Stamp Act, 1763–1765.* Princeton, NJ: Princeton University Press, 1982. Traces George Grenville's brief career as Chancellor of the Exchequer and the ideas behind the origins of the Stamp Act.

Countryman, Edward. *The American Revolution.* New York: Hill & Wang, 1985. Discusses the role of the Stamp Act in helping foment the Revolution.

Ferling, John. *A Leap in the Dark: The Struggle to Create the American Republic.* New York: Oxford University Press, 2003. Ferling's *Leap in the Dark* is one of the best recent comprehensive histories of the American Revolution.

Holton, Woody. *Forced Founders: Indians, Debtors, Slaves, and the Making of the American Revolution in Virginia.* Chapel Hill: University of North Carolina Press, 1999. Holton touches on the Stamp Act, but the main idea behind his book is that some people were coerced into participating in the Revolution.

Jennings, Francis. *Empire of Fortune: Crowns, Colonies, and Tribes in the Seven Years War in America.* New York: Norton, 1988. Jennings ends his tome with a discussion of the colonial resistance to the Stamp Act.

Maier, Pauline. *From Resistance to Revolution: Colonial Radicals and the Development of Opposition to Great Britain, 1765–1776.* New York: Knopf, 1972. Maier points out that the Stamp Act was not the first thing that engendered colonial resistance, but perhaps it resulted in the first widespread resistance.

Middlekauff, Robert. *The Glorious Cause: The American Revolution, 1763–1789.* Revised edition. New York: Oxford University Press, 2005. Middlekauff's is one of the most thorough treatments of the American Revolution.

Morgan, Edmund S., and Helen M. Morgan. *The Stamp Act Crisis: Prologue to Revolution.* Chapel Hill: The University of North Carolina Press, 1963. Morgan and Morgan examine the Stamp Act and the colonial response.

Nash, Gary B. *The Unknown American Revolution: The Unruly Birth of American Democracy and the Struggle to Create America.* New York: Viking, 2005. The Stamp Act is featured in Nash's book.

Shy, John. *Toward Lexington: The Role of the British Army in the Coming of the American Revolution.* Princeton, NJ: Princeton University Press, 1965. Shy discusses the role of the British Army during the French and Indian War, the postwar decision to maintain an army in North America, and the friction between colonists and British soldiers.

Wood, Gordon S. *The American Revolution: A History.* New York: Modern Library, 2003. A recent and brief history of the American Revolution.

World Wide Web

"Colonial America: Stamp Act, 1765." http://www.u-s-history.com/pages/h642.html. This article traces the history of the Stamp Act from its inception to it repeal.

"Parliament Enacts the Stamp Act." http://www.history.com/this-day-in-history.do?action=Article&id=7068. History Channel "This Day in History" piece that provides a good overview of the Stamp Act.

"The Stamp Act." http://www.ushistory.org/declaration/related/stampact.htm. Article on the Stamp Act.

"The Stamp Act." http://americanrevwar.homestead.com/files/stamp.htm. Article about the Stamp Act with images of the stamps.

Multimedia Sources

The History Channel Presents the Revolution. A&E Home Video, 2006. 4 DVDs. 600 minutes. Recreations and historical analysis of the Revolution, including the effect of the Stamp Act.

Liberty! The American Revolution. PBS, 1997. 3 DVDs. 360 minutes. This presentation used narration, documents, and reenactments. It includes a good portion on the Stamp Act.

85. Townshend Acts (1767)

A year after the repeal of the Stamp Act, which would have imposed a tax on all printed material, the British government again sought to raise revenue from the colonies. Reasoning that the Stamp Act failed because the colonists resented "external taxes," Charles Townshend, the Chancellor of the Exchequer, proposed a set of "internal taxes." Taking the forms of duties on the importation of glass, lead, paint, paper, and tea, the Townshend Acts were supposed to pay the salaries of royal governors and to defray the costs of defending the colonies. The acts also called for stepped-up enforcement of laws regarding smuggling. At first, the colonial response was muted. While the colonists resented the Townshend Acts, they had always thought that England had a right to charge duties. Philadelphia lawyer John Dickinson published a set of editorials known as *Letters from a Pennsylvania Farmer.* More moderate than some of his revolutionary contemporaries, Dickinson argued that Parliament could collect duties, but not for the purpose of generating revenue. In other words, Dickinson argued the Townshend Acts were, in fact, a tax. In Massachusetts, political activist Sam Adams and attorney James Otis drafted a circular letter protesting the Townshend Acts. In response, the royal governor dissolved the assembly. The assembly defied the governor by meeting anyway. The most effective protest undertaken by colonists was economic. Colonists refused to purchase English imports, opting for homespun clothing, homemade paper, and unpainted houses. They also boycotted local merchants who sold British goods. Pressured by English merchants, Parliament rescinded the Townshend Acts in March 1770, with the exception of the tax on tea.

TERM PAPER SUGGESTIONS

1. Discuss the reasoning of Charles Townshend. How did he differentiate between "external" and "internal" taxes?

2. Examine the writings of John Dickinson and Samuel Adams. Do they agree on their objectives? Do they agree on the means of achieving those objectives?
3. Examine the nonimportation movement as a means of political protest. Did it seem to be more effective than the writings of John Dickinson and the circular letter of Adams and Otis?
4. One of the purposes of the Townsend Acts was to provide a means for paying royal governors. Why was this an important measure? Who was paying them before?
5. Discuss the role of English merchants in the revocation of the Townshend Acts. Why were they able to exert pressure on Parliament?

ALTERNATIVE TERM PAPER SUGGESTIONS

1. It is 1767 and you are a colonist who is upset with the Townshend Acts. You have been reading Dickinson's *Letters from a Pennsylvania Farmer.* Many of your friends are confused as to whether the Townshend Acts are taxes or duties. Prepare a PowerPoint presentation that illustrates the difference for them.
2. It is 1768 and you are a radio talk show host. The largest merchant in your city is importing and selling goods that are charged duties under the Townshend Acts. Prepare a podcast that is designed to convince your listeners not to patronize this merchant's establishment.

SUGGESTED SOURCES

Primary Sources

"Boston Non-Importation Agreement, August 1, 1768." http://avalon.law.yale.edu/18th_century/boston_non_importation_1768.asp. This source and the next one are the texts for the nonimportation agreements for two key American ports.

"Charleston Non-Importation Agreement; July 22, 1769." http://avalon.law.yale.edu/18th_century/charleston_non_impotation_1769.asp. This source and the preceding one are the texts for the nonimportation agreements for two key American ports.

Dickinson, John. *Letters from a Pennsylvania Farmer.* New York: The Outlook Company, 1903. Contains all of Dickinson's letters that encouraged the colonists to protest the Townsend Acts. Available at both Google Books and the Internet Archive at www.archive.org.

"Great Britain: Parliament—The Townshend Act, November 20, 1767." http://avalon.law.yale.edu/18th_century/townsend_act_1767.asp. This is the text of the Townshend Act.

"Massachusetts Circular Letter to the Colonial Legislatures; February 11, 1768." http://avalon.law.yale.edu/18th_century/mass_circ_let_1768.asp. This is the text of the circular letter drafted by Samuel Adams and James Otis.

Secondary Sources

Countryman, Edward. *The American Revolution.* New York: Hill & Wang, 1985. A short history of the American Revolution.

Ferling, John. *A Leap in the Dark: The Struggle to Create the American Republic.* New York: Oxford University Press, 2003. One of the best recent comprehensive histories of the American Revolution.

Middlekauff, Robert. *The Glorious Cause: The American Revolution, 1763–1789.* Revised edition. New York: Oxford University Press, 2005. Middlekauff's is one of the most thorough treatments of the American Revolution.

Nash, Gary B. *The Unknown American Revolution: The Unruly Birth of American Democracy and the Struggle to Create America.* New York: Viking, 2005. A recent history of the American Revolution.

Thomas, Peter D. G. *The Townshend Duties Crisis: The Second Phase of the American Revolution, 1767–1773.* New York: Oxford University Press, 1987. A good summary of the Townshend Acts and the colonial response.

Wood, Gordon S. *The American Revolution: A History.* New York: Modern Library, 2003. A good brief history of the American Revolution.

World Wide Web

"The Patriot Resource: The Townshend Acts." http://www.patriotresource.com/events/townshend.html. Article and chronology about the Acts.

"The Townshend Acts." http://americanrevwar.homestead.com/files/town.htm. Article about the Townshend Acts

Multimedia Sources

The History Channel Presents the Revolution. A&E Home Video, 2006. 4 DVDs. 600 minutes. Uses re-creations and historical analysis and includes a section on colonial opposition to the Townshend Acts.

Liberty! The American Revolution. PBS, 1997. 3 DVDs. 360 minutes. This PBS presentation uses historical documents and reenactments to illustrate events from the American Revolution.

86. Spanish Build Missions in California (1768)

In the 1760s, fearful that the Russians would move down the Pacific coast and occupy Alta California, the Spanish set about settling the region. However, lacking a sufficient number of soldiers and unable to find colonists willing to settle there, the Spanish chose to employ an old strategy. They would turn California's natives into Spaniards through the process of missionization. The mission process had been attempted by the Spanish in the sixteenth and seventeenth centuries in what are now Florida, New Mexico, and Texas, but had little success in making native peoples into Hispanics. The process of establishing the first missions was entrusted to Fray Junipero Serra. Usually accompanied by soldiers who established a nearby *presidio* (fort), the friars used the pomp of the mass and trade goods to attract the interest of the Indians. Once "converted" (the quality of the conversions was always questionable), native people were forced to reside at the mission and had to adopt a regimented lifestyle. Native people who resisted could find themselves slaves who were whipped and chained. The Franciscans forced the Indians to build the missions themselves, erect fences, perform agricultural labor, and tend domesticated animals. The missions were to some degree economic successes. In 1775, for example, California mission herds had 427 cattle, which had grown to 95,000 thirty years later. However, while the friars' livestock prospered, living in the missions exposed native people to European disease. The native population between San Diego and San Francisco was thought to be 72,000 at the time the first mission was founded in 1769. When Spanish rule ended in 1821, there were only 18,000.

TERM PAPER SUGGESTIONS

1. Why did the Spanish choose to try and make native people into Hispanics? This strategy had been attempted before and failed.

2. Was the Spanish fear that the Russians would soon begin to colonize California realistic?
3. Examine the process of conversion among California mission Indians. Were these true conversions?
4. Examine the factors that contributed to the ballooning of the mission's livestock herds.

ALTERNATIVE TERM PAPER SUGGESTIONS

1. It is 1769 and you are accompanying some of the first friars to Alta California. In order to impress the natives and make them more amenable to conversion, you have been asked to prepare a PowerPoint presentation that will fascinate them.
2. It is 1769 and you are a native person. Prepare a podcast giving the native point of view of the missions.

SUGGESTED SOURCES

Primary Source

"Original Sources." http://www.ca-missions.org/links.html#orig. Contains links to hundreds of primary sources on the missions.

Secondary Sources

Haas, Lisabeth. *Conquests and Historical Identities in California, 1769–1936.* Berkeley: University of California Press, 1995. A history of California that begins with the mission period.

Hackel, Steven W. *Children of Coyote, Missionaries of St. Francis: Indian-Spanish Relations in Colonial California, 1769–1850.* Chapel Hill: University of North Carolina Press, 2005. A good account of the often strained relationships between California's native peoples and the Franciscans.

Phillips, George Harwood. *Chiefs and Challengers: Indian Resistance and Cooperation in Southern California.* Berkeley: University of California Press, 1975. A history of Native Americans in California from the Spanish occupation to the mid-nineteenth century.

Phillips, George Harwood. *Indians and Intruders in Central California, 1769–1849.* Norman: University of Oklahoma Press, 1993. A good history of California's Indians under Spanish and, later, Mexican rule.

World Wide Web

"California Missions." http://missions.bgmm.com/. Offers a map of the missions, links to each mission, and a brief history of each.

"California Missions: A Virtual Tour." http://www.californiamissions.com/. This large site contains histories of the missions, images, and even music.

"California Missions Foundation." http://www.californiamissionsfoundation.org/home.html. This is an organization that seeks to preserve the missions. Their well-done Web site has histories of each of the missions.

"California Missions Studies Association." http://www.ca-missions.org/. This is the Web site of an organization that seeks to preserve the California missions. It has links to articles and images.

Multimedia Sources

The Missions of California. Shannon & Company, 2007. 1 DVD. 60 minutes. This is a tour of all 21 California missions.

Saints and Sinners of the California Missions. A&E Home Video, 1998. 1 DVD. 50 Minutes. A brief retelling of the story of Spanish priests and soldiers who founded the California missions.

87. Tea Act (1773)

By 1773 relations between Great Britain and the colonies in North America had entered a lull. The lull was broken when Parliament attempted to bail out one of the largest companies in England, the East India Company. While the East India Company was in dire financial straits, it did have one notable asset: 17 million pounds of tea sitting in its warehouses. In order to keep the company from going under, Parliament waived the duties they normally paid on the importation of its tea to North America. By not having to pay the duties, the East India Company could underprice even the smuggled Dutch tea that most colonists drank. The Sons of Liberty, an organization that fostered resistance to British taxes and duties, promoted the notion that the Tea Act was some sort of trick on the part of the British to get Americans to drink their tea. The Sons of Liberty staged protests in the port cities of Charleston, Philadelphia, and New York. The East India Company unloaded their cargo of tea in Charleston, but in Philadelphia and New York mobs forced the ships to depart without unloading their cargo. In Boston, however, Governor Thomas Hutchinson forbade any ship from leaving without discharging its cargo. The captain of an East India Company ship remained in port, refusing to unload his ship, fearful that Boston mobs would riot. Governor Hutchinson set a deadline of December 17 for the ship to be unloaded. On December 16, the Sons of Liberty, many of them disguised as Indians, boarded the vessel and, during what came to be known as the Boston Tea Party, cast 342 chests of East India Company tea into Boston Harbor.

TERM PAPER SUGGESTIONS

1. Why did the colonists see some sort of plot in the Tea Act? They were, after all, going to be able to pay less for Dutch teas that they had been smuggling in.
2. Why did Parliament take measures such as the Tea Act to rescue the East India Company?
3. Compare and contrast the actions of Sons of Liberty in Charleston, New York, and Philadelphia with their actions in Boston. Why was the response in Boston comparatively more violent? Were the Sons of Liberty entirely at fault?
4. Discuss the ruling of Governor Thomas Hutchinson in forbidding ships to leave the port of Boston without discharging their cargo. Was Hutchinson attempting to provoke a confrontation?
5. Discuss the reaction throughout the colonies to the Boston Tea Party? Did most colonies initially approve or disapprove of the Tea Party? Did they later change their minds, and if so, why?

ALTERNATIVE TERM PAPER SUGGESTIONS

1. It is 1773 and you are the captain of an East India Company ship that has arrived at the port of Boston. You cannot unload your cargo of tea because a mob, led by the Sons of Liberty, is dockside, threatening to riot if you attempt to unload your cargo. On the other hand, you learn you cannot leave port without unloading the tea because the governor of Massachusetts will put you in jail. Prepare an appeal to the governor as to why you should be allowed to leave port.

2. It is 1773 and you are the minister of propaganda for the Sons of Liberty. You have recently been challenged to explain why people should avoid English tea. After all, it will be cheaper than Dutch teas. Prepare a podcast to explain the position of the Sons of Liberty.

SUGGESTED SOURCES

Primary Sources

"Association of the Sons of Liberty in New York; December 15, 1773." http://avalon.law.yale.edu/18th_century/assoc_sons_ny_1773.asp. Decision of the New York Sons of Liberty to Protest the Tea Act.

"Boston Tea Party: Eyewitness Account by a Participant." http://www.historyplace.com/unitedstates/revolution/teaparty.htm. This is a participant's account of his actions during and immediately after the Boston Tea Party.

"The Tea Act: British Parliament—1773." http://ahp.gatech.edu/tea_act_bp_1773.html. This is the text of the Tea Act.

Secondary Sources

Ferling, John. *A Leap in the Dark: The Struggle to Create the American Republic.* New York: Oxford University Press, 2003. Ferling's *Leap in the Dark* is one of the best recent comprehensive histories of the American Revolution.

Ketchum, Richard. *Divided Loyalties, How the American Revolution came to New York.* New York: Holt, 2002. The Tea Act is commonly associated with Boston (no doubt because of the famous Tea Party), but Ketchum reminds us it sparked protests in New York as well.

Middlekauff, Robert. *The Glorious Cause: The American Revolution, 1763–1789.* Revised edition. New York: Oxford University Press, 2005. Middlekauff's is one of the most thorough treatments of the American Revolution.

Nash, Gary B. *The Unknown American Revolution: The Unruly Birth of American Democracy and the Struggle to Create America.* New York: Viking, 2005. Another of the newer histories of the American Revolution.

Young, Alfred F. *The Shoemaker and the Tea Party: Memory and the American Revolution.* Boston: Beacon Press, 1999. Young's interesting book looks at the role of an ordinary person, Boston shoemaker George Robert Twelves Hewes, in historic events like the Boston Tea Party.

World Wide Web

"Boston Tea Party Historical Society." http://www.boston-tea-party.org/. This Web site contains links to firsthand accounts and articles about the Boston Tea Party.

"Colonial America: Tea Act, May 10, 1773." http://www.u-s-history.com/pages/h1248.html. Explains the importance of the Tea Act in encouraging colonial resistance.

"The Tea Act." http://www.ushistory.org/declaration/related/teaact.htm. Summary of the Tea Act.

Multimedia Sources

The History Channel Presents the Revolution. A&E Home Video, 2006. 4 DVDs. 600 minutes. Looks at the American Revolution, including the Boston Tea Party.

Liberty! The American Revolution. PBS, 1997. 3 DVDs. 360 minutes. This PBS series includes a reenactment of the Boston Tea Party and its effects.

88. Coercive Acts (1774)

Shocked by the Boston Tea Party (1773), Parliament passed a series of acts to punish Boston. Known collectively as the Coercive Acts (colonists referred to them as the Intolerable Acts), they were meant to punish Boston, tighten British control over the colony of Massachusetts, and protect British officials. The first and most severe of these acts, the Boston Port Act closed Boston's port and forbade its reopening until the city reimbursed the East India Company for the tea destroyed in the Boston Tea Party. In May 1774, Parliament passed the Administration of Justice Act and the Massachusetts Government Act. The Administration of Justice Act specified that British officials or soldiers who killed a colonist in the performance of his duties would stand trial in England (the colonists called this the Murder Act). The Massachusetts Government Act replaced the colony's elected representatives and sheriffs with appointees by the royal governor. In addition, town meetings were restricted to one a year. In June, Parliament added the Quartering Act to Boston's burdens, requiring the local government to house British troops, in private homes if need be. Finally in October, Parliament passed the Quebec Act, which recognized the Catholic Church in Quebec. New Englanders took it as proof that Parliament did not recognize their sacrifices during the French and Indian War. Parliament though the Coercive Acts would make an example of Boston and isolate the city from the other colonies. Instead, the Coercive Acts became the impetus for the first Continental Congress.

TERM PAPER SUGGESTIONS

1. After examining earlier events, explain why the Administration of Justice Act would have been so upsetting to the colonists.
2. Examine Boston's economy in the 1770s, and then discuss why the Boston Port Act was so devastating to this city.
3. Examine the Massachusetts Government Act. How did it tie into colonists' fears that they had a lack of representation?
4. Discuss the provisions of the Quartering Act and why it offended the colonists.
5. The Quebec Act seems to have very little to do with Boston or the Tea party. Why did it upset the colonists?

ALTERNATIVE TERM PAPER SUGGESTIONS

1. It is 1774 and you are a resident of Boston. Knowing that you are a very persuasive person, your fellow citizens have asked you to travel to England and convince Parliament *not* to enact the Coercive Acts. Prepare a PowerPoint presentation designed to change the minds of Parliament. Good luck.
2. It is 1774 and you are a radio talk show host in Boston. The city has just learned about the Boston Port Act. You know your audience will call in and they will be upset. Prepare a set of talking points and attempt to calm them down.

SUGGESTED SOURCES

Primary Sources

The following sites contain the texts of the five acts that were known collectively as the Coercive Acts.

"Great Britain: Parliament—The Administration of Justice Act; May 20, 1774." http://avalon.law.yale.edu/18th_century/admin_of_justice_act.asp.

"Great Britain: Parliament—The Boston Port Act: March 31, 1774." http://avalon.law.yale.edu/18th_century/boston_port_act.asp.

"Great Britain: Parliament—The Massachusetts Government Act; May 20, 1774." http://avalon.law.yale.edu/18th_century/mass_gov_act.asp.

"Great Britain: Parliament—The Quartering Act; June 2, 1774." http://avalon.law.yale.edu/18th_century/quartering_act_1774.asp.

"Great Britain: Parliament—The Quebec Act: October 7, 1774." http://avalon.law.yale.edu/18th_century/quebec_act_1774.asp.

The following sites are the reactions of different communities in the colonies to the Coercive Acts.

"Circular Letter of the Boston Committee of Correspondence; May 13, 1774." http://avalon.law.yale.edu/18th_century/circ_let_boston_1774.asp.

"Letter from the New York Committee of Fifty-One to the Boston Committee of Correspondence; May 23, 1774." http://avalon.law.yale.edu/18th_century/letter_ny_comm_1774.asp.

"Letter from Lieutenant-Governor Colden to the Earl of Dartmouth; June 1, 1774." http://avalon.law.yale.edu/18th_century/letter_colden_dartmouth_1774.asp.

"Proceedings of Farmington, Connecticut, on the Boston Port Act; May 19, 1774." http://avalon.law.yale.edu/18th_century/proc_farm_ct_1774.asp.

"Proceedings of the Inhabitants of Philadelphia; June 18, 1774." http://avalon.law.yale.edu/18th_century/proc_in_pa_1774.asp.

Secondary Sources

Ammerman, David. *In the Common Cause: American Response to the Coercive Acts of 1774.* Charlotte: University Press of Virginia, 1974. Ammerman points out that the Coercive Acts helped unite colonies against Great Britain.

Countryman, Edward. *The American Revolution.* New York: Hill & Wang, 1985. A brief history of the American Revolution.

Ferling, John. *A Leap in the Dark: The Struggle to Create the American Republic.* New York: Oxford University Press, 2003. Ferling's *Leap in the Dark* is one of the best recent comprehensive histories of the American Revolution

Middlekauff, Robert. *The Glorious Cause: The American Revolution, 1763–1789.* Revised edition. New York: Oxford University Press, 2005. Middlekauff's is one of the most thorough treatments of the American Revolution.

Nash, Gary B. *The Unknown American Revolution: The Unruly Birth of American Democracy and the Struggle to Create America.* New York: Viking, 2005. Another of the newer histories of the American Revolution.

Wood, Gordon S. *The American Revolution: A History.* New York: Modern Library, 2003. A brief history of the American Revolution.

Young, Alfred F. *The Shoemaker and the Tea Party: Memory and the American Revolution.* Boston: Beacon Press, 1999. This very interesting book focuses on one participant in the Boston Tea Party, and how Americans chose to remember the Revolution.

World Wide Web

"The Coercive Acts." http://countrystudies.us/united-states/history-26.htm. Overview of the Coercive Acts.

Multimedia Sources

The History Channel Presents the Revolution. A&E Home Video, 2006. 4 DVDs. 600 minutes. Discusses the Coercive Acts.

Liberty! The American Revolution. PBS, 1997. 3 DVDs. 360 minutes. This PBS presentation covers the Revolution, including the Coercive Acts.

89. First Continental Congress (1774)

The Coercive Acts (1774) generated sympathy for the City of Boston throughout the colonies. In response to the Boston crisis, the colonies called the First Continental Congress, which met in Philadelphia on September 5, 1774. Twelve colonies sent 57 representatives, who quickly approved the Suffolk Resolves (named for the county around Boston). The Suffolk Resolves argued against the legality of the Coercive Acts, called upon Massachusetts citizens to arm themselves, and urged economic retaliation against Great Britain. The Congress also passed the Declaration of American Rights, which allowed that Parliament could regulate trade, but denied it had the right to intervene in the internal affairs of the colonies, which should be handled by their own elected assemblies. The most important act of the first Congress was the formation of the Continental Association. The Association planned to wage economic war against England by enforcing a nonimportation movement throughout the colonies. Committees would be formed throughout the colonies to enforce a boycott of British goods. While these committees lacked legal authority, merchants who did not comply with the boycotts faced the prospect of losing customers. Congress agreed to meet again in 1775 and assess the results of the nonimportation movement. If the nonimportation movement did not have the desired effect of Parliament repealing the Coercive Acts, Congress then planned to enact a nonexportation act in an effort to deprive British manufacturers of the American raw materials they needed. However, when Congress met again in May 1775, they faced a drastically different situation.

TERM PAPER SUGGESTIONS

1. Examine and discuss the Suffolk Resolves. Were citizens in the vicinity of Boston really considering armed resistance at this early date?
2. Discuss the Declaration of American Rights that the first Continental Congress approved of in 1774, with the Declaration of Independence two years later. What changed in those two years to produce two different declarations?
3. Discuss the Continental Association. Why did Congress think that economic coercion would work? Was it really aimed at Parliament, or was it an attempt to influence Parliament's constituents?
4. Discuss the actions that local committees took to enforce the rules of the Continental Association. Were they effective?

ALTERNATIVE TERM PAPER SUGGESTIONS

1. It is 1774 and you have been appointed by the Continental Congress to impress on Parliament the effects that an American nonexportation movement will have on Britain and British manufacturers should it be put into effect. Prepare a PowerPoint presentation and try to convey to the British that they face an economic calamity if the Americans are forced to do this. Give examples of specific commodities that will be denied to the British.
2. It is 1774 and you are the leader of a local committee of the Continental Association. You have discovered that the firm of Smith & Jones is selling British goods. Prepare a broadside designed to convince their would-be customers to go elsewhere.

SUGGESTED SOURCES

Primary Sources

"The Association of the Virginia Convention; August 1–6, 1774." http://avalon.law.yale.edu/18th_century/assoc_of_va_conv_1774.asp. This is the text of Virginia's nonimportation resolves.

"Declarations and Resolves of the First Continental Congress; October 14, 1774." http://avalon.law.yale.edu/18th_century/resolves.asp. This document argues that American colonists possess the same rights as Englishmen and complaints against specific acts of the Crown and Parliament.

"Journals of the Continental Congress—The Articles of Association; October 20, 1774." http://avalon.law.yale.edu/18th_century/contcong_10-20-74.asp. This document established the Continental Association and provides guidelines for local chapters of the Association.

"Journals of the Continental Congress, 1774–1789." http://memory.loc.gov/ammem/amlaw/lwjclink.html. This Library of Congress Web site has the records of the Continental Congress in 34 volumes.

Secondary Sources

Countryman, Edward. *The American Revolution.* New York: Hill & Wang, 1985. A short history of the Revolution.

Ferling, John. *A Leap in the Dark: The Struggle to Create the American Republic.* New York: Oxford University Press, 2003. Ferling's *Leap in the Dark* is one of the best recent comprehensive histories of the American Revolution.

Middlekauff, Robert. *The Glorious Cause: The American Revolution, 1763–1789.* Revised edition. New York: Oxford University Press, 2005. Middlekauff's is one of the most thorough treatments of the American Revolution.

Nash, Gary B. *The Unknown American Revolution: The Unruly Birth of American Democracy and the Struggle to Create America.* New York: Viking, 2005. A newer history of the American Revolution.

Wood, Gordon S. *The American Revolution: A History.* New York: Modern Library, 2003. A brief history of the American Revolution.

World Wide Web

"The American Revolution: Continental Congress." http://www.americanrevolution.com/ContinentalCongress.htm. Article about the Congress with links to sources.

Multimedia Sources

The History Channel Presents the Revolution. A&E Home Video, 2006. 4 DVDs. 600 minutes. Includes an account of the First Continental Congress.

Liberty! The American Revolution. PBS, 1997. 3 DVDs. 360 minutes. This PBS presentation looks at the actions of the First Continental Congress.

90. Skirmishes at Lexington and Concord (1775)

In the months after the Continental Congress had adjourned in 1774 in Philadelphia, local Committees of Safety began organizing militias and training them. They also began to gather military supplies. In Boston, General Thomas Gage learned that the Boston Committee of Safety had stored military supplies in the village of Concord, 20 miles outside Boston. He also learned that patriot leaders Samuel Adams and John Hancock were there. On the evening of April 18, 1775, 700 British troops formed on Boston Common and set out for Concord. The British had been watched by the Boston Committee of Safety, and they sent out riders, including silversmith Paul Revere, to warn the villages of Lexington and Concord. The British had to go through Lexington in order to reach Concord. The British entered Lexington just after dawn on April 19 and found a contingent of 70 minutemen on the green. Outnumbered by the British ten to one, the minutemen probably meant only to make a show of force. Ordered to disperse by British officers, some of the minutemen began to move off the green when someone—no one knew who—fired a shot. The British responded with a volley that killed several minutemen. When the British reached Concord they discovered that Adams and Hancock had fled and the military supplies had been moved. During the march back to Boston, the British found themselves under constant fire and suffered three times as many casualties as the Americans. The American Revolution had become a shooting war.

TERM PAPER SUGGESTIONS

1. Discuss the role of the Committees of Safety. What were their activities and how did they help foment resistance to the British?

2. Discuss the warning system set up to let the residents of Lexington and Concord know the British were coming.
3. Given that the British outnumbered the Lexington minutemen by a factor of ten to one, why do you think they were there? Does the notion of a "show of force" make sense in this context?
4. Discuss British evaluations of the effectiveness of American minutemen before and after the battles of Lexington and Concord.

ALTERNATIVE TERM PAPER SUGGESTIONS

1. It is 1775 and you are a British officer in Boston. General Gage knows there are all kinds of spies in Boston and that it would be difficult to march on Lexington and Concord without somebody noticing and warning the two towns. He has tasked you with developing a plan by which a good number of troops can leave Boston without attracting too much attention.
2. It is 1775 and you are a radio news reporter. Prepare a podcast as if you were on the scene of the Battles of Lexington and Concord.

SUGGESTED SOURCES

Primary Source

"Depositions Concerning Lexington and Concord, April, 1775." http://lcweb2.loc.gov/learn/features/timeline/amrev/shots/concern.html. Eyewitness accounts of the Battles of Lexington and Concord.

Secondary Sources

Countryman, Edward. *The American Revolution.* New York: Hill & Wang, 1985. A brief history of the Revolution.

Ferling, John. *A Leap in the Dark: The Struggle to Create the American Republic.* New York: Oxford University Press, 2003. Ferling's *Leap in the Dark* is one of the best recent comprehensive histories of the American Revolution.

Fisher, David Hackett. *Paul Revere's Ride.* New York: Oxford University Press, 1994. An interesting account about the origins of the Revolution in Boston as well as a detailed account of Paul Revere's ride and the clash between British troops and colonial minutemen at Lexington and Concord.

Gross, Robert A. *The Minutemen and Their World.* New York: Hill & Wang, 1976. A very readable detailed account of Lexington and Concord.

Maier, Pauline. *American Scripture: Making the Declaration of Independence.* New York: Knopf, 1997. Maier points out there were elements in Congress who hoped that the colonies and Great Britain could reconcile, even after Lexington and Concord.

Middlekauff, Robert. *The Glorious Cause: The American Revolution, 1763–1789.* Revised edition. New York: Oxford University Press, 2005. Middlekauff's is one of the most thorough treatments of the American Revolution.

Nash, Gary B. *The Unknown American Revolution: The Unruly Birth of American Democracy and the Struggle to Create America.* New York: Viking, 2005. A newer history of the American Revolution.

Wood, Gordon S. *The American Revolution: A History.* New York: Modern Library, 2003. A brief history of the American Revolution.

World Wide Web

"Lexington and Concord." http://americanrevwar.homestead.com/files/LEXCON.HTM. Narrative and illustrations of the battles of Lexington and Concord.

"The Patriot Resource: The Shot Heard 'Round the World." http://www.patriotresource.com/battles/lexington.html. Offers an outline and timeline of events at Lexington and Concord.

Multimedia Sources

The History Channel Presents the Revolution. A&E Home Video, 2006. 4 DVDs. 600 minutes. Uses period illustrations, narrations, and reenactments to illustrate Lexington and Concord.

Liberty! The American Revolution. PBS, 1997. 3 DVDs. 360 minutes. Uses period illustrations, narrations, and reenactments to illustrate Lexington and Concord.

91. Thomas Paine Publishes *Common Sense* (1776)

After the Battles of Lexington and Concord, Americans fought the British throughout the remainder of the year 1775. The Continental Army was formed and besieged Boston, fighting the Battle of Bunker Hill in the process. Americans captured the British post of Ticonderoga in New York State and launched an unsuccessful invasion of Canada. For his part, King George III issued a proclamation, declaring the colonies in rebellion. Despite the fighting, only a few colonists considered independence, believing the rift with England could be repaired. In 1775 Thomas Paine migrated from England to America. Paine had not been a successful man. He had been a corset maker and twice fired from his job as a tax collector. He once went into business as a tobacconist, but ran the shop into debt in only a few months. Paine arrived in Philadelphia intending to start a school for young ladies. The school did not materialize, but Paine, intrigued by American politics, involved himself in the Revolutionary struggle. His 46-page pamphlet, *Common Sense,* appeared in February 1776 and was an immediate best seller, selling 150,000 copies in three months. Written in everyday language, Paine argued that islands should not govern continents and noted that British interests were not the same as American interests. Paine also shifted the focus of American ire from Parliament to the king, declaring him a "royal brute." The popularity of *Common Sense* led many Americans to consider independence for the first time.

TERM PAPER SUGGESTIONS

1. Read *Common Sense.* What do you think is Paine's most persuasive argument for America severing its ties to England, and why?
2. Who seems to be Paine's audience? Why do you think *Common Sense* was so popular when it appeared in 1776?
3. Paine spends a lot of time in *Common Sense* discussing nature. How does he relate nature to governments?
4. Paine is also the author of another famous pamphlet from the American Revolution, *The American Crisis.* Compare and contrast this work to *Common Sense.*

ALTERNATIVE TERM PAPER SUGGESTIONS

1. It is 1776 and you are the publisher of Paine's *Common Sense.* You are uncertain whether this new pamphlet will sell. To try and boost sales, you will devise a full-page newspaper ad designed to attract attention to Paine's work.

2. It is 1776 and you are a newspaper reporter. You have landed an interview with Thomas Paine. Prepare a list of questions that you plan to ask him.

SUGGESTED SOURCES

Primary Sources

Paine, Thomas. *Common Sense*. http://www.bartleby.com/133/. Full text of Paine's *Common Sense*

Paine, Thomas. *Common Sense and Related Writings*. Ed. Thomas P. Slaughter. Boston: Bedford/St. Martin's, 2001. Contains excerpts of *Common Sense* and other revolutionary era writings of Paine.

Secondary Sources

Countryman, Edward. *The American Revolution*. New York: Hill & Wang, 1985. A short history of the Revolution.

Ferling, John. *A Leap in the Dark: The Struggle to Create the American Republic*. New York: Oxford University Press, 2003. Ferling's *Leap in the Dark* is one of the best recent comprehensive histories of the American Revolution.

Liell, Scott. *46 Pages: Thomas Paine, Common Sense, and the Turning Point to Independence*. Philadelphia: Running Press, 2003. Liell includes the text of *Common Sense* in his book, but he also examines how Paine's writings affected the thinking of the founders regarding independence.

Maier, Pauline. *American Scripture: Making the Declaration of Independence*. New York: Knopf, 1997. Maier discusses the role that Paine played in helping to foster calls for American independence.

Middlekauff, Robert. *The Glorious Cause: The American Revolution, 1763–1789*. Revised edition. New York: Oxford University Press, 2005. Middlekauff's is one of the most thorough treatments of the American Revolution.

Nash, Gary B. *The Unknown American Revolution: The Unruly Birth of American Democracy and the Struggle to Create America*. New York: Viking, 2005. Nash discusses Paine as one of the more radical figures of the American Revolution.

Nelson, Craig. *Thomas Paine: Enlightenment, Revolution, and the Birth of Modern Nations*. New York: Penguin Books, 2007. Discusses the influence of Paine and American Independence on other nations throughout the world.

World Wide Web

"Thomas Paine." http://www.ushistory.org/PAINE/. Offers a short biography of Thomas Paine and links to several of his writings.

Multimedia Sources

The History Channel Presents the Revolution. A&E Home Video, 2006. 4 DVDs. 600 minutes. This presentation discusses Thomas Paine and his influence.

Liberty! The American Revolution. PBS, 1997. 3 DVDs. 360 minutes. This PBS presentation discusses Thomas Paine and his influence.

92. Declaration of Independence (1776)

The success of Thomas Paine's *Common Sense* in 1776 helped propel the notion of independence. Politicians began considering the question, as being independent would make it easier for America to obtain foreign assistance in their war against England and would give political leaders a legal basis for their authority. On June 7, Virginia representative Richard Henry Lee proposed that the United States should detach itself from England. Lee's motion was adopted by Congress on July 2. Congress had appointed a five-man committee to develop a public explanation for America's need to separate itself from Great Britain. Overthrowing a king in the eighteenth century was a radical act, and some explanation was thought to be in order. The committee gave the task of writing the Declaration to John Adams and Thomas Jefferson, and Adams deferred to Jefferson, who he thought was the superior writer. The first portion of the Declaration of Independence rested heavily on the contract theory of government that had been developed by English political theorist John Locke. In short, the contract theory states that citizens owe government their loyalty so long as the government protects them. When government withdraws that protection, the contract is voided and the people may form a government that will address their needs. The second part of the Declaration of Independence consists of a list of grievances against King George III. This was necessary because the Americans had to justify to the world why they were choosing to rebel against the king.

TERM PAPER SUGGESTIONS

1. Many scholars have noted the influence of the English political philosopher John Locke on the Declaration of Independence. How does Locke's contract theory of government fit into the Declaration?
2. Examine the second part of the Declaration of Independence, the list of grievances. Attempt to identify specific incidents that Jefferson is referring to. Does he exaggerate anywhere in his list of grievances?
3. How would declaring independence have helped legitimatize the authority of American political leaders?
4. Was the Declaration of Independence a radical document? If so, do we still consider it radical today?

ALTERNATIVE TERM PAPER SUGGESTIONS

1. It is 1776 and you are a reporter for a major newspaper in Philadelphia. You have landed an interview with Thomas Jefferson. Prepare a list of ten questions that you will ask during the interview.
2. It is 1776 and you are a radio talk show host. The Declaration of Independence has just been published, and many Americans have questions. The Declaration is the topic of your show. Prepare a list of questions that you expect from your listeners, and prepare your answers as well.

SUGGESTED SOURCES

Primary Sources

"The Charters of Freedom: The Declaration of Independence." http://www.archives.gov/exhibits/charters/declaration.html. This National Archives Web site contains images and transcripts of the Declaration

"The Declaration of Independence Home Page." http://www.duke.edu/eng169s2/group1/lex3/firstpge.htm. This Duke University Web site contains transcripts of the rough draft of the Declaration, the copy that was considered by the committee, and the final version.

"Journals of the Continental Congress, 1774–1789." http://memory.loc.gov/ammem/amlaw/lwjclink.html. This Library of Congress Web site has the records of the Continental Congress in 34 volumes.

"Primary Documents in American History: Declaration of Independence." http://www.loc.gov/rr/program/bib/ourdocs/DeclarInd.html. This

Library of Congress Web site contains images and transcripts, as well as a timeline of the drafting and publication of the Declaration.

Secondary Sources

Ellis, Joseph J. *What Did the Declaration Declare?* Boston: Bedford/St. Martin's, 1999. Essays by five scholars regarding the declaration.

Ferling, John. *A Leap in the Dark: The Struggle to Create the American Republic.* New York: Oxford University Press, 2003. Ferling's *Leap in the Dark* is one of the best recent comprehensive histories of the American Revolution

Maier, Pauline. *American Scripture: Making the Declaration of Independence.* New York: Knopf, 1997. Perhaps the best account of the drafting of the Declaration.

Middlekauff, Robert. *The Glorious Cause: The American Revolution, 1763–1789.* Revised edition. New York: Oxford University Press, 2005. Middlekauff's is one of the most thorough treatments of the American Revolution.

Nash, Gary B. *The Unknown American Revolution: The Unruly Birth of American Democracy and the Struggle to Create America.* New York: Viking, 2005. Nash discusses the effects of the Revolution on different segments of American society, including slaves, Indians, and women.

Wood, Gordon S. *The American Revolution: A History.* New York: Modern Library, 2003. A brief history of the Revolution.

Wood, Gordon S. *The Creation of the American Republic, 1776–1787.* Chapel Hill: University of North Carolina Press, 1969. Wood's dense tome includes a section regarding the Declaration of Independence.

World Wide Web

"The Declaration of Independence." http://www.ushistory.org/declaration/. Contains images and facts about the declaration.

"Declaration of Independence." http://colonialhall.com/histdocs/declaration/. Offers a line by line explanation and analysis of the grievances listed in the Declaration.

"NOVA: Saving the National Treasures." http://www.pbs.org/wgbh/nova/charters/. This PBS Web site examines the damage that time and imperfect preservation techniques have done to the Declaration.

Multimedia Sources

Both of these programs look at the history of the Declaration and the efforts to preserve the document itself.

Save Our History: The Declaration of Independence. A&E Television Networks, 2008. 1 DVD. 50 Minutes.

Saving the National Treasures. Boston: WGBH-PBS, 2007. 1 DVD. 60 minutes.

93. American Victory at Saratoga Results in an Alliance with France (1777)

In 1777, English General John Burgoyne hatched a plan he thought could end the American Revolution. Believing that New England was the hotbed of the Revolution, Burgoyne proposed to move his army south from Montreal, down the Lake Champlain–Hudson River Valley corridor, while General William Howe in New York City advanced north up the Hudson with his army. In this way, the British would isolate New England from the rest of the colonies. In the early summer of 1777, Burgoyne moved south with 7,000 men, thinking that General Howe was moving north. However, a lack of communication meant that Howe did not know he was to go north up the Hudson. Instead, Howe attacked Philadelphia and seized control of the city. Slowed by having to cut a road through the wilderness and to make allowances for a large baggage train, Burgoyne advanced slowly south. Burgoyne had his sole success of the campaign when he seized Fort Ticonderoga in July. Burgoyne's slow pace meant that his army was expending their supplies too quickly. American militia frustrated British foraging parties. By October, Burgoyne had less than 6,000 men and was unable to break through American forces at Saratoga, which was commanded by Horatio Gates. Lacking provisions, Burgoyne surrendered his army. Saratoga, however, had consequences far beyond the battlefield. The victory convinced the French, who had been surreptitiously shipping military supplies to the Americans, to openly enter the war on their side. The presence of the French Army and the French Navy would be critical to later American victories.

TERM PAPER SUGGESTIONS

1. Examine General Burgoyne's idea that New England could be severed from the rest of the colonies. Assuming that his plan did work, would it really have had the effect of ending the Revolution?
2. Discuss the lack of coordination between Burgoyne and Howe. Was this really all their fault? What could each commander have done differently to improve communication between New York City and Montreal in 1777?
3. Discuss the laws in Burgoyne's plan. How did his unfamiliarity with the terrain of upstate New York contribute to his defeat?
4. Discuss the effect that Saratoga had on the American alliance with France? Why did the victory at Saratoga make the French more willing to openly, rather than covertly, support the United States?
5. The victory at Saratoga created some strife among the upper echelon of the Continental Army. Supporters of Horatio Gates argued that he, rather than George Washington, should be the commander of the Continental Army. Would Gates have been a better commander than Washington?

ALTERNATIVE TERM PAPER SUGGESTIONS

1. It is 1777 and you are an officer in the Continental Army. General Gates has ordered you to attend a parley to discuss the surrender of the British Army. Your job is to prepare a PowerPoint presentation that will be shown to the British officers. Using period maps, your goal is to convince the British that their position is hopeless and they have no choice but to surrender.
2. It is 1777 and you are an aide to the American ambassador to France, Benjamin Franklin. Franklin has ordered you to prepare an iMovie, illustrating the American victory at Saratoga for his French hosts.

SUGGESTED SOURCES

Primary Sources

"Articles of Convention Between Lieutenant-General Burgoyne and Major General Gates; October 16, 1777." http://avalon.law.yale.edu/18th_century/burgoyne_gates.asp. This is the text of Burgoyne's surrender to Gates.

"Plan of the Treaties with France of 1778." http://avalon.law.yale.edu/18th_century/fr1778p.asp. This is the text of the treaty signed between the United States and France.

Secondary Sources

Ferling, John. *A Leap in the Dark: The Struggle to Create the American Republic.* New York: Oxford University Press, 2003. Ferling's *Leap in the Dark* is one of the best recent comprehensive histories of the American Revolution.

Ketchum, Richard M. *Saratoga: Turning Point of America's Revolutionary War.* New York: Holt, 1997. Ketchum examines the battle and its effects beyond the battlefield.

Middlekauff, Robert. *The Glorious Cause: The American Revolution, 1763–1789.* Revised edition. New York: Oxford University Press, 2005. Middlekauff's is one of the most thorough treatments of the American Revolution.

Mintz, Max M. *The Generals of Saratoga: John Burgoyne and Horatio Gates.* New Haven, CT: Yale University Press, 1990. Mintz offers short biographies and looks at the strategies of the two rival commanders at Saratoga.

Schiff, Stacy. *A Great Improvisation: Franklin, France, and the Birth of America.* New York: Henry Holt, 2005. Mainly about Franklin's diplomatic efforts in France, Schiff argues that the American victory at Saratoga was a key part in securing overt French support.

World Wide Web

"The Battle of Freeman's Farm." http://www.britishbattles.com/battle-freemans-farm.htm. This is considered the first battle of Saratoga. This site contains maps, images, and a narrative of the battle.

"The Battle of Saratoga: September 19, 1777." http://www.americanrevolution.com/BattleofSaratoga.htm. This site contains a narrative of the battle, as well as maps and images.

"The Battle of Saratoga 1777." http://www.britishbattles.com/battle-saratoga.htm. Contains maps, images, and a narrative of the battle.

"Saratoga: National Historical Park." http://www.nps.gov/sara/. This National Parks Service Web site has images and information about the battles.

Multimedia Sources

Both of these presentations delve into the battle of Saratoga.

The History Channel Presents the Revolution. A&E Home Video, 2006. 4 DVDs. 600 minutes.

Liberty! The American Revolution. PBS, 1997. 3 DVDs. 360 minutes.

94. Congress Adopts the Articles of Confederation (1781)

For the first several years of its existence, the United States lacked a governing structure. The Articles of Confederation had been proposed in 1777, but it was not until 1781, when Maryland finally dropped its objections to the Articles, that they became the governing document of the United States, a scant four months before the victory at Yorktown. Part of Virginia Representative Richard Henry Lee's motion for a Declaration of Independence in June 1776 included a proposal for a confederation. The Articles were drafted in July 1776 but not approved by Congress until November 1777. Maryland held out until 1781, refusing to ratify until other states dropped their western land clams. The Articles contained several weaknesses. The Confederation was, in effect, a grouping of autonomous states. The Articles had no provision for a national judiciary and no chief executive. Decisions dealing with war, peace, or finances required the approval of nine states. Under the articles, Congress was empowered to conduct foreign policy, declare war, and settle disputes among the states. Yet while Congress had the authority to declare war, it did not have power to raise an army or to impose taxes to pay for an army. It could only ask the states to supply troops and money. The primary reason for the articles prescribing a weak central government lay in Americans' recent experience with the British government, which resulted in a reluctance to hand over too much power to Congress or any other strong central authority.

TERM PAPER SUGGESTIONS

1. Congress functioned (after a fashion) for several years without the Articles. Were the Articles truly needed during the Revolution?

2. Why did Maryland hold out on approving the Articles?
3. In the years after the American Revolution, and before the adoption of the Constitution, Congress under the Articles of Confederation did have a few achievements. Do some research and discuss these achievements.
4. What were the primary weaknesses of the Articles of Confederation?

ALTERNATIVE TERM PAPER SUGGESTIONS

1. It is 1787 and Americans are debating whether to replace the Articles with the Constitution. Create a PowerPoint presentation that uses a side-by-side comparison of the two documents.
2. It is 1782 and Congress has asked you to improve the Articles. The only sources you have to work with are the proposed drafts by Benjamin Franklin and John Dickinson, as well as Thomas Jefferson's comments on the Articles (see under "Primary Sources"). Using these documents, see whether you can improve the Articles. Good luck.

SUGGESTED SOURCES

Primary Sources

"Articles of Confederation: March 1, 1781." http://avalon.law.yale.edu/18th_century/artconf.asp. This Yale University Web site has the text of the Articles, proposed drafts by Benjamin Franklin and John Dickinson, as well as Thomas Jefferson's comments on the Articles.

"U.S. Constitution Online: The Articles of Confederation." http://www.usconstitution.net/articles.html. Contains a transcript of the Articles and a comparison of the Articles and the Constitution.

Secondary Sources

Ferling, John. *A Leap in the Dark: The Struggle to Create the American Republic.* New York: Oxford University Press, 2003. Ferling's *Leap in the Dark* is one of the best recent comprehensive histories of the American Revolution.

Main, Jackson Turner. *The Antifederalists: Critics of the Constitution, 1781–1788.* New York: University of North Carolina Press, 1961. Main looks at the supporters of the Articles of Confederation, even after it became clear that they did not work.

Middlekauff, Robert. *The Glorious Cause: The American Revolution, 1763–1789.* Revised edition. New York: Oxford University Press, 2005. Middlekauff's is one of the most thorough treatments of the American Revolution.

Wood, Gordon S. *The Creation of the American Republic, 1776–1787.* Chapel Hill: University of North Carolina Press, 1969. Wood has a good section on the Articles of Confederation.

World Wide Web

"Primary Documents in American History: The Articles of Confederation." http://www.loc.gov/rr/program/bib/ourdocs/articles.html. This Library of Congress Web site contains images and links to other sources.

Multimedia Sources

Both of these presentations have brief discussions of the Articles of Confederation.

The History Channel Presents the Revolution. A&E Home Video, 2006. 4 DVDs. 600 minutes.

Liberty! The American Revolution. PBS, 1997. 3 DVDs. 360 minutes. This PBS presentation uses documents, narrative, and reenactments to tell the story of the American Revolution.

A New Nation (1776–1815). Schlessinger Media, 2002. 1 DVD. 30 minutes. Covers the Articles of Confederation and the Constitution.

95. Battle of Yorktown (1781)

After their failures to put down the Revolution in the North, the British shifted their efforts south, believing they would have greater loyalist support. At first, the British were very successful forcing the surrender of Charleston and defeating an army under Horatio Gates at Camden, South Carolina. Nathaniel Greene took command of the Continental Army in the south and fought a war of attrition with British General Charles Cornwallis. In August 1781, Cornwallis's army, needing rest and resupply, retired to Yorktown on the York River. Cornwallis assumed that the British navy would evacuate him and his men. However, the French navy controlled Chesapeake Bay, denying the British access to the York River. George Washington and the bulk of the Continental Army were encamped outside New York City when he learned that Cornwallis was trapped at Yorktown. Leaving a few men to tend fires to make the British think the Continental Army was still outside New York, Washington began a forced march toward Yorktown. The battle of Yorktown was conducted as a siege with the Continental Army and their French allies digging trenches that moved their artillery closer to the British positions every day. Running out of supplies, and realizing that he could not be evacuated, Cornwallis surrendered on October 19, 1781, but did not attend the surrender ceremony. The battle of Yorktown set off a period of cautious optimism in the colonies. Many hoped the war was now over. King George III wished to continue the war, but in February 1782, Parliament effectively ended the conflict by refusing to fund the war any longer.

TERM PAPER SUGGESTIONS

1. Some historians have described Nathaniel Greene's Continental Army in the South as a "fugitive army." What do they mean by that?
2. The British army in the South had a number of runaway slaves who attached themselves to the army. During the battle of Yorktown, Cornwallis, in order to preserve supplies, forced many of these slaves to leave. What happened to them?
3. Discuss the march the Continental Army made from New York to Yorktown. What measures did the Continentals take to deceive the British as to their whereabouts?
4. Americans were guardedly optimistic that the war was over after the battle of Yorktown, but they could not be absolutely sure it was over. Why?

ALTERNATIVE TERM PAPER SUGGESTIONS

1. It is October 19, 1781, and you are a radio newscaster at Yorktown. Using accounts of the British surrender, make a podcast and describe the scene for your listeners.
2. It is November 1781 and you are an editorial writer for an American newspaper. The question everyone wants to know, is the war really over? Compose an editorial with your opinion.

SUGGESTED SOURCES

Primary Sources

"Articles of Capitulation; October 18, 1781." http://avalon.law.yale.edu/18th_century/art_of_cap_1781.asp. These are the terms for the British surrender at Yorktown.

Fitzpatrick, John C., ed. *The Writings of George Washington from the Original Manuscript Sources.* 39 volumes. Washington, DC: GPO, 1931–1944. http://etext.lib.virginia.edu/washington/fitzpatrick/index.html. Fitzpatrick's edition of Washington's papers contains mainly documents that originated with Washington.

"The George Washington Papers at the Library of Congress, 1741–1799." http://lcweb2.loc.gov/ammem/gwhtml/gwhome.html. This Web site is home to the largest collection of George Washington papers. It features images of the original documents and transcriptions of them.

Martin, Joseph Plumb. *A Narrative of a Revolutionary Soldier: Some of the Adventures, Dangers, and Sufferings, of Joseph Plumb Martin.* New York: Signet, 2001. Originally published in 1830, this is one of the few Revolutionary War narratives written by an enlisted man. Martin was present for the battle of Yorktown and the British surrender.

"The Papers of George Washington." http://gwpapers.virginia.edu/. The University of Virginia's George Washington Papers project, begun in 1969, will eventually include documents originating with Washington as well as correspondence to him. As of March 2009, this project has published Washington's papers up to 1793.

Secondary Sources

Ketchum, Richard M. *Victory at Yorktown: The Campaign That Won the Revolution.* New York: Macmillan, 2004. A good account of the battle of Yorktown.

Middlekauff, Robert. *The Glorious Cause: The American Revolution, 1763–1789.* Revised edition. New York: Oxford University Press, 2005. Middlekauff's is one of the most thorough treatments of the American Revolution.

World Wide Web

"The Battle of Yorktown 1781." http://www.britishbattles.com/battle-yorktown.htm. This site contains maps, images, and a narrative of the battle of Yorktown.

"Yorktown Battlefield." http://www.nps.gov/york/. This National Park Service Web site offers neoformation about the 1781 battlefield.

Multimedia Sources

All three of these presentations cover the battle of Yorktown.

The History Channel Presents the Revolution. A&E Home Video, 2006. 4 DVDs. 600 minutes.

The History Channel Presents Washington the Warrior. A&E Home Video, 2006. 1 DVD.

Liberty! The American Revolution. PBS, 1997. 3 DVDs. 360 minutes.

96. Treaty of Paris Ends the American Revolution (1783)

In February 1782, the English Parliament refused the request of King George III for funds to prosecute the war in America. The war effectively over, American representatives met with their British counterparts in Paris. The most active members of the American contingent were Benjamin Franklin, John Adams, and John Jay. Congress instructed the delegation to follow the instructions of the French. The treaty of alliance between the United States and France forbade the signing of a separate peace agreement. The French, however, were allied to the Spanish, whereas the United States was not. Realizing that French and American interests were not the same, Franklin and Jay decided to pursue negotiations without the French. The most important provision of the treaty was that England recognized American independence. The treaty also established boundaries, with the American westward boundary being set at the Mississippi River. Americans also promised to pay prewar debts to British merchants, while England promised to promptly withdraw its troops. American loyalists were to be unmolested, and slaves in British custody were to be returned to their American owners. Many of these provisions were not honored, however. Americans did not promptly repay their prewar debts, and, in response, the British still occupied

American forts in the Old Northwest. When the British evacuated Charleston and New York City, they took many slaves with them in defiance of the treaty. Congress, it turned out, could do little to protect Loyalists in the United States, and many were forced out by their neighbors. Many of the provisions that were not honored in the Treaty of Paris would not be resolved until the Jay Treaty in 1795.

TERM PAPER SUGGESTIONS

1. Discuss the political mood in England after the battle of Saratoga. King George III wished to continue the war, but Parliament did not. Did Parliament think the war was unwinnable or did they think it was too costly? Or both?
2. Examine Benjamin Franklin's strategy in negotiating with the British. Did he really want Canada when he brought it up during meetings with British representatives? Or was it a gambit to get something else?
3. Franklin and Jay tended to ignore their instructions from the Continental Congress. Given the outcome of the negotiations, was this a good or bad thing for the United States?
4. The United States either did not or could not honor the provisions of the treaty that required that British merchants be paid prewar debts and that former Loyalists remained unmolested. Why did they not do these things?
5. Great Britain either did not or could not honor the provisions of the treaty that required slaves in their control to be returned to their American owners and that they withdraw from American soil. Why did they not do these things?

ALTERNATIVE TERM PAPER SUGGESTIONS

1. You are a British officer in Charleston, South Carolina, in 1783. In accordance with the Treaty of Paris, your military unit has boarded ships to leave. However, your unit also takes a good number of American slaves with you. When you arrive in Halifax, Nova Scotia, your commander approaches you. He has tasked you to draft a report explaining why your unit did not attempt to return the slaves to their American owners.
2. It is 1782, and the King is upset that Parliament has refused to further fund the war. He is sending you to Parliament and he wants you to change

their mind. Prepare a PowerPoint presentation that outlines to Parliament the enormous strategic and economic value of the colonies to the British Empire, and why they should endeavor to keep them.

SUGGESTED SOURCES

Primary Sources

"British-American Diplomacy: The Paris Peace Treaty 1783 and Associated Documents." http://avalon.law.yale.edu/subject_menus/parismen.asp. This Yale University Web site contains the text of the Treaty of Paris, plus other agreements.

"The Papers of Benjamin Franklin." http://franklinpapers.org/franklin/framedVolumes.jsp. One of the American envoys during the peace talks, Franklin refers to the negotiations in his papers.

Secondary Sources

Countryman, Edward. *The American Revolution.* New York: Hill & Wang, 1985. Discusses the terms of the treaty that ended the American Revolution.

Ferling, John. *A Leap in the Dark: The Struggle to Create the American Republic.* New York: Oxford University Press, 2003. Ferling's *Leap in the Dark* is one of the best recent comprehensive histories of the American Revolution.

Middlekauff, Robert. *The Glorious Cause: The American Revolution, 1763–1789.* Revised edition. New York: Oxford University Press, 2005. Middlekauff's is one of the most thorough treatments of the American Revolution.

Nash, Gary B. *The Unknown American Revolution: The Unruly Birth of American Democracy and the Struggle to Create America.* New York: Viking, 2005. Discusses the effects of the treaty.

Wood, Gordon S. *The American Revolution: A History.* New York: Modern Library, 2003. This very compact history discusses the 1783 Treaty of Paris.

World Wide Web

"Primary Documents in American History: Treaty of Paris, 1783." http://www.loc.gov/rr/program/bib/ourdocs/paris.html. This Library of Congress Web site contains images and links to other sources.

"Treaty of Paris, 1783." http://www.state.gov/r/pa/ho/time/ar/14313.htm. This is a State Department summary of the treaty.

"Treaty of Paris, 1783." http://www.ourdocuments.gov/doc.php?flash=true &doc=6. Has a synopsis of the treaty.

Multimedia Source

"Treaty of Paris signed." http://www.history.com/this-day-in-history.do?action =VideoArticle&id=5315. Brief online video about the Treaty of Paris.

97. Spain Interferes with U.S. Navigation of the Mississippi River (1785)

Spain had allied itself with the French, but not the Americans, during the American Revolution. Spanish troops acquitted themselves well during their service in America, advancing from Louisiana into British-held West Florida and Florida. When England and the United States signed the 1783 Treaty of Paris, the Spanish, because they were not allies of the United States, had no part in it. However, they were affected by the territorial cessions that Great Britain made to the United States. The Spanish claimed much of present-day Alabama and Mississippi as well as portions of present-day Tennessee. In addition, the Spanish periodically closed the Mississippi River to American navigation. This was a very serious matter for Americans living west of the Appalachian Mountains because the Mississippi was the only means they could use to move their crops or other produce to markets. Spain also made things difficult for Americans in the South by encouraging Cherokee, Choctaw, Chickasaw, and Creek Indians to resist American westward expansion. In addition, Spain provided material aid to native peoples by providing them with powder and shot.

However, American frontiersmen destroyed many Indian villages. With the native allies scattered, and the British withdrawing from the old Northwest, the Spanish sought terms with the Americans. In the 1795 Treaty of San Lorenzo (also known as Pinckney's Treaty) the United States and Spain agreed on a southern border at the 31st parallel and free navigation of the Mississippi River and granted Americans the right to deposit goods at New Orleans.

TERM PAPER SUGGESTIONS

1. Spain was an ally of France during the Revolution, at a time when France was allied to the United States. Why were they left out of the treaty negotiations?
2. The United States and Spain had overlapping claims. What Native American peoples did the Spanish recruit to harass the Americans? What were the motivations of native peoples?
3. The Spanish also attempted to create or encourage the creation of breakaway republics such as the Miro district in western Tennessee. Examine the history of these efforts.
4. Perhaps the key issues to Americans west of the Mississippi were free navigation of the Mississippi River and access to the port of New Orleans. Why were these issues so important?
5. Discuss the provisions of Pinckney's Treaty. Compare the public reception of this treaty with that of the contemporaneous Jay Treaty. What accounted for the difference in the way the American public responded to these two treaties?

ALTERNATIVE TERM PAPER SUGGESTIONS

1. It is 1785 and you live on the American frontier. You and your neighbors have attempted to ship some of your products to New Orleans, only to find that the Spanish have closed the port to Americans. Your community thinks that Congress is not doing enough about this issue. You have been appointed to go to Congress and impress on them the importance of opening the Mississippi to American commerce. Prepare a PowerPoint presentation so that Congress can understand the importance of the Mississippi to Americans in the West.
2. It is 1795 and the terms of Pinckney's Treaty have just been announced. You are a radio talk show host. Prepare a podcast that will inform your listeners what the terms of the treaty are. Prepare a list of questions you expect from your listeners.

SUGGESTED SOURCES

Primary Source

"Treaty of Friendship, Limits, and Navigation with Spain: Hunter Miller's Notes." http://avalon.law.yale.edu/18th_century/sp1795n.asp. This site contains the text of Pinckney's Treaty with Spain.

Secondary Source

Weber, David J. *The Spanish Frontier in North America.* New Haven, CT: Yale University Press, 1994. Weber looks at Spanish tensions with the new American nation.

World Wide Web

"Spain, the United States & the American Frontier: Historias Paralclas." http://www.loc.gov/rr/hispanic/frontiers/meetingeng.html. This Library of Congress Web site, which deals with the Spanish presence in the Americas, is a work in progress.

98. Shays's Rebellion (1786)

In the 1780s, Massachusetts had a large war debt left over from the Revolution. To pay the debt, the government levied steep poll and land taxes on its citizens. These taxes were especially onerous to farmers in western Massachusetts, who, while land rich, often had little in the way of cash. When Massachusetts did not provide paper money as a means of payment in 1786, some 1,200 farmers revolted in western Massachusetts. Led by Daniel Shays, a former captain in the Continental Army, the rebels invaded courthouses to prevent courts from ordering foreclosure proceedings as a means of collecting back taxes. What Shays and his men wanted was the right to pay in kind, to use their crops as currency since the government did not provide paper money, and "stay laws," that would give debtors an extended time to pay their taxes. Shays and his men advanced on the Springfield arsenal but were turned back. However, the reports that the state government received in Boston gave the impression of a mob run amok. Massachusetts turned to the central government for help, but without an army, or the ability to raise one, Congress told Massachusetts officials they would have to put down the rebellion themselves. Eventually, Massachusetts sent 4,000 militiamen to quell the revolt. However, Shays's Rebellion made an important unexpected contribution. The weak response of the central government caused people to wonder whether perhaps the Articles of Confederation should be strengthened and the federal government given more power.

TERM PAPER SUGGESTIONS

1. Discuss the actions of the Massachusetts state government. Did they provoke the crisis? What could they have done differently?
2. Discuss the significance of Congress not assisting Massachusetts during Shays's Rebellion. Compare and contrast the actions of the federal government during Shays's Rebellion with their actions during the Whiskey Rebellion a decade later.
3. Shays's Rebellion was not the only issue that caused many Americans to start thinking that a stronger central government was needed. What were some of the other issues at the time that made Americans reconsider the idea of a strong central government?
4. Discuss the economic situation of farmers in western Massachusetts. Many of them purchased land and prospered during the Revolution. How did their situation change so abruptly?

ALTERNATIVE TERM PAPER SUGGESTIONS

1. It is 1786 and you are a radio talk show host in Boston. You are reporting on Shays's Rebellion. You expect a number of your listeners to call in. Prepare a list of remarks you expect from your listeners, with five approving of the rebellion and five opposing the rebellion. Prepare your responses in podcast form.
2. It is 1786 and Daniel Shays has asked you to be his public information officer. You are to prepare PowerPoint presentations that will be uploaded to the Web. The purpose is to convince the public that Shays and his men are not a mob as the press in eastern Massachusetts has portrayed them. Your job is to inform the public about the grievances of Shays and his men and to generate public sympathy for them.

SUGGESTED SOURCES

Primary Sources

"George Washington Lesson Plans: Lesson Two." http://lcweb2.loc.gov/learn/lessons/gw/gw2.html. Links to Washington's correspondence concerning Shays' Rebellion.

"Government Under the Articles of Confederation." http://lcweb2.loc.gov/learn/collections/madison/history2.html. This links to letters of James Madison concerning Shays's Rebellion.

"Jefferson's Service to the New Nation." http://frontiers.loc.gov/learn/collections/thomas/history4.html. Jefferson's writings concerning the rebellion.

Secondary Sources

Richards, Leonard L. *Shays's Rebellion: The American Revolution's Final Battle.* Philadelphia: University of Pennsylvania Press, 2002. Richards views Shays's Rebellion as a sort of continuation of the American Revolution.

Szatmary, David P. *Shays' Rebellion: The Making of an Agrarian Insurrection.* Amherst: University of Massachusetts Press, 1980. Argues that Massachusetts authorities unthinkingly prompted the revolt.

World Wide Web

"Shays Rebellion." http://www.nps.gov/spar/historyculture/shays-rebellion.htm. This National Parks Service Web site discusses Shays's attack on the Springfield Armory.

"Shays' Rebellion: America's First Civil War." http://www.actualreality.tv/production.html?production=shays. Homepage for the History Channel production.

Multimedia Sources

The History Channel Presents the Revolution. A&E Home Video, 2006. 4 DVDs. 600 minutes. Re-creations and historical analysis.

Liberty! The American Revolution. PBS, 1997. 3 DVDs. 360 minutes. Documents and reenactments.

Ten Days that Unexpectedly Changed America. History Channel, 2006. 3 DVDs. 460 minutes. Shays's Rebellion is one of the ten days that the producers of this series argue changed America. This program uses narration, interviews with historians, and animation.

99. Constitutional Convention (1787)

Shays's Rebellion in western Massachusetts in 1786 helped prompt calls for a stronger government. In 1786, nine states were invited to attend the Annapolis, Maryland, convention to foster interstate cooperation.

Only five states sent delegates, however, but Alexander Hamilton proposed they meet in Philadelphia in May 1787 to consider measures to strengthen the federal government. The delegates agreed to keep the proceedings secret and decided not to revise the Articles of Confederation, but to start from scratch. Two plans were advanced. One, proposed by James Madison of Virginia, called for a bicameral legislature—that is, more than one house—an executive and a federal judiciary. Representation in both houses in Madison's scheme would be proportional to a state's population. This would have placed small states at a disadvantage. William Paterson proposed a plan that differed in that it gave each state, regardless of size or population, only one vote. The two sides disagreed, but Roger Sherman of Connecticut crafted the Great Compromise. Under this compromise, each state receives equal representation in the Senate, but proportional representation in the House. The other sticking point concerned slavery. Southern politicians wanted slaves to count for representation, but not taxes, whereas northern politicians thought they should count for tax assessments but not for representation. After much debate, the two sides agreed that for proposes of representation free residents would be counted exactly while "all other persons" (the word slavery does not appear in the Constitution) would be counted as three-fifths of a person.

TERM PAPER SUGGESTIONS

1. Discuss the provisions of Madison's Virginia Plan. What elements of his plan are still part of our government today? Which portions of his plan did not become part of the Constitution?
2. Discuss William Paterson's New Jersey Plan. Which elements of his plan are recognizable in our Constitution today? Which states favored his plan and why?
3. Discuss the three-fifth's compromise. What may have happened if northern delegates simply refused to accommodate the South over the slavery issue?
4. Why did the convention scrap the Articles of Confederation? Why did they keep their proceedings a secret?

ALTERNATIVE TERM PAPER SUGGESTIONS

1. It is 1787 and you are a reporter for a Philadelphia newspaper. The Constitutional Convention is in town, and they have locked all the doors and windows

of Independence Hall and are holding all of their meetings in secret. Your editor orders you to infiltrate the Convention and find out what they are doing. Write out a plan as to how you will do this.

2. It is 1787 and the Constitutional Convention has just ended. You are a radio talk show host in Philadelphia. Prepare a podcast explaining the provisions of the new Constitution to your audience.

SUGGESTED SOURCES

Primary Sources

"The American Constitution—A Documentary Record." http://avalon.law.yale.edu/subject_menus/constpap.asp. This site contains many of the influences on the U.S. Constitution, from the Magna Carta in 1215 to the Kentucky Resolution of 1799.

"Notes on the Debates in the Federal Convention." http://avalon.law.yale.edu/subject_menus/debcont.asp. This site has James Madison's notes on the Constitutional Convention.

"Variant Texts of the Plan Presented by William Patterson—Text A." http://avalon.law.yale.edu/18th_century/patexta.asp. This site contains variations of the New Jersey Plan that was presented to the Constitutional Convention.

"Variant Texts of the Virginia Plan, Presented by Edmund Randolph to the Federal Convention, May 29, 1787." http://avalon.law.yale.edu/18th_century/vatexta.asp. This site contains different versions of the Virginia Plan that was presented to the Constitutional Convention.

Secondary Sources

Bowen, Catherine Drinker. *Miracle at Philadelphia: The Story of the Constitutional Convention, May to September, 1787.* Boston: Little, Brown, 1966. Straightforward historical account of the Constitutional Convention.

Countryman, Edward, ed. *What Did the Constitution Mean to Early Americans?* Boston: Bedford/St. Martin's, 1999. Contains five essays by different historians examining what Americans thought of their new Constitution.

World Wide Web

"The Constitutional Convention of 1787." http://www.law.umkc.edu/faculty/projects/ftrials/conlaw/convention1787.html. Contains essays, images, and documents related to the convention.

Multimedia Sources

Both of these programs contain segments on the Constitutional convention.

The History Channel Presents the Revolution. A&E Home Video, 2006. 4 DVDs. 600 minutes.

Liberty! The American Revolution. PBS, 1997. 3 DVDs. 360 minutes. Documents and reenactments.

100. Constitution Is Ratified (1787–1791)

After having drafted the Constitution in 1787, the men who backed it now had to convince the country to ratify it. The publication of the Constitution set off an intense political argument throughout America. Ratification required the approval of nine states. The supporters of the Constitution called themselves the Federalists, in part because they did not want to be called the Nationalists. In other words, they wanted to deflect the notion they favored excessive centralization. Most other supporters were commercial farmers or residents concentrated in port cities such as Charleston, Philadelphia, New York, and Boston. Their opponents became known as the anti-Federalists, a moniker hung on them by the press. Most of their support came from backcountry farmers and state politicians. The Federalists were far more organized than the anti-Federalists and quickly secured approval for the Constitution in ratification conventions in most of the small states and Pennsylvania. However, the large states of New York and Virginia were holdouts. Technically, the Constitution could have gone into effect without them (ratification required the approval of nine states), but the Federalists realized that without these two states the new federal government would be greatly weakened. The tide was turned in these states by the *Federalist Papers,* a series of 85 essays that made the case for the Constitution. The *Federalist Papers* appeared in American newspapers and was authored by Alexander Hamilton, James Madison, and John Jay. Anti-Federalists also published editorials, though not as widely. New York's and Virginia's ratification conventions agreed to approve the Constitution with the proviso that the Bill of Rights, which are the first ten amendments to the Constitution, be added.

TERM PAPER SUGGESTIONS

1. Today it seems strange that there was a good deal of opposition to the proposed Constitution. Discuss the positions of the anti-Federalists. Were their concerns justified?
2. Pick what you think is the most persuasive of the *Federalist Papers.* Why is it the most persuasive?
3. Pick what you think is the most persuasive of the *Anti-Federalist Papers.* Why do you find it persuasive, and how would our government be different today if the nation had followed the author's line of argument?
4. Why did several of the states insist on a Bill of Rights? Why was one not included in the original version of the Constitution?
5. What is the least persuasive of the *Federalist Papers?* Where does the argument fall short?

ALTERNATIVE TERM PAPER SUGGESTIONS

1. It is 1789 and you are a political operative for the anti-Federalists. Your job is to sow uncertainty about the adoption of the Constitution. As part of your job, you travel the country, speaking to various groups. Prepare a PowerPoint presentation that you will show in order to turn your audience against the Constitution.
2. It is 1789 and you are a political operative for the Federalists. Your job is to encourage people to support the adoption of the Constitution. Prepare a PowerPoint presentation that you will show to audiences in an effort to get them to support the Constitution.

SUGGESTED SOURCES

Primary Sources

Hamilton, Alexander, James Madison, and John Jay. *The Federalist.* Ed. Jack N. Rakove. Boston: Bedford/St. Martin's, 2003. This collection offers some of the key Federalist Papers and analysis of each editorial and its effect.

Ketcham, Ralph. *The Anti-Federalist Papers and the Constitutional Convention Debates.* New York: Mentor, 1986. This is a collection of anti-Federalist responses to the Federalist Papers.

Rakove, Jack N. *Declaring Rights: A Brief History with Documents.* Boston: Bedford/St. Martin's, 1998. Rakove examines British and colonial notions of rights, and looks at the adoption of the Bill of Rights.

Secondary Sources

Holton, Woody. *Unruly Americans and the Origins of the Constitution.* New York: Hill & Wang, 2007. Holton argues that it was the response of ordinary Americans that prompted changes in the Constitution, such as a Bill of Rights.

Main, Jackson Turner. *The Anti-Federalists: Critics of the Constitution, 1781–1788.* Chapel Hill: University of North Carolina Press, 1961. Main discusses the primary opponents of the Constitution and their arguments against ratification.

Rakove, Jack N. *Original Meanings: Politics and Ideas in the Making of the Constitution.* New York: Vintage, 1997. Seeks to explain the original intent of the Framers.

World Wide Web

"Anti-Federalist Papers." http://www.constitution.org/afp/afp.htm. This site offers a few of the anti-Federalist rebuttals to the *Federalist Papers.*

"Documents from the Continental Congress and the Constitutional Convention." http://lcweb2.loc.gov/ammem/collections/continental/. This Library of Congress Web site has a timeline and documents.

"The Federalist Papers." http://avalon.law.yale.edu/subject_menus/fed.asp. The complete *Federalist Papers.*

Multimedia Sources

Both of these presentations contain brief segments regarding the ratification of the Constitution.

The History Channel Presents the Revolution. A&E Home Video, 2006. 4 DVDs. 600 minutes.

Liberty ! The American Revolution. PBS, 1997. 3 DVDs. 360 minutes.

Index

About the Author

ROGER M. CARPENTER is Assistant Professor of History at the University of Louisiana at Monroe. He is the author of *The Renewed, the Destroyed, and the Remade: The Three Thought Worlds of the Huron and the Iroquois, 1609–1650* (2004).